Praise for *Blood Strangers*

"*Blood Strangers*, Kathy Briccetti's long personal journey to reclaim her family's past, illuminates how the secrets of closed adoption can linger, haunting subsequent generations. Only when she succeeds at piecing the puzzle of her family back together does she seem to find complete peace with herself, proof perhaps that hindsight about one's origins is not only enlightening but necessary."

—Jean A. S. Strauss, author of *Birthright: The Guide to Search and Reunion for Adoptees, Birthparents, and Adoptive Parents*

"Kathy Briccetti has written a moving, lyrical, and deeply satisfying book about the search for her extended family. Part memoir, part genealogical detective story, part reflection on the changing American family, *Blood Strangers* is a wonderful reminder of how the ties that bind us can transcend time and distance."

—Frances Dinkelspiel, author of *Towers of Gold: How One Jewish Immigrant Named Isaias Hellman Created California*

"Abortion and adoption, stepfathers and sperm donors, birth mothers, marriage and divorce—it's all here in *Blood Strangers*, a fine and fascinating memoir about the complicated love between parents and children in a modern American family."

—Beth J. Harpaz, author of *Finding Annie Farrell* and *The Girls in the Van*

"Told with clearheaded eloquence, Kathy Briccetti's story easily transcends its particulars, compelling in their own right—fatherlessness, adoption, same-sex parenting—to explore such universal issues as belonging and identity. Readers of various experiences will get swept up in her dogged quest for connection."

—Sarah Saffian, author of *Ithaka: A Daughter's Memoir of Being Found*

"*Blood Strangers* is a story of hard-earned wisdom, forgiveness, and the unending search for self. In our culture of absent fathers, it fills in a vivid spot in the mosaic."

—Mark Matousek, author of *The Boy He Left Behind: A Man's Search for His Lost Father*

Blood Strangers

A Memoir

Katherine A. Briccetti

Heyday Books, Berkeley, California

The publishers are grateful to the BayTree Fund for the support that made this book possible.

Library of Congress Cataloging-in-Publication Data

Briccetti, Katherine A., 1957-
Blood strangers : a memoir / Katherine A. Briccetti.
p. cm.
ISBN 978-1-59714-130-7 (pbk. : alk. paper)
1. Briccetti, Katherine A., 1957- 2. Briccetti, Katherine A., 1957--Family. 3. Fathers and daughters--United States--Biography. 4. Lesbian mothers--United States--Biography. 5. Absentee fathers--United States-- Biography. 6. Adoptees--United States--Biography. 7. Birthparents--United States--Identification. I. Title.
HQ755.86.B74 2010
306.874'2092--dc22
[B]

200905001

Cover photograph courtesy of the author.
Book Design: Lorraine Rath
Printing and Binding: Thomson-Shore, Dexter, MI

Orders, inquiries, and correspondence should be addressed to:
Heyday Books
P. O. Box 9145, Berkeley, CA 94709
(510) 549-3564, Fax (510) 549-1889
www.heydaybooks.com

Printed in the United States of America

Heyday Books is committed to preserving ancient forests and natural resources. We elected to print this title on 100% post consumer recycled paper, processed chlorine free. As a result, for this printing, we have saved:

21 Trees (40' tall and 6-8" diameter)
7 Million BTUs of Total Energy
1,976 Pounds of Greenhouse Gases
9,519 Gallons of Wastewater
578 Pounds of Solid Waste

Heyday Books made this paper choice because our printer, Thomson-Shore, Inc., is a member of Green Press Initiative, a nonprofit program dedicated to supporting authors, publishers, and suppliers in their efforts to reduce their use of fiber obtained from endangered forests.

For more information, visit www.greenpressinitiative.org

Environmental impact estimates were made using the Environmental Defense Paper Calculator. For more information visit: www.papercalculator.org.

10 9 8 7 6 5 4 3 2 1

In memory of my four grandmothers

Martha Rose Terborgh "Conway"
Hazel "Cyrus Manfred"
Joan Filardi Briccetti
Mavis Foster Shaver

And with love to both of my fathers

For my mother

Note to Readers: To protect the privacy of some of the people who appear in this book, I have changed their names and invented some locations. I have altered the identifying characteristics of the sperm donor. For flow and dramatic effect, I have also turned a phone call and two letters into face-to-face conversations and merged two trips into one without changing the content of events. I took notes during my travels and after conversations in order to remember details and essence. In any given situation, we know that people remember events differently, and although I'm sure my family will have somewhat varying versions of this story, I'm confident they will appreciate the veracity of my experience.

Prelude

My left foot bowed in when I was born, its toes reaching for their mates on the other side. A month later, when the foot hadn't turned back naturally, the pediatrician fitted me with a baby-sized leather and metal brace that attached around my waist like a belt, holstered my leg, and over the next six or seven months guided my foot into its proper place. I wore the brace twenty-four hours a day, scraping it across the floor as I learned to crawl. It wasn't a burden. My mother says I seemed to accept that it was just part of life.

That year, 1957, my parents lived in the converted army barracks that constituted the married student housing at Indiana University. Mom had finished her coursework for her master's in music the year she was pregnant with me, and after I was born, she began practicing six hours a day for her violin recital the following spring. During my waking hours—when my father was in the practice hall with his cello and not pushing me around campus in my stroller while humming pieces of music—my mother slipped me into a bouncy seat hanging from the doorframe so she could practice. There I jumped, she tells me, up and down and around in circles, my metal sole clunking on the linoleum like a faulty metronome.

For most of my life, I have danced to a discordant beat as I searched for the rhythm of my family and my place in it.

PART I

"If we cannot name our own we are cut off at the root,
our hold on our lives as fragile as seed in a wind."

Dorothy Allison

ONE

Blueprints

I am drawn to fathers and sons because my two boys were conceived with the sperm of a stranger. When people refer to Benjamin and Daniel's "father," I correct them. "The donor," I say, not meaning to be rude, but needing to make the distinction. "No dad in this family."

In the summer of 2005, my younger son Daniel and I waited in the San Francisco airport to board a plane to Kentucky to visit my own father, a man I hardly knew, a man whom I had lost and then found again. Now we visited every few years, trying to make up for lost time, trying to settle into our adult relationship, a relationship that defied easy definition.

Standing at the gate with my ten-year-old, I found myself staring at a teenage boy and a man ahead of us, the boy hunched over an electronic game, the father resting his arm across his son's shoulder, fingers grazing his neck. Not taking my eyes off the teenager, I smoothed my boy's silky hair, watching the future my sons would not have. The future I once believed I had stolen from them.

When the boy looked up from the game, his father turned the caress into a playful squeeze, a jostle almost, as if remembering how men are supposed to show their affection for one another.

Sometimes when my sons brush away my embraces, when they think they're too big for them, like a halfback I charge them and grab them in a quick, rough hug, pretending it's nothing more than a tackle. Absurd as it may sound, I even find myself grunting when I accost them, my voice deepening in my imitation of a male-bonding ritual.

Waiting in line to board the plane, I remembered a conversation I'd had with Daniel on a walk home from kindergarten years before.

"Hey," I'd said, as we turned the corner on our block in Berkeley. "How do you feel about not having a dad?" I wanted to keep it light, not project my anxiety onto him, make it sound like, "Did you feed the dog this morning?"

"Um..." Daniel paused. "Sometimes good and sometimes bad."

Uh-oh. Here we go. In preschool, having two moms had made Daniel an object of envy, but maybe by kindergarten two moms were no longer enough to make up for the absence of a father.

"Okay," I said, preparing myself. "What's the bad thing about not having a dad?"

"The bad is because you can climb up on a dad and he can lift you really high."

I stifled a laugh. "You mean like Uncle Mike does?"

"Yeah. I can touch the ceiling when he lifts me."

"All right." I prepared for the rest. "What else?"

"That's all."

That was all? The only bad thing about not having a dad was not having someone to climb on? I wanted to believe him, desperately wanted this to be true, but I feared he was old enough to know what might hurt my feelings. He might have been holding back, protecting me.

"What about the good?" I asked as we neared our house. Instead of looking over at him, I stared at the jacaranda I'd planted next to the sidewalk the year before, noted its growth. "What's good about not having a dad?"

"It's good because they're meaner. Jack told me his dad is meaner than his mom."

All right. Score another for two moms.

"You're like the dad."

I felt as if I might stumble on the sidewalk. "I'm like the dad?"

"Yeah, you're meaner than Mama."

I smiled, but something stung inside my chest. I knew he meant "stricter" when he said "meaner," and he had me pegged. I am the heavy, the alpha female in our pack. I holler more, and louder, than Pam does. Too often I overrule her, and then she and I argue over how to share authority.

"But you know I love you, right?" I asked Daniel. It was lame, but I was desperate. I wanted to be known as the mom who let him wrap his arms and legs around her like a koala cub and who kissed the warm spot in the soft hollow of his neck. The mom who played basketball in the driveway and pitched baseballs at the park. I needed to be acknowledged as a Good Mom. Did he appreciate any of this?

"Yeah, I know, Mommy," he said, glancing up and grinning. "You love me."

I was saved.

"But you're still meaner."

I sometimes wonder whether my family's legacy, what feels like an invisible blueprint, has influenced my choices, however unconsciously, and led me to create two children who will not grow up with the man whose genes they share. Their relationship with their biological father—if they ever meet him—will mirror my relationship with mine: lost opportunity for anything deeper than simple acquaintance.

My children are the third generation in our family to be adopted in some fashion and the third generation to grow up without their father. These repetitions fascinate me. I'm attracted by the pattern: the thirty-year spread between each of these events—from the nineteen thirties to the sixties to the nineties—the numbers suggesting a type of balance, or symmetry, like a repeating design in a quilt. Granted, the three adoptions were of different types—traditional, step-parent, and second-parent—but the threads of father absence woven throughout bind us together.

It wasn't until the man in the airport smiled at his son that I could see their resemblance. The father was balding, and his eyes were rounder than his son's, but when they smiled at each other, there was no questioning their kinship. Their lips and the creases in their chins were identical. I'd have been embarrassed if they'd turned and found me intruding on this intimate moment, but I was riveted.

Around that time, whenever I caught my reflection in store windows, I saw my mother. Although she was dark-haired and I was blonde, I had her plank-like body and eyes that disappeared when I smiled, and at forty-seven, my face was becoming hers. Our lips—reedy lines when we concentrated—were the same. More and more often now, usually when I'm being silly with my boys, I catch myself saying something in exactly the tone my mother would use. Even though she's still enjoying her earthly incarnation, I feel as if I'm channeling her spirit. If women turn into their mothers at a certain stage, do men turn into their fathers? My sons share many of my family's physical characteristics, but they must also resemble the donor, whose photograph we've never seen. Both boys inherited my fair skin and blonde hair, and Daniel got my mother's wide, round eyes, but I don't recognize my eldest's steeply vaulted Mr. Spock eyebrows. These may have come from his biological father. The need for my sons to compare themselves to this man, the need to see themselves reflected in him, might become important when they reach adolescence—when they try to figure out who they are, where they belong, which man they came from.

I'm beginning to understand how repeating ruptures across generations have affected me and my children as well as to recognize the ways we've broken free of the blueprint. And I'm realizing something else: how losing, in different ways, both my father and my stepfather has shaped me, perhaps made me tougher, more resilient, dogged in my pursuits. I better understand now my continuing drive toward reunions—beginning with a Greyhound bus trip at sixteen to meet my father again. It's the mélange of my genetic make-up and early experiences that propelled me toward years of detective work, drove the decade-long search for my father's birth mother, and impelled me to travel from my Berkeley home to Texas and Missouri to meet missing kin. During those journeys, I would uncover the secret my mystery grandfather took to his grave, and I would finally find the grandmother I never knew.

A woman behind the teenage boy in line shifted her weight. The boy's father spoke to her, and she handed him a boarding pass. It took me a moment to realize that she was the mother; she had been invisible to me, standing in line behind them. I realized that this could be me in a few years: redundant, unnecessary when the need for Mommy is less passionate, when I'm no longer the center of my sons' universe, when my sons might turn their attention to the missing man. Perhaps there will be one more search that will take place in this family; perhaps my sons will set off on their own quests to find their father.

Once, running errands on Solano Avenue in Berkeley when Benjamin was about five, we passed the donor on the sidewalk—or a man who could have been the donor. According to the file from the sperm bank, he was the right height and body type, and something about his eyes made me inhale sharply. I don't remember if it was the hue of blue, matching Ben's perfectly, or if it was their almond shape and particular slope, but I felt for a second as if I was looking into my son's eyes. The man's glance at Benjamin lingered a beat too long, and I tightened my grip on my boy's hand. I didn't want to meet the donor—for I was convinced in that instant that it was him—yet. I turned my back on the man, hurried Benjamin to the car, and nudged him into his car seat.

If, when they turn eighteen, my sons decide to locate the man who helped us make two marvelous boys, if they feel they lack a piece of their identity, or if they just want to know what he looks like, the sperm bank will release his name, and they can go looking for him. I have mixed feelings about this possibility. I don't want to find him if he's an out-of-work, four-times-divorced, drug-addicted deadbeat dad who'll show up at our house every Friday night wanting to hang out for the weekend. I don't want to be disappointed by him, and I don't want my boys to wish they'd never looked for him.

On the other hand, because we can tell from the notes in his file that more than likely he's a decent guy, I hope they do find our donor, so we can get a look at him, so we can study photos of him as a boy, which I'd like to place side by side with those of my sons at parallel ages. And I want to find him so that I can wrap my arms around him, the man who gave us the gift of our children, and ask him just one question: How can I ever thank you?

Since each donor is allowed ten offspring, my sons could have eight half-siblings scattered around the country, girls and boys sharing half of their genes. Someday I'd love to see what these kids look like, what characteristics they share, as well as how each is unique. Sometimes I imagine an odd gathering in a park in the hills east of San Francisco: tofu hotdogs grilling on a barbeque, badminton players' shouts ricocheting off eucalyptus trees, and all the kids and adults in red T-shirts with the inscription *Family Reunion of Donor 042-75.*

At the airport, a voice through the speaker called our row. I lifted my carry-on bag and slung it over my shoulder. Daniel picked up his backpack, slipped his hand in mine, and together we boarded the plane.

TWO

Leaving

When I was three and a half years old, my mother tossed suitcases and a cardboard box of toys into the trunk of her Chevy Corvair and slammed it shut. With care, she placed her violin case on the floor of the back seat and then called to my brother and me. The magnolia in the front yard of our Kentucky home still clenched its flame-shaped buds, new leaves glowing like green embers, and, in its shade, my father bent his stalky frame to embrace me. When his smooth cheek brushed mine, I filled up on his Daddy smell—spicy mouthwash and the musty velvet and rosin scent he carried from his cello case. He patted my back, lingering a second before unfolding and standing again. I grabbed his legs, and with my cheek felt his knees jutting against the soft fabric of his slacks.

"Come on, honey," he said, peeling back my fingers from around his shins. "Be a good girl and get in the car." He spoke as if my little brother, my mother, and I were heading to the park for the day, but something in his voice was off. I climbed into the front while Michael, not quite two years old, settled onto the back seat, the car's lap belts dangling like abandoned playground swings. Perched on my knees, I pressed my forehead to the side window as my mother backed the car down our driveway.

"I'll let you know when we get a place," she called out her open window, her stone jaw contradicting the flowery lilt of her voice. Eyes hard, she was already a hundred miles away. I swiveled to catch a last glimpse of my father through the back window, a cloudy oval framing the moment. His hands in his pockets, he stood fixed at the end of the drive, swaying slightly. His face vanished into the shadows cast by the magnolia, and as the car headed down Oakdale Street toward the expressway, my father slowly shrank, then disappeared.

This is how it might have happened. But somewhere along the way, I had forgotten this scene, this leaving, and the vanished memory melded into a child's confabulation: the belief, the never-doubted knowledge, that *he* had left *us*. Perhaps I forgot this parting because it was too painful to hold on to, or I simply forgot it just like I forgot the other events of my first three or four years. I do remember the apartment in New Jersey we moved to, and can still conjure up images from that time—a neighbor girl teaching me how to tie my shoes on the steps of our brick apartment building and the mail carrier bringing me a snow cone maker, the prize for winning a coloring contest. However, the scene of our leaving escaped me entirely, happy memories trumping sad ones.

It would be nearly forty years before I learned what happened that day, when I finally rectified the mistaken belief that had in many ways set the course of my life, when I finally understood the circumstances of the parting. Even though it might be equally painful to a child, to be left is not the same as leaving, and although I know the truth now, the ghost of that old, distorted belief refuses to vanish.

In our apartment in New Jersey near my grandparents' home, I knelt on a phone book on a kitchen chair coloring a picture of Cinderella's rag dress. My mother, her back to me, snipped the ends off green beans with a pair of red-handled kitchen scissors, the pointy bean ends disappearing into the sink, the neatly clipped sections landing in a colander. A bacon-draped meatloaf sizzled in the oven. I colored

Cinderella's hair yellow like my own and the coals in her fireplace a bold red-orange, working to stay within the lines. I pressed hard with the crayon, risking a break, but wanted the colors deep.

"Mommy, where's Daddy?"

She turned toward me, her colorless lips pulling down slightly at the corners. "I told you. He's at our old house, in Burlsville." I couldn't tell if she was sad or angry. So far she'd been careful with us, as if we might break, and I feared the same about her.

"Why didn't he come with us?"

She returned to the sink, inhaling deeply. Her back straightened. "It's just better this way."

The crayon slipped, giving Cinderella a bloody foot. I had an urge to tear the picture out of the coloring book, ball it up, and throw it at my mother's back. I wanted to pound on her legs with my fists; instead I scratched at the red-orange wax with my fingernails. My bottom lip trembled and my tears threatened my mother's calm.

"There's no need to cry," she said, turning to pet my head. "Let's think of all the things we can be grateful for. Let me see what you've colored."

This forget-the-bad-and-concentrate-on-the-good attitude she'd inherited from her parents, although it was meant to comfort, sent me on my way to a lifelong pattern, for better or worse, of pushing aside painful feelings. Adults at that time did not sit down with children and acknowledge their feelings, so no one sat me on their lap and said, "This must be hard on you, not seeing your Daddy. I bet you're wondering what's going on. Maybe you feel sad or scared." There was the belief that if you ignore painful feelings they would go away. My mother didn't have the shelves of parenting books I can find in bookstores now. She didn't know how to guide herself, much less her children, through such a loss.

At the kitchen table, I scribbled over the Cinderella picture with the crayon in my fist. My stomach squeezed in on itself and burned. I put the crayon down and turned to a clean page.

* * *

The first summer after leaving Kentucky, the three of us whizzed along the interstate on the way back to my father's house for a visit, my brother Michael and I kneeling on the back seat, ignoring the imaginary line we'd set moments before to delineate each other's territory. Giving high-pitched voices to my Barbie dolls, we manipulated them into splits and bent their cracking knees backward in impossible contortions.

Mom was quiet on this trip, and we knew we should be, too. But we had begun to fight for her attention, and when our arguing turned to whining, she shushed us. She distracted us briefly with nursery rhymes but soon fell into her reverie again. When we began to kick each other, and one of us bumped the back of her seat, she swatted at the air behind her and threatened to pull over.

"Be a big girl," she pleaded, turning soft again. "I need your help on this trip."

I raised my finger at Michael and shook it. "Be good," I said.

We exited at a grassy rest area somewhere between our new home in New Jersey and our old home in Kentucky, the designated spot for the transfer of us children. Mom slowed the car and then eased to a stop. Checking the mirror, she ran her fingers through her short hair but left her lipstick in her purse.

"All right. There's Daddy. Hop out." She lifted a plaid canvas suitcase from the trunk and took Michael's hand. Holding onto her wrist above the suitcase handle, I clutched both Barbies in my other fist. Unlike the nebulous memories and speculations so far, this next sensation I remember with utter clarity. I can still feel the gravel crunching under the spare soles of my white canvas sneakers as we shuffled from one car to the other.

This is where my memories begin.

During our visit to our father's house, I ran barefoot on scorching sidewalks and damp grass, caught fireflies, and fled from Honk, my father's pet goose, an unpredictable beast that pecked at my chest and chased me from his territory in the side yard. Michael and I played cowboys, riding a life-sized stuffed toy bear on wheels, which bellowed when we yanked a cord under its belly. At this house, classical music faded in and out on the scratchy kitchen radio, punctuated by soft bursts of static. All of this distracted me from our family that wasn't a family anymore.

The following summer we met my father's new wife, Ursula, a woman with wiry onyx hair pulled into a ball at the nape. She painted with watercolors at an easel next to a bay window, laughed a smoker's laugh, and taught me to make fresh lemonade. But I didn't stay inside much; it was easier to be outside, to become lost in childhood games. I ran around with a summer pal, free to explore the small town, and when she wasn't available, I straddled my father's porch swing like a pony, riding it sideways, my bare feet slithering across the slick cement.

Because she represented my mother's replacement, meeting Ursula could have precipitated my childhood confusion, making me think that my father had left us for her. Since my mother was still single—had not yet replaced *him*—in my five-year-old's mind, Ursula could have been the reason he had abandoned his family. It was easier to hold my father responsible for the rupture, since he was the absent one. Plus, it was too risky to fault my mother, my only remaining parent. If I had turned my child's anger on her, I could have made her disappear, too.

Two years later, my father sent me a black-and-white snapshot of an infant with wide, happy eyes and a toothy grin, a perfect Gerber baby peering over the top of her playpen, his new daughter. *My* replacement. I ran the scalloped edges of the photograph over my lips and then placed it in my jewelry box underneath the ballerina that twirled to wind-up music. I took my time straightening the knickknacks on my bureau, squaring them at precise angles, setting them right. It was here that my father, Cyrus Manfred, truly began to disappear, leaving me with only hazy impressions, not of a person but of a hodgepodge of murky sensations: his scent and the feel of fabric on my cheek.

THREE

Slatch

Like an early warning system, the roar of an Alfa Romeo engine announced the stranger's arrival from blocks away. A minute later, he was a cartoon blur, zooming into our driveway, screeching to a stop, ratcheting the car's parking brake, hopping out of the convertible and slamming the car door behind him before sprinting up the steps.

"Hey, kids," he said as he knelt next to Michael and me and pinched our cheeks between thumb and knuckle. "I've heard a lot about you."

He leaped up to greet my mother. "They're beautiful." He smiled as if they shared a secret, and then briefly cupped her jaw in his palm, a motion so filled with tenderness that it startled me. Now eight, I recognized the same mistiness in her eyes that I saw when she tucked me in at night, when she smoothed the bangs off my face and pulled the sheet to my chin.

A rose flush surfaced on her tanned face, highlighting her model-like cheekbones. "Say hello to Mr. Briccetti," she said, stepping back slightly at the same time his hand dropped from her jaw. "He's the conductor of the orchestra."

The man's raven beard, wild eyebrows, and baby-fine hair the color and silky sheen of coffee beans placed him far outside my realm of experience. His compact, sinewy body was foreign; the men in Mom's family, my grandfather and uncle, were tall and lanky, almost bony. My father Cyrus was too. Our family had descended from fair-skinned, thick-haired northern Europeans, while this man was olive-skinned with a nose like a raptor's beak. He stood a couple of inches shorter than Mom's five feet, nine inches, and when he began to telephone our house regularly, Michael or I would shout, "Mom! The man with the beard is on the phone!"

For three summers, Michael and I had visited our father in Kentucky, but after moving to Florida, where Mom was teaching music in the public schools and playing in a symphony orchestra, our routine changed. Instead, that summer Michael and I were shuttled off to overnight camp in Massachusetts. Although we didn't know it yet, the visits with our father were over.

When we returned from camp, Mr. Briccetti packed the four of us into his forest green sports car, the "zoom-zoom car," as my brother called it. We sped for St. Pete Beach, convertible top down, towels and sand toys stowed in the tiny trunk, the four of us wearing flip-flops of different colors, Mom's fluttering silk scarf emblazoned with a map of the world. Michael and I sat stuffed into the gap behind the bucket seats, meant for two grocery sacks, not two children. We rode, the wind whipping my ghost-white hair into my eyes and mouth. Looking over Mr. Briccetti's shoulder, I watched the speedometer climb to sixty on city streets and to eighty, then ninety, on the interstate. Tiny bumps in the road jolted me, making my rear end fly off the ledge and thump back down. I clutched the back of Mom's seat until my hands stiffened. Like a carnival ride, it was frightening and thrilling at the same time.

Stuck behind a driver following the speed limit, Mr. Briccetti pounded the horn with his fist. "Idiot!" he shouted. "Get out of my way!" His voice was thunder; he was a lightning strike, and I dreaded his anger ever directed at me. At the bridge tollbooth he slowed, then sped through without paying, making me check over my shoulder for the police I imagined speeding after us. When the tires squealed on corners, I worried about crashing, but he projected such an indefatigable air of confidence that for a time I, too, believed we were invincible.

At the beach, he spread out a blanket. While Michael and I sat on one corner playing with our beach toys, he lay on his side next to Mom and told jokes that made her laugh so hard she finally begged him to stop. On the way home, he stopped the car, set me on his lap, and let me turn the leather-wrapped steering wheel the last couple of blocks. His scent was different from my father's, which I was beginning to forget. This man was a musky intermingling of cigarettes, mints, and Old Spice, and I was temporarily sheltered in his embrace.

Mr. Briccetti bought True Blue menthol cigarettes by the carton and went nowhere without a pack in his breast pocket. In the first professional photograph of him I saw, he posed in his tuxedo, cradling his conductor's baton in one hand and a burning cigarette in the other, a curl of smoke wafting up beside his face. To me, a gangly, towheaded eight-year-old who hadn't grown into her new teeth yet, Thomas Briccetti was a movie star.

After a year of "dating" our family, the man with the beard stood in front of a judge and twenty guests lining the living room of a symphony benefactor's sprawling ranch house and married my mother. To the wedding, Mr. Briccetti wore a black suit and skinny black tie, and both he and Michael sported matching white carnation boutonnières. Mr. Briccetti had shaved his beard several weeks before and looked even younger with his Florida tan, his sculpted cheekbones. Posing for photos, he cupped a cigarette behind his hand.

To this, her second wedding, my mother wore a glossy knee-length dress the color of lime sherbet. When she folded her long legs and crouched to hug me after the ceremony, the scent of her body powder merged with a perfume I didn't recognize. She had visited the beauty parlor that morning, flipping the ends of her Jackie

Kennedy hairstyle into wide, soft curls, accentuating the natural wave above her forehead. In photographs taken that day, her head is thrown back in laughter; she is a coal-haired beauty with sanguine painted lips standing side by side with her new husband—his arm around her waist possessively, she half a head taller in her pumps.

During the ceremony, when the guests formed a large semicircle around the room, Michael nuzzled into a corner of the couch and scowled, refusing to stand or join the wedding party next to the fireplace. Whether registering his protest or just too shy to put himself in front of an audience, I don't know. He doesn't remember doing this, even when I remind him of the photographs. As for me, I knew my role well that day—how to evoke smiles, nods of approval, pats on my head. My brother's reticence made me look even better, and I took advantage of it. Clutching in my white-gloved hands a tightly bound bouquet of daisies and carnations, I flanked my mother, proud to stand with her on this stage while at the same time unsure what it all meant. Lifting one patent leather shoe behind me, I polished it on a lacy anklet. Afterward, as the photographer's flashbulbs popped in front of us, I beamed in pretend beatification while Michael hugged our mother's hip with his cheek and clutched her waist with a skinny arm, trying, I imagine now, to repossess her.

Behind my Good Girl persona, I was aching. I hadn't seen my father in almost a year. I feared he was forgetting me, like I was forgetting him. A girl who would forget her father was evil, and at this wedding, I was a traitor. By standing next to my mother during the ceremony, I was consenting to this event. Even though part of me knew that this wedding was a good idea because it would make my mother happy, I also realized that this new man was not only stealing my mother's attention from me, he was banishing the ghost of my father.

At nine, I understood that my mother deserved this happiness. But I must have also silently questioned why we never mentioned my father. Perhaps she thought it would be easier on us if we all just forgot him, pretended he'd never existed. When I become annoyed at her today for a minor slight, my irritation may be rooted more deeply than I'm aware. Even though I understand that child custody was often awarded to mothers back then, and that my mother was trained to keep her feelings private, to ignore the negative and focus on the positive, I still wonder how I might make her pay, might hold her responsible for that first loss.

One photograph from the ceremony made it into my mother's wedding album despite my unflattering expression. Of all the photos from that day, it may be the most accurate expression of my true feelings, for instead of recording untainted happiness, it captures me with a hazy stare and half-smile. Studying it now, I see myself as I must have been: waiting. Waiting during the lull, the slatch between my past and my future, between one father and the other.

FOUR

Leaving a Mark

I used to find it paradoxical that the term "birth mother" is two words while "stepmother" and "stepfather" are one. Ever since I began searching for my grandmother and devouring adoption stories, I thought it should be the reverse. *Birthmother. Step-father.* But now it makes sense that the term "birth mother," since it often applies to a mother who has relinquished a child, would be composed of two separate words, the white space between the words as much of a void as the distance between mother and child.

And looking back on my relationship with my stepfather, I believe that the single compound word—"stepfather"—a word containing no hyphens, is apt. He is the man who raised me, the man who became my father, the man whom I call Dad.

After the wedding, we moved to a larger house in St. Petersburg near Crescent Lake where Michael and I climbed the banyan trees that rimmed its banks and played hide-and-seek amongst the trees' ropy trunks. On weekends, the four of us took our boat to an inlet of St. Pete Bay, where Mom and our new father taught Michael and me to water-ski.

In our own yard, the avocado tree—a giant's umbrella—was so huge Dad hung rope swings from two of its branches, and Michael and I sold its fruit from a red wagon we pulled up and down the block. On Saturday mornings, instead of watching cartoons, Michael joined Dad in his study for piano lessons. In my mother's study every week, I clicked open my violin case and breathed in the familiar scent of old varnished wood. Finding my cube of rosin in its velvet-lined compartment, I took my time rubbing it back and forth across my bow like I'd seen her do so many times. Then, studying my image in the mirror, I mimicked her stance, her posture, her wrists, everything straight yet supple.

But, as our lessons progressed, I couldn't learn vibrato, the violin's chin rest rubbed raw a spot on my collarbone, and my fingers were disloyal, behaving as if they belonged to someone else. More and more, my mother would stare out the window and quietly sigh.

I found the music of my peers and played the Monkees, Herman's Hermits, and the Beach Boys on my plastic stereo. The teenage babysitter who watched us during our parents' evening rehearsals and concerts called her younger sister on the phone one night. "Bring the Beatles albums over here; this chick will dig them."

One season, Dad conducted Donizetti's opera *The Elixir of Love* and Michael and I joined the cast as extras, playing Italian street urchins. Since Mom played in the orchestra, the four of us attended rehearsals and performances together, Michael and I heading off to work with our parents instead of being put to bed by a babysitter. On the night of the first dress rehearsal, backstage in the women's dressing room, the singers in the chorus fawned over Michael and me. Someone tucked my shoulder-length hair under a cap to make me look like a boy and helped me change into my raggedy costume. The women applied our makeup, darkening our fair skin to the shade of our new father's, and finishing with dirty smudges across our cheeks.

"Leave your watch at home," Dad had warned me at dinner one night. "We're not playing around up on that stage. If you forget, I'll punish you." He wasn't smiling, but I couldn't believe he was serious.

I hadn't warranted such a threat; I was a good kid who did what she was told without too much back talk. I was still intimidated by him, would have obeyed him no matter what. "This is important to me," he said by way of explanation when I pouted at the table. "You're my kid, and you'll reflect badly on me if you screw up."

He was taking possession of me, and while I needed to be his child, I also opposed the ruse. He wasn't my real father; I wasn't really his child. I didn't belong to him in the way I belonged to Cyrus, on a cellular level. But because Cyrus was only a shadow father to me, I needed to be claimed by my new father. I both resisted the change of ownership and consented to it, too.

During each performance, as Michael and I mingled with chorus members on stage, a hot air balloon descended from above, and the man playing the peddler climbed out. Watching for our father's cue—eyebrows lifted and a slight nod at us—Michael and I broke from the townspeople to chase each other around the peddler, nudging and taunting the man selling the elixir of love. Each night, in character, he scowled and brushed us dirty orphans away.

After the opera's run ended, Dad called me into the living room, where he was removing a reel of audio tape from its box and snapping it into place on the reel-to-reel machine. "Listen to this, Kithi," he said, calling me by my family nickname. We all had them: monikers that had sprung from our silly talk, the way our family had of speaking in code, changing all vowels to the short "i" sound so that our names became choppy, two-syllable absurdities. I was Kithi, Mike was Miki, Dad was Ditti, and Mom became Mimi.

"Kithi, come listen to this," he said, wrapping the end of the tape around the large empty reel and taking up the slack by spinning it with his fingers. He adjusted the dial, and the numbers on the counter whirled. He slowed the tape to a stop, clicked the dial, and music filled the room. I recognized the passage leading up to our cue.

"Listen," he said. "Right here." And, after a few measures more, I heard it. A sound from the audience: at first a rumble, then distinguishable laughter. It ended quickly, and the music took over again.

"Cool," I said, looking up at him.

He was watching my face, and when I smiled he did, too. "You're a star, honey."

I giggled. "Oh, Ditti, no, I'm not."

"Ah, but to me, my darling, you are." He pulled me into an embrace, and I let him hold me. Submitting felt wrong and right at the same time.

In 1968, Mom and Dad got jobs with the Indianapolis Symphony Orchestra. That summer they sold the ski boat and we moved to Indiana just before I began the sixth grade. Our new house, a four-bedroom brick Colonial previously owned by the S. S. Kresge five-and-dime family, was shaded by giant magnolia and catalpa trees on a half-acre lot. Inside, Michael and I found a closet hidden under the stairs, a basement with a maze of dark, connecting rooms, and a dusty, hot attic with pull-down steps in which we found fifty-year-old *National Geographic* and *Good Housekeeping* magazines. It was a house with depth, history, and roots.

Playing outside one afternoon soon after moving in, I came across a freshly poured section of cement in the sidewalk in front of our house. Once certain I wasn't being watched, I slipped beneath the string barrier and stepped into a corner of the square, letting my sneakers sink into the gritty sludge. Excited by my naughtiness—I imagined a police officer catching me, marching me to the front door to face my parents' shame—I ran off the sidewalk into the grass, wiping my soles clean, leaving my secret behind.

In this new place, no one knew Mr. Briccetti wasn't my true father. But when I called him Dad, it evoked funny stares—me, a tall, skinny, fair girl and him, a short man with Italian features. "You sure don't look like your father," classmates said, leaving me mute. Except for the best friend I had left behind in Florida, who was also adopted by her stepfather, had changed her surname, and had lost touch with her father, I knew no one whose parents had even divorced. I avoided using the word "stepfather" because it suggested an abnormality, an oddity. To confess that I had a stepfather made me feel illegitimate.

Eventually, I would refer to Cyrus Manfred as my *real* father. I did this even though I barely knew him, even though I hadn't seen him in years, even though my stepfather felt like my real father. Now, when I need to, I refer to Cyrus as my "biological father." But it's a cumbersome title, too clinical, too much like "sperm donor." He'd been my father until I was eight. Then he became something else, and for a long time I didn't know what that was.

Our dinner table in Indianapolis became my father's second stage. One night, opera diva Joan Sutherland joined us for dinner, and Mom served a huge platter of spaghetti, using Dad's mother's spaghetti sauce recipe, the aroma of Italian sausage and garlic filling the huge house. Dad poured from bottles of Bolla Valpolicella, and I placed on the table a basket containing a loaf of crusty bread wrapped in a cloth napkin. The conversations at the table were dynamic and loud, like the music he made.

After dinner, Dad scooted his chair back from the head of the table, crossed one leg over the other, and waited for our attention. It was almost as if he were tapping his baton on his music stand, directing the eyes of the musicians to him.

"Did you hear about the viola player who dreamed he was performing the *Messiah*?" he asked, his voice rising with the anticipation of the laughs he'd receive. "And when he woke up, sure enough he was?" He laughed along with his audience, his tongue pressed against his teeth in a *thh-thh-thh* sputter. My father, the consummate performer, always on stage, soaked up admiration like it was the sustenance he needed to live. I was proud to be the daughter of this interesting and important man. I never tired of his jokes, his repertoire, no matter how many times I heard it.

One afternoon, when Dad had been shut up in his study all day humming bars of music over and over, composing pieces on the piano, I heard his voice over the music on the tape player.

"Porco miseria! Disgraziado!" The only Italian I remember today is the profane.

"Incompetent! *Santa Maria!*" he shouted into the phone. A half hour later, he emerged from his room, carrying a small box into the kitchen. He had impaled his credit card with an oversized metal screw and was now placing it in a cardboard box and taping it shut for mailing. He and my mother laughed like conspirators, but I wasn't sure what to make of the symbol he had invented. I knew it meant "screw you," and that he had fashioned it in anger. I knew that his method of protest was unique. I knew *he* was incomparable.

Occasionally his anger was directed at Michael and me, but more often, he teased us, his aggression spilling out more passively, in a more socially acceptable manner. "Oh, Kithi," he said the day I found a twenty-dollar bill on the empty sidewalk near our house. "I saw an old woman walking back and forth today with her head down. Poor thing had a cane, and she was sobbing." His eventual smile gave him away, but the joking had dashed my excitement, evoked guilt instead. Being teased felt like being tickled—an aggressive, not loving, action. While tickling felt unpleasant, unbearable even, to my body, teasing was hurtful to my soul.

During those years, Michael and I were grounded for "talking back" to our parents. Theirs was a zero-tolerance parenting plan, and "disrespect for one's elders" carried stiff fines: missing dinner, losing privileges, extra jobs. Even being sad was discouraged. Dad's favorite line was "Don't be a poo-poo sport." He teased at these times, too, thinking he could snap me out of a bad mood. Trying to be good, I put on a false smile, but occasionally I pouted and refused to speak. So our cycle persisted; the more he tried to lighten me up, the more I ended up feeling sad and misunderstood.

I never once, even in anger, reminded him that he wasn't my real father. I was too afraid of his reaction, and at this time he was morphing into my real father anyway, since there was no other. But when he frustrated or angered me, I silently raged. You shouldn't be teasing me; you have no right.

On the first Christmas in the new house, Michael and I, now nine and eleven, burst out of our rooms at the appointed hour, slid down the banister, and took our places on the couch. "Come on, Ditti!" we shouted. Dad had risen early, as he often did, to begin working in his study, a sun porch adjacent to the living room where he studied music he would be rehearsing with the orchestra, taught conducting students, and composed his own music. His studio was an organized mess: piles of musical scores, reel-to-reel tapes in boxes, and hotrod magazines stacked against the walls. Shavings from the electric eraser he used on musical scores littered the carpet. On his desk sat more piles of music, and, in an orange juice can decorated with macaroni and glitter I had made for him in school, a handful of batons protruded like pick-up sticks.

In her quilted robe, Mom tapped lightly on Dad's studio door. "Be right there," he said. His metronome ticked out a steady beat, which I matched by slapping my terrycloth slipper against my sole. Michael moved to the tree, shaking boxes until Mom called him away. The three of us stared at the door, willing it to open.

Finally, Mom threw open Dad's door. "It's Christmas," she said. "The kids are waiting; are you joining us or not?"

He appeared a few minutes later, taking on the role of Santa and distributing gifts with gusto. However, despite the excitement of the morning, I could not shake the feeling that we'd interfered with something more important.

FIVE

Rupture

More women than men research their family trees, and more women seek reunion with kin lost to adoption. We are specially wired for social bonding, but I often wonder what makes some of us become searchers when others are not so compelled. The extra thrust must come not only from our biology but also from the particular pattern of experiences that shape us. At times throughout my life, I could have been accused of having tunnel vision, so focused were my searches for biological connection.

In the spring of 1970, when I was twelve, I received a bulky business envelope with extra eight-cent stamps from my grandfather in New Jersey. I carefully unfolded four slick Photostat pages that my mother's father had taped together, and I spread out the paper puzzle on my bedroom floor. Behind my closed door, I blasted a Supremes album from my record player's speakers.

"Wow!" I whispered, not knowing that the document I'd asked him for—the Partial Genealogy of the Conway Family—was at that moment sparking what would become an obsession with bloodlines, a compulsion to search for those who shared my genes.

Instead of a sketch of a huge tree, or the more typical espalier turned on its side, Grandpa's hand-drawn diagram of the Conway descendants resembled a multilayered box kite. It soared back up through ten generations of American men with my grandfather's surname, their wives' names joined to theirs like redundant appendages. At the bottom, I found my generation: my brother, my cousins, and me. Even though I didn't share this surname, my mother's maiden name, I felt linked to these people. Finally, I could see from whom I'd come and to whom I belonged.

We were from England I learned as I studied the poster-sized family tree; the first Conway had emigrated from Bath in the 1600s. My sixth-grade teacher had matched our class with European pen pals, and I'd been writing to a girl in England for nearly a year. I played with the idea that she and I could be related, too.

Soon after, my grandfather sent Grandma Rose's family tree, but this more modest sketch fit on one sheet of paper. Grandma's parents, born in Holland, headed the chart, and I felt an immediate bond to this country of wooden shoes and tulips because, after all, weren't all the Dutch blonde like me? Studying both family trees, I became part of something old, established, rooted in history and over time. Like shoe prints in cement, they connected me to something permanent.

But studying my mother's family trees also reminded me of what I lacked: the other half, my biological father's side. I remembered a grandmother in Kentucky, a chilly, dark room with trinkets covering every surface, but I couldn't summon her face or name. I started to sketch another branch, adding Cyrus Manfred's name, but, frustrated by the blank spots above his, I put it aside. Even then, though, I knew that one day I would fill them in.

At the same time I began to feel drawn to my ancestors, I felt increasing—burgeoning adolescent—estrangement from the people I lived with. In turn, this feeling only fed the desire to search the past, these polar urges reinforcing each other. My family's idiosyncrasies added a unique flavor to my yearning.

Every night at the dinner table in Indianapolis, my parents and brother spoke to each other in musical code, humming bars of music and talking about how their practicing had gone that day. "You know that passage in the Dvořák that goes *da da dee dum* and then repeats?" my father would say, and Mom and Michael would nod or join the humming. Michael had continued studying piano after I'd quit squeaking my bow across my violin's strings, and he had added the trumpet to his list of talents as well. He had appeared in a second opera when we still lived in Florida, but that time there was no part for me so I sat in the audience. In Puccini's *Suor Angelica,* Michael played an angel, the young child of the soprano. Fitting, I thought, my sibling rivalry smoldering. From center stage, dressed in a white gown that matched his ghostly hair, in time to the downbeats of our father's baton, he slowly descended the steps of a riser while his stage mother wept at his feet. From my seat in the auditorium, I prayed that he'd trip and tumble off the riser.

I was convinced that Michael had taken over center stage in our house, too. Listening to them at the table, I longed to join the conversation but had no entry point; I lacked the vocabulary, the common experience. I was beginning to take on the role of outsider. I had formed my own self-fulfilling prophecy.

In my second year of high school, I taught myself a cheer by watching the cheerleaders at basketball games. I had never considered actually trying out for a cheerleading spot; I knew I lacked the prerequisites: coordination, popularity, and large enough breasts. I'm embarrassed to admit that I once dreamed about being a cheerleader, but back then I yearned to fill out the uniform, if for nothing else but to catch the eye of a hunky football player on whom I had a terribly-out-of-my-league crush. But I was not brave enough to have performed in front of a crowd; I believed I would only make a fool of myself.

Instead, I held my own tryouts at home, just to see if I could do it, memorize a whole cheer. I also must have hoped that my performance, not exactly musical but close enough, might finally gain me entrance into my family's private club. For three weeks after school I practiced in the driveway, whispering the words to myself so that no one would hear me until I knew the cheer perfectly. It had a long series of arm bends, thigh slaps, and kicks, some of which I still remember today. Finally, one afternoon, I nailed it.

That night before dinner, I gathered my family around me in the kitchen. "Okay everybody, watch this," I said. "I know this cheer all the way through now."

"Charge!" I shouted, my voice too loud for the room. "C! H!—A, R, G, E!" My arms flew, I kicked with precision, and finished the cheer with a hop in place, not one missed step.

But instead of applauding when I finished, my mother, father, and brother exploded in laughter, first little sputters and then, after exchanging glances, a crescendo of howls. "You didn't get the rhythm right, sweetie," my father said, snorting.

Rhythm? I'd copied the cheerleaders exactly. I left the kitchen, raced upstairs to my bedroom, and, in a flood of self-pity, threw myself across my bed. I swiped at tears and pounded my fist on the mattress. *Go to hell, all of you. I don't need you.*

I don't remember if I conjured up a typical teenager's fantasy at that moment—that I'd been abducted by aliens in human form, or switched at birth with another baby, or secretly adopted, and my distraught birth parents, the only ones who could ever understand me, were out there somewhere searching for me. Nor do I remember pining for my biological father, nor believing that he would not have also made fun of my attempts at a cheer. At that time, I rarely thought about him, had pushed my memories of him so far back he existed only as a shade, as intangible as a silhouette. But I did believe that, because my brother was more musically talented than I was, there was no way I belonged with these people.

For years, when people asked me why, coming from a family of musicians, I didn't play an instrument, I forced a smile. "I'm the audience in my family," I'd say, pretending I no longer held any bitterness about it.

The fall of my junior year, Dad left his study one evening to escort me to my high school's father-daughter dance, where he whirled me around the cafeteria floor to recorded ballroom music. I hadn't known he could dance, that he knew the steps to the polka and the waltz. Even though I was taller than he by an inch, and slouched to compensate, I was proud to be on his arm and grateful for the rare attention from him. But, stiff and clumsy, I stepped on his feet—mine were bigger than his. "Kithi, my sweet, just bounce on your toes and I'll lead you," he said, pulling me, his lumbering daughter, across the shiny linoleum, slick with wax. We could not have been more mismatched, and this only fostered my sense that something was missing, that there was a hole that needed filling.

One night, in hushed voices, my parents argued behind Dad's closed study door. I knew that Mom had been increasingly annoyed at his self-absorption, his habit of jumping into the shower as soon as she called us all to dinner, that he didn't have time for any of us. I couldn't hear what they were arguing over that night, only that they were disagreeing, and that Mom was shushing him, reminding him to keep his voice down so that we wouldn't hear them. But I had heard, and had come into the living room on the pretense of needing an encyclopedia, plopping on the loveseat with volume M open on my lap in case I was caught eavesdropping. Sitting there, I realized that Mom had become quieter recently. She didn't laugh as often, and the lines around her mouth were more firmly set. Mom and Dad no longer cuddled on the loveseat, and I couldn't remember when I had last seen them kiss or embrace. Dad did not leave his study except for meals, or when he was commuting to a second conducting job in Ft. Wayne, where he rented a small house, leaving us several days a week.

While my parents argued, I rolled out of the loveseat and replaced the encyclopedia. From another shelf I pulled down our copy of *Who's Who in America*. Like I had before, I scanned the list of symphony orchestra conductors for my father's name. I wanted to find the words that had pleased me so much when I'd first found them. It was reassurance I needed, and I found it quickly: Katherine Briccetti. Daughter.

The following spring, I stood at the doorway of my father's study. After each of his visits, a few more of his belongings—the denim jacket he always hung on the coat tree in the hall, the tin of spicy mints on the ledge above the kitchen sink, the clay ashtray I made for him in fourth grade that he kept on his desk—had disappeared. I wasn't home the day the movers came for his piano. And I wasn't there the morning he backed a U-Haul truck into the driveway, loaded it with the rest of the furniture from his study, and drove away. I don't think we ever said good-bye. At a time when I needed to push away from my parents and prepare to leave home, Dad had beat me out the door.

I gazed into his empty study, staring at sunlight striking newly bared carpet, three potted plants left behind on windowsills, and a small blue pencil sharpener lying on its side in a corner. I picked up the pencil sharpener and took it to my room. There, I opened my jewelry box and placed it carefully inside.

My parents sold the big brick house, and Mom bought a smaller house two blocks away. Mike—as he now wanted to be called—was living with Dad in Ft. Wayne because Mom could no longer handle his teenage rebellion: ignoring her rules, breaking curfew. Even though I had fought hard with my brother, I missed him. We'd experienced two huge events together—losing our birth father and accepting a replacement father into our lives. Now we were losing our family again. This time, though, we did it apart.

Mom and I wrapped dishes in newspaper the day before our move. My best friend, Nancy, had helped us for a few hours but had gone home for dinner. Alone together, Mom and I ordered a pizza. She poured grape juice into two paper cups and handed me one. I held it up and tapped hers gently with it. She smiled. "To a new start," she said. "This garden was too big for me anyway."

On my last trip to the new house, I pulled a red wagon filled with my mother's African violets, which had decorated the windowsills in several rooms of our big house. The wagon rattled over an uneven square of sidewalk in front, and I stopped to see what had caused the racket. The rear wheels had just passed over the impressions of two sneakers, and I remembered that day, soon after we'd moved in, when I had sunk my feet into wet concrete in front of our new house and left my mark.

SIX

In Search of the Missing

My clogs clunked on the stairs of the Greyhound bus, the engine hissing to life beneath my feet. I paused to let my eyes adjust to the dim interior as stale odors hinted at lingering ghosts of past riders. That summer of 1974, before my senior year in high school, I was returning to Kentucky to meet my father, Cyrus Manfred, again.

I claimed a spot near the front of the bus so the driver could keep an eye on me, and tossed my macramé shoulder bag onto the adjacent seat, hoping to give the impression it was occupied. It was my first solo trip, and I prayed that a chatty woman with foul breath or a creepy man with roaming hands would not sit next to me. I flipped open *Catcher in the Rye* and hid behind its pages. I didn't want to see the Indianapolis bus station disappear behind me, the men sleeping on benches, the fast-food wrappers whirling in the gutter as we sped away. I didn't want to see my mother climbing into her car to drive back home.

Inside the station, I had hugged Mom with more fervor than usual. "I'll go out myself," I said. I'd left her for summer camp before, but this parting was different. I was seeking something she couldn't provide: the other half of me. My aching throat—dammed tears—kept me from squeezing out a good-bye. Our family didn't weep at partings. Instead I had waved, and then turned to go.

When I finally looked up, rows of Indiana corn had softened into a blur against the backdrop of a cloudless sky, and with the sun almost at its zenith, the stalks radiated a shimmering vapor. Past the fields of corn, hay rolls like giant cinnamon buns dotted the farmlands of southern Indiana, and finally the bus drummed over the bridge spanning the Ohio River, bringing us into Kentucky.

I abandoned my book and stared at the dual images in my window. Sometimes I focused on my reflection, watching myself weave a clump of long hair between my fingers. Other times, I stared beyond the window at the alien countryside, stared at this place that might have been my home had things gone differently. And I pondered my own duality: in one place I was a stepdaughter, a member of the pack, and well known; in another I was a daughter in pedigree only, simply a visitor. If my parents had worked it out, or endured an unhappy marriage for us kids, I might have been raised in Kentucky, could have had a Southern accent, would have had an entirely different life. But riding the bus, I couldn't imagine that alternative life; my own was too large and overshadowed it.

At the same time that I felt like two people, I also felt as if I were less than one. I knew my stepfather as well as any daughter knows her father, but I didn't know the man who had made me, who was the reason I was alive, and whose absence had formed a void in me. It's human nature to seek wholeness; our perceptual systems are programmed to see and hear the gestalt when given only pieces, so I imagine our emotional systems are similarly encoded. My family tree research, pen pals, and the silver P.O.W. bracelet I wore were precursors, but this bus trip was the first physical manifestation of that drive in me.

The bus driver downshifted. Turning to look through the windshield of the bus, I spotted the omnipresent mirage a hundred yards ahead on the pavement—the illusion of something there but forever out of reach. I twirled my silver bracelet. On it was etched the name of a stranger, an American soldier named Charles Shelton who had disappeared in Vietnam in 1965, the year my stepfather had entered our lives. I had been attracted to the plight of men missing in action, and the television images—the four children, for example, running across the tarmac into their father's arms after his release from a P.O.W. camp—haunted me.

My affinity, though, lay with the families whose men did not return home, the M.I.A.s. All of my high school friends wore bracelets I'd sold them, and every month I set up a booth at the local mall to distribute literature and sell bracelets to strangers. I'd churned out letters to my representatives, and to Presidents Nixon, Ford, and Carter, demanding an accounting of the missing men. I mailed letters to the editors of the *Indianapolis Star* and *Indianapolis News* calling for action and wrote to television celebrities begging them to mention the M.I.A.s in public because, for reasons unknown to me then, the missing men, fatherless children, and wives in limbo touched me at my core.

It's clear to me now that I was pouring energy into locating missing fathers because I had lost two of my own. Wearing the bracelet, demanding that the government search for our missing soldiers, was the symbol—and my rehearsal—for finding my first father again. When my letters to the editor were published, when my voice was heard, I felt a touch of power. I felt, too, the first aches of my own longing for reunion.

Deeper into Kentucky, the bus passed tobacco plants undulating like a green sea, islands of cranberry red barns and dull silver silos rising up every few miles and, later, in horse farm country, creosote-painted fences delineating territory as if drawn with a permanent marker. I was hyperaware of these boundaries, of the notion of "mine" and "not mine," of not belonging, of being far from home. I didn't know what I'd say to my father when I arrived, couldn't imagine embracing him or even shaking his hand. I didn't know whether his family had rituals that were strange to me, like bowing heads at the dinner table and saying grace.

My Grandma Rose, my mother's mother, had kept in touch with my father. When I started asking about him, she had been the one to tell me that he lived only one state, and a five-hour bus ride, away. Before I made the trip, Cyrus and I exchanged a few letters and talked briefly on the phone once, each of us waiting for the other to speak, neither of us knowing what to say. What if, when we finally met, I didn't like him or if he didn't like me? I didn't know how his children would treat me, whether they would make room for me, share our father, or fight me for him.

Staring out the windshield at the mirage on the road, I remembered another trip I'd taken in search of the missing. The summer after eighth grade, Mom had picked me up from camp in Massachusetts, and I'd begged her to detour to a tiny Presbyterian Church cemetery in Plymouth, Connecticut.

Grandma Rose had spurred this side-trip, too. "I heard somewhere that we might be descended from a Mayflower passenger," she had mentioned the previous fall. "On my mother's side." This had hooked me, and I was sucked into the world of genealogy detective work. I found the family trees my grandfather had sent me earlier and set out to fill in the empty branches at their crowns.

Over the years that I researched my family history, I would come across no one else my age doing something similar. Most of the genealogists I corresponded with were retired or worked as records clerks in small-town government offices. While it pleased my grandmother to see me so interested in our family's roots, I sensed there was something deeper than my need to please, deeper than a hobbyist's interest, that was compelling me, inciting my curiosity, feeding my yearning to know where I came from.

About the size of a house trailer, the Plymouth, Connecticut, cemetery was enclosed by a waist-high wrought-iron fence sprouting lethal-looking spear points. I plodded carefully over the uneven ground. With each step, the prickly grass found its way past my sandals' soles, poking the tender skin of my arches. There was no breeze, no shade.

"They all died so young." My mother was scanning the carved headstones one row over. Most were small, flat markers rounded at the top and decorated with winged cherubs, urns, and willows. But some rows held towering obelisks or larger monuments surrounded by their own iron fences.

"Look at this," Mom said, pausing to read headstones. "There's a group of children over here. That's so sad." She wiped perspiration from her forehead with the back of her hand and continued to stroll down her row. "What are we looking for again?" She carried my bulging manila envelope for me. I carried a sheaf of blank paper and a black crayon.

"Anyone with the last name Cook," I said. "I need birthdates so I can get birth certificates. Then I can tell who their parents were, and that'll give me another generation to add to our tree." I knelt down to study a lichen-covered marker. "I'm really close to finding the link to the Mayflower guy, Francis Cooke. Just one more generation. Wouldn't it be neat to belong to the Society of Mayflower Descendants?"

My mother shrugged. "I guess so."

"Most of these people," she continued, "the adults at least, were born in England and died here. Didn't Grandma's parents come from Holland?"

"Her father's side did," I answered. "But her mother's mother is the one who might be related to the Mayflower passenger." I enjoyed our reversed roles, my teaching *her* something. "Your dad's ancestors came from Bath, England. Isn't it amazing that they left their families and their country to come here?" I was titillated, intrigued by whatever it was that would cause a pull that strong, a pull to uproot, travel so far away, and start over.

"Here they are!" I shouted. A trio of crows lifted off from the top of a willow tree behind the church, squawking as they swooped away. "It looks like four Cooks are buried right here." I knelt at the first marker. "This is so cool; it's the Lamarcus guy I was looking for. And his parents are here, too!" I felt a quiver of excitement in my gut. "This is just what I was looking for." I placed a clean sheet of paper over the stone and rubbed furiously with my black crayon, creating an odd piece of graveyard art.

"If you say so," Mom said, laughing. "I can't keep it all straight." She leaned over and picked a sticky burr off her sock.

The bus pulled into the tiny depot in Burlsville, Kentucky, and I peeked out the tinted window searching for the family in the photo I'd tucked between the pages of my novel. The ride had lulled me to the point of sleepiness, but as I stood in the aisle waiting for the door to open, my heart flopped around inside my chest as if loosened from its moorings.

I stepped down from the air-conditioned bus and squinted through a white-hot glare, my forearms tingling under the sun's rays. Across the street, in the shade of maple trees, a man climbed out of a sand-colored VW camper van, its luster long gone. He approached, a tiny bounce in his walk, and stood in front of me. I recognized him from the photograph but did not remember him.

"Hey there," my father said.

His right hand, stuck in his pocket, jiggled change like my grandpa's did. His shoulder-length sable hair was graying at the temples, and a side part accentuated his receding hairline. His nose, large for his face, mirrored mine. He was lanky and fair-skinned, like me, and before I dropped my gaze to my feet I noticed a shaving cut on his chin.

I'd hoped to feel a jolt of recognition, an immediate connection to him, the sense that I knew him, had always known him. I had fantasized about our reunion, our own made-for-television movie: We embrace then pull back to stare meaningfully into each other's faces, he gingerly touching my face and whispering something like, "Never again will you be lost to me." And with tears streaming down my youthful face, I would say, "Daddy, I missed you." But it didn't happen that way. After eight years apart, we were strangers. I could have been meeting a host family from an exchange program in another country. I couldn't speak their language, and I knew already that I would embarrass myself by committing social and cultural blunders.

When I looked up again, he smiled. I realize only now that he must have been as anxious as I was. He had the burden of being the thoughtful and cautious adult, needing to be gentle with me, not moving too fast, not scaring me away. It's difficult to imagine, though, what it feels like to see your child again after an eight-year separation. I think of birth mothers reuniting with their young adult children and parents whose kidnapped children show up years later, completely different people from when last seen.

"Hi," I said softly, giving him a quick, waist-high wave, and then, uneasy with the intimacy, turned my gaze to the van across the street.

When he leaned over to pick up the green paisley suitcase I had decorated with fluorescent daisy stickers, I detected something both familiar and strange about his scent. It was unlike my stepfather's Certs-cigarettes-Old Spice scent, but not entirely alien. It grazed a place in my memory long dormant.

Cyrus's wife, Ursula, sat in the passenger seat of the van with her arm flat on the window ledge, a lit cigarette between her first two fingers. She squinted at a trail of smoke curling around her face. "Hey, Kathy," she said, smiling. I waved.

Cyrus slid open the side door, revealing my three young half-siblings seated on a side-facing bench. I climbed in, and during the five-minute ride back to their house, Sarah, Cody, and Melissa gaped at me, their instant big sister. No one spoke. Cyrus stole glances in the rearview mirror as he drove just under the speed limit, turning the wheel with great deliberation. Although my insides were roiling—I wanted, *needed*, them to like me—I worked hard at looking collected, as if this were something a sixteen-year-old did every day, visiting blood strangers.

Inside the house I hadn't seen in eight years, the only thing I recognized was the toy bear on wheels parked in a corner of the living room. I knew its stiff, bristle-like fur and musty odor even before I reached it.

"Mike and I used to ride this bear," I said, running my hand across its back. The fur had worn away in spots, leaving smooth patches of leather skin. The bear had been mine first. With a surge of envy, I wanted it to be mine again. I was sure he would pass on the bear to one of my half-siblings and not to me, and, like the time I received the photograph of my baby half-sister, Sarah, I felt as if I had been displaced. I recognized the familiar tug toward self-pity, the sadness of being dropped from number-one daughter to faraway, possibly forgotten daughter. It was a revival of the old haunting curse of abandonment that I was attached to then. It had become the Story of My Life.

The bear was a toy that I had been made to share with my half-siblings, just as I had been made to share our father with them. Actually, I hadn't shared it and him but had given up both the bear and my father completely. Before I even touched it, I remembered the feel of the bear's back, the way brushing its hair one way felt smooth, while brushing it the other way, against its natural nap, felt wrong.

Ursula had grown up in Tennessee, and her voice pealed with the melody and timbre of the Blue Ridge Mountains. Ten years younger than her forty-three-year-old husband, she still painted watercolors at an easel at the bay window in the dining room, walked barefoot, and laughed unabashedly with her gravelly smoker's voice. Now her children's artwork covered the refrigerator, and her own fruit bowl still life hung in a homemade wooden frame on the wall above the kitchen hutch.

I wanted to major in education when I went to college the following year, and I listened carefully to her stories about teaching in a one-room schoolhouse in Tennessee before she married.

"You don't learn how to be a good teacher in college," she said, drawing deeply on a cigarette. "You just need to take the kids outside and let them run around and ask questions."

"You didn't get in trouble for not making them sit in their seats and learn the multiplication tables?"

"God no! My boss knew I did things my way. Some of the parents complained, but I don't care what people think about me. That's never stopped me." Her kinky curls shook as she tipped her head back in laughter.

While she sometimes shocked me with her cavalier words, I was in awe of her. I wanted to teach in a one-room schoolhouse, too, paint landscapes with watercolors, and not care what people thought of me. Unrestrained by convention, she was so unlike my mother, so unlike me. The difference was intoxicating.

Raised in Missouri, Cyrus Manfred spoke with only a trace of the accent his second wife and three Kentucky-born children possessed. In the letters he'd written to me after we'd reconnected—always scribbled on motel stationery collected on past vacations—he used dashes instead of commas and periods, and his thoughts bounced around in a free-for-all on the page. He signed his letters "Love—Cyrus."

Unsure what to call him in person, I waited until he was in earshot before speaking. I considered addressing him as Cyrus, but that seemed wrong; I was too young to call him by his first name. But there was no way I could call him Dad. That name was reserved for the man who had taken his place.

"By golly, we're all here," he said as we found places at the table for dinner. I soon learned that my father, who taught music at the university in an adjacent town, exaggerated his goofiness, saying things like "Golly" and "Hecky, gosh, darn." He loved inventing puns, and he often fell into the Southern helping-verb habit, saying things like, "We do enjoy seeing you all" and "I can see that you are tired." He also tended to eschew contractions. "I will be quiet now so you all can visit a mite bit." When he concentrated, he placed his palms together in a gesture that resembled praying and then brought his fingertips to his lips.

He didn't sit at the table for long but soon jumped up and strode around the room, hanging on every word, raising his eyebrows and laughing without sound while covering his mouth with a hand to contain his exuberance.

A popular babysitter at home, I was more comfortable around my half-siblings than my father and Ursula. The three of them followed me wherever I went, Melissa waiting outside the bathroom until I reappeared each time. At four, the age I had been when I lost our father, Melissa had gained another big sister in whose lap she could sit and into whose face she could stare with the pure love of that age. Sarah and I danced to Jackson Five songs in her room, and we all swung on the swing set in the backyard, the four of us squeezing into the bench swing made for two, and I quizzed them about their schools, their friends, and their lives without me.

Many years later, when I asked Ursula what she remembered about my first visit, she told me that I'd laughed a lot. Giggled, I think she said. This surprised me since I'd remembered mostly solemn, weighty moments from that time. She must have been recalling the nervous laughter that I expelled—still do—the noise that sounds like laughter but is really just edgy energy, beats of staccato exhalations spitting out of me.

During my visit, Cyrus paced, hands in pockets, humming pieces of classical music. Studying him over the next few days, I recognized character traits we shared, like fidgetiness and a tendency to fill quiet spaces with too much talking. And we both waved at people, even when they stood within speaking distance.

But he remained an enigma, floating on our group's periphery, watching and listening. Our attempts at conversations, father and daughter, were bumbling. I questioned whether we'd ever be comfortable with each other and, doubting we would, felt regret settling its weight inside me. I couldn't have articulated the feeling then, but I had been robbed, my father had been stolen from me, and this visit served as a reminder of what I had lost.

Parting at the bus station in Burlsville, I promised I would visit again, would bring Mike the next time, would continue writing letters. I hugged my siblings one by one, then Ursula, and finally Cyrus. "Hope you come back," Cyrus said, "real soon." His tone pulled at a place in my memory I could not locate. As I stepped away from the group, I waved good-bye, looking only at my father. He waved, too, backing up to join his family as I turned and crossed the street.

On the bus ride home, I twirled my P.O.W. bracelet and replayed scenes from my visit, remembering how seven-year-old Cody had appraised me, not quite sure what to make of the appearance of this third sister. I thought about how the kids and I had walked the couple of blocks downtown where murky memories from summers past niggled at my consciousness. On the bus, I scribbled in my diary about the two sisters and brother I had met. "They loved me!" I wrote. "They treated me like they have loved me their entire lives. And I love them the same way."

It had been easy to fall in love with my half-siblings; they were innocent of any blame over the ruptures in my life. My relationships with the adults, though, were complicated by obscured memories of loss, by misconstructions I'd built to protect myself, by mysterious feelings rooted in the past. Although Ursula had been kind, had treated me like the adult I thought I was, I didn't write in my diary about gaining a stepmother. Ursula didn't feel in any way like a mother but more like an adult pal, like the mothers whose children I babysat for. And of Cyrus, who I could see was elated to have me in his house again, I wrote, "He doesn't feel like my father. I don't know him."

It would have been different if I had understood, as I do now that I'm a parent, the depth of his feelings about my visit. Of the ambivalence he must have felt: elation at our reunion and cutting pain at the lost time, the daughter stolen from *him*. Had I known this then, had I this adult perspective, it might have allowed me a quicker connection to him. It might not have taken as long for us to become comfortable in each other's company. Maybe we could have found our way to a different adult relationship, one that felt less like an uncle-and-niece connection and more like a father-and-daughter bond. But I was sixteen, and, like most sixteen-year-olds, my empathy skills were embryonic. I couldn't see too far past my own orbit.

On the trip home, I realized it was the siblings I had gained from this reunion. We could start fresh, unmarked by years of close, rivalrous contact, absent even the normal conflicts within families. This was something I couldn't do with Cyrus. It would take much more to repair our bond.

SEVEN

Fighting Gravity

On a visit to Dad's house in Ft. Wayne during my first year in college, he and I climbed onto his motorcycle and headed to a restaurant for dinner. He'd given me his helmet, and he drove without one, his hair flapping in a deranged dance in front of me while I concentrated on keeping the huge helmet from bumping into his head every time he shifted. Whether he was driving my mother's boxy Chevy Impala, his Alfa Romeo, or this thundering Suzuki motorcycle, he raced over roads as if running from something. I feared he would die a relatively young man in a horrific traffic accident. As we sped around town that night, I was afraid we'd tip over, and on every turn I leaned out, pulling against gravity.

"Lean with me, don't fight it!" he shouted over the roar of the engine.

At first I resisted, but then I tried it and felt the ease with which we turned, the way we were connected to the road, the way the rumble of the engine vibrated my bones. For a moment, he and I were in sync. For once, I was not the scared little girl, afraid of being pulled over by a police officer or tipping over and scraping flesh against pavement. I held onto my father's waist, braced the helmet against his shoulder, and let the speed take us away.

The farms bordering Ball State University in Muncie, Indiana, were lush in summer, but after the leaves dropped, the land turned rough and barren, cornfield stubble accentuating the flatness. In winter, vistas turned gray and white like an old, grainy movie.

I brought my genealogy folder with me when I moved to college in 1975, and when I had time between classes, I visited the dank basement of the main library, searching the *Mayflower Index* for names in our family. During high school, I'd continued to work on my mother's family tree, and each time I uncovered a name that belonged on it, a charge of adrenaline spiked through me. It was like a drug, a rush of something chemical, when I opened my mail and found a copy of an 1856 birth certificate, a hand-lettered baptism record, or a page photocopied from the 1920 census. Discovering a new ancestor to add to our family tree always felt as if I'd won a prize. In the library that winter, hunkered inside a study carrel and sheltered from the Midwest winds, I was making connections on paper, connections linking me to the past, making up for the broken links of the present. I needed to feel as if I belonged somewhere. I needed to feel the deep security of being attached to the earth. I needed to feel the pull of gravity.

Because I wanted to explore my adopted family's tree, too, I interviewed my Grandma Briccetti for a college history paper. Grandma wrote back a long letter answering all of my questions about her Italian immigrant family, and while I enjoyed her stories—her grandparents believed the streets of America would be paved in gold, for example—they did not captivate me like the ones I'd heard about my biological relatives. I had laid claim to my mother's family history; it felt richer and somehow more important to my young woman's consciousness. My mother's mother, Grandma Rose, had told me stories about an ancestor who was sent to prison in Missouri for helping slaves escape, and she shared other tales about my great-great-grandfather, a physician, who had been in Ford's Theatre the night Lincoln was assassinated. In my grandparents' house in New Jersey, I had seen the heavy, ornate sword he had carried in the Civil War. In a peculiar way, I was proud of my ancestors even though our connection was simply an accidental biological link.

In college that first year, I worked my way down several generations in the *Mayflower Index*, hoping to bridge the gap between the Mayflower's Francis Cooke and the great-great-greats at the top of my mother's family tree. I wanted to make the connection so I could please Grandma Rose, so I could impress my family with my research skills, and so I could join the General Society of Mayflower Descendants. That appealed to me then, having that way to describe myself to others, wearing that badge of belonging. At the time, I longed for membership in a club, even if it excluded others based on a random toss of the DNA dice, because I needed to prove my worth, my legitimacy.

I came within one generation, but ultimately could not connect the final link to Francis Cooke of the Mayflower. At the end of my first year in college, I placed the papers back into their folder, slipped it into a trunk with my keepsakes, and moved on to other interests. This folder has come with me every time I have moved to a new home. It now lies in the box that contains the paper trail from my search for my missing grandmother and the photographs of my father Cyrus's birth family.

The summer after my freshman year of college, I returned home to work as a day camp counselor with low-income kids at parks in Indianapolis. My boyfriend, a junior, had returned to his home in New Jersey to work for the summer as well. Before school ended, I'd been nauseated, and then I missed a period in June. At eight o'clock one morning, I told my mother I was headed to the mall with my best friend, Nancy, who instead drove me to a clinic for a pregnancy test. We were home before the mall stores opened, but Mom didn't challenge my lie. All day I pretended to read a novel, and at four o'clock that afternoon, I snuck upstairs.

"That test was positive." A nurse's voice over the phone was gentle but distant.

"What does that mean?" For a second, I hoped positive meant positive outcome—nothing to worry about.

"It means you're pregnant."

Balancing on the edge of my mother's bed, I strangled my index finger with the curly phone cord until it turned purple. I'd paid attention in biology class, knew how babies were made. I must have convinced myself that it wouldn't happen to me because only girls who slept around got pregnant. But I knew better. It had been a year of regular sex with my boyfriend, my first lover: in a dorm room, in a friend's house trailer, on a bunk bed in a frat house. "If you don't want something to happen, just don't think about it" had been my mantra of denial. My mother and I had never spoken about birth control; I didn't know how to get it. At the time, sex was not a topic open for discussion in our family, or in most of my friends' families either.

I asked the clinic nurse for my options, and she responded as if she were reading from a script. "You can relinquish the child for adoption—I have referrals here—or abortion is legal during the first trimester." She paused. "Or you can keep it, of course."

I'd finished a year of college and planned to go back in the fall. I wasn't ready to be a mother. I wanted to finish school, to teach, and I wanted children when I was older, when I could earn enough to support them, when I was mature enough to raise them.

I thanked the nurse, hung up the phone, and stared at the crosshatch pattern on the lampshade until it blurred. I covered my face with my hands but didn't cry. I'd read that abortions made women crazy with regret, that they never really got over them. I hadn't heard yet that relinquishing a baby for adoption did the same, or worse, to birth mothers. I didn't know that birth mothers suffered nightmares, phobias, and depression, or that those who had little choice in the matter had the most unresolved grief. I'd heard that an abortion would emotionally scar me for life, that my grief would be all-consuming, endless. Abortion was something I would never be able to talk about, not even with my husband, it was so shameful a secret. It was an act that, if one believed certain religious doctrines, would damn me to hell and cause me so much guilt I'd wish I were dead.

I had not wanted this pregnancy. I still remember today the acidic fear of becoming pregnant and the tearful relief that came each time I found the monthly stain in my underwear. I wanted the boyfriend. I wanted to be loved. I wanted the status I believed the sexual relationship gave me. But I did not want a baby, not even unconsciously, I can say now with authority. I didn't need to create another being in order to feel worthy or important or to get attention. Rather than a girl who needed a baby to feel whole, I was still the girl who needed her parents in order to feel whole.

There was an embryo inside me, a seahorse-looking organism, not a baby, I reasoned. I knew the difference between zygote, embryo, and fetus—viable human and potential human. I tried to ban from my memory the photographs of late-term fetuses that pro-life militants would push in the faces of women entering abortion clinics. Their cruelty angered me and made me empathize even more with the pregnant women. The protesters had no right to terrorize; they had no right to dictate anyone else's life.

But it was the *potential* of a baby inside me that gave me pause. I could have a son or daughter the following spring. I could be a mother, and this would make me a different person. It would give me membership in a small and special group, give me a certain clout. It would also make me a slut, a teenage mother, a stupid girl. I would shame my family, and I would be mortified to be seen pushing a baby carriage around our neighborhood.

Over the years, I've occasionally calculated how old my son or daughter would be. A few times, I'd run into someone around that age and imagine he or she was mine, the baby I gave away all those years ago. For a moment, I was a birth mother on the lookout for her lost child. But then I returned to a real place and understood that my longing was displaced. I did not spend months imagining my child in utero, nor did I name her, push her out of me, watch her disappear through a doorway. I gave up the *idea* of a child, not an actual baby.

"We could get married," my boyfriend said when I called him. "I guess I love you." He sounded bored. "Or do you want to get an abortion? I'd have to borrow the money." I suspected he'd been through it before.

"What if I go ahead and have the baby, then give it up for adoption?" I asked.

He paused a moment. "I don't like that idea."

I didn't know why he was opposed to adoption. Maybe he'd been adopted. Maybe he was afraid I'd change my mind and at twenty he'd be stuck with a kid. *I should make him marry me,* I thought. It was his mistake, too. I wanted him to suffer with me. But I didn't want to marry someone who didn't love me; I didn't want to do that to myself or my child.

After the call with my boyfriend, I didn't struggle long with the decision. I knew I could never grow a baby inside me and then hand over my child to a stranger. Instead of hurting from the disconnect that an abortion would bring, it was more painful to imagine the disconnect of relinquishing my child. I believe my decision was both selfless and selfish: my child might have struggled with a rootlessness greater than my own, and I would surely have grieved that lost piece of myself. I could imagine missing all of that time, feeling that so much had been lost. I could imagine our bittersweet reunion. And, sitting on my mother's bed with my face in my hands, that is what made the tears form.

I told Mom at dinner that night, and I imagined that her pained expression reflected revulsion and shame. "What do you want to do?" she asked, her voice soft. I told her my plan and she nodded slowly.

"I don't want to tell Dad," I said. I hadn't seen him since my visit to Ft. Wayne eight months earlier, but we'd exchanged a few letters and talked on the phone once in a while. I didn't want him to know what I'd done. I was the one who was ashamed.

The next day my mother sat in a waiting room as a social worker ushered me into a consultation room to sign consent forms. Then, lying on an examination table, my heels digging into stirrups cushioned with oven mitts, I lost myself in the ceiling tiles, connecting the tiny holes into unique constellations. A nurse lightly cupped her hand in my palm, and I flinched when the machine kicked on behind me.

Afterward I rested on a couchette and a nurse handed me a glass of orange juice. "Your mother just asked about you," she said. "She looked worried." When I reentered the waiting room, Mom sprang from the chair. Her face was pallid and strained. "Are you all right?" she whispered. She enfolded me in her arms and pulled me close. Relief, not regret, flooded my body.

I spent my sophomore year tutoring a first-grader, performing in college plays, and writing for the school paper, but it wasn't enough. By junior year, I had a part-time job off-campus and a boyfriend at home in Indianapolis who took me to Fleetwood Mac and Chicago concerts, but it wasn't enough. My discontent grew, and although I didn't know what it was that I wanted, I began to suspect it wasn't in Indiana.

On a benumbing morning in December of my junior year, the air stinging my face and freezing my nostril hairs into sharp pins, I stumbled over mounds of snow from sidewalk to crosswalk. Clumps of ice wedged inside my scuffed Earth Shoes. I swore at the cold, the snow, and the wretched farm town in the middle of nowhere. I hated the evenness, the colorlessness, the tedium. So, instead of heading for my theater class, I detoured past boxy brick buildings toward the one I needed, picked my way up its icy steps, and pushed open its heavy iron doors. I found the counselor who had scheduled my classes each of the three years.

"I'm quitting school," I said, and, just like that, three weeks before Christmas 1977, I was a college dropout.

When I called her later, Mom said, "If you need to do this, I trust you." When I reached Dad in Omaha, where he then lived, he made me list my reasons, quizzed me on my plans, read the customary line of the parent: Are you sure you can't tough it out? I had expected opposite reactions, but my parents had flip-flopped on this, the most important decision I'd ever made. It surprised me, momentarily unbalanced my world.

Ever since Mom had had to cancel a family vacation out West because she'd needed shoulder surgery two summers before, I'd wanted to see the bewitching state with its long coast and persimmon sunsets.

"I'm going to California," I said.

EIGHT

Uprooting

Four days after Christmas at Mom's house in Indianapolis, I heaved my suitcases and framed backpack into the trunk of her Chevy Impala. Cinereous snow lay in half-melted heaps, and a feeble light penetrated the taut canopy of clouds. I kicked a chunk of gritty snow off the car's wheel well and climbed into the back seat. Grandma Rose, visiting from New Jersey for Christmas, settled onto the front seat, and Anne, a friend of Mom's from the orchestra, joined me in the back.

I realize now that Mom had filled the car for a reason. Anne, who wore fat bell-bottom jeans and her hair to her waist, told funny stories on the way to the train station in Chicago, distracting my mother from her mission: dropping me off at a terminal again. Letting me go. On their way back home to Indianapolis, when my seat was empty, Anne and Grandma's presence would comfort Mom.

When we arrived in downtown Chicago, Mom parked across the street from a massive brick building. Through my window I stared up at the foot-high letters above its door. UNION STATION. This was what I wanted, I reminded myself, to be on my own, making decisions, controlling my own life. But as the four of us lifted my luggage out of the trunk and the frigid air hit my lungs, I had trouble breathing.

Inside the station I tipped my head back to gawk at the cathedral dome a football field away. A weak sun pushed its way through vaulted skylights near the ceiling, providing a dull gray glow. A horde of brightly dressed travelers surged around us carrying suitcases, boxes, and odd-shaped packages.

How did I get here? I'd been miserable fifty miles from home; it made no sense to take off for California, the farthest place I could afford to go. Although I didn't recognize the irony then, I was trying to cure a case of loneliness by going off by myself. The crush of people in the station, the humming voices echoing off the high ceiling, and the blur of swirling colors, all of it threatened to suffocate me. There, in the middle of the teeming room, I was totally alone.

A labyrinth of tunnels shot off in four directions. Passengers disappeared into and emerged from the tubes. I sensed urgency everywhere. People knew where they were going. When I found the tunnel that led to the California Zephyr, I glanced at my mother.

"Walk with me?"

"Of course."

Hoisting my backpack, she fell in beside me while Anne and Grandma followed with my goldenrod overnight bag and matching medium-sized suitcase. I lugged the largest suitcase, filled with turtlenecks, corduroy slacks, a plaid wool blanket, and paperback novels. It banged against my leg with each step.

As we rounded the tunnel's final bend, I stopped, causing Grandma and Anne to nearly bump into me. In front of me, a dozen trains, lined up parallel, stood ready to pull out. Steam hissed from beneath the engines and floated upward, hugging the huge machines and turning the tableau a misty black and white.

"I guess this is it," I said, turning to the group, my words rushing to beat the tears. "Bye."

I gave Anne a quick hug, and she whispered into my ear. "Hey, man, I think what you're doing is totally radical."

Grandma Rose gave me a tight squeeze. "Have a safe trip, hon-bun."

Finally, I turned to Mom.

"Call me when you get to Omaha?" she said, embracing me. We parted and I reached for the bulging backpack. She held on to it a moment longer, then finally surrendered it.

I lifted the backpack onto my shoulders and, balancing two hard suitcases, an overnight bag, and a shoulder purse, made my way to the train alone, swaying under the weight. When I reached the step stool next to the door of the last car, I pivoted. Through the steam churned out by the engines, I could just distinguish three figures, their hands held high, waving like grasses in a soft wind. The image was blurry, the soft focus of a movie camera. I set my cases on the platform and jerked an arm up in a last wave that caused their movements to quicken in response. I handed my suitcases up to the steward and climbed the steps.

After the train cleared the station, its screechy acceleration pulled me back into the seat, and I stared out the window at the backs of sooty wood shacks and frozen clothes pulling on disorderly lines. I felt a dizzy euphoria. In eight hours, I'd stop off in Omaha to visit my father, but then what would I do in California? I didn't know if I was leaving home for good, or if I would return in a couple of months when my money ran out. I both worshipped and feared the freedom.

The train picked up speed, obscuring the near view and throwing distant images into relief. Gazing at frosted fields, I fingered the locket around my neck. When she was sixteen, Grandma Rose had traveled by train from the plains of Alberta to Oberlin College in Ohio, and the locket, shaped like a coat of arms, had been a gift from her mother. When I'd turned sixteen, Grandma Rose had given it to me. Unclasping it on the train, I peeked at the tiny photos of my grandparents from their college yearbook. My grandmother had made a journey like this. Away from home. Toward her future. If she could do it, I told myself, so could I.

Looking back, the train trip at twenty was a bold act of separation from my family. Like my grandmother's, it was a journey to establish my adult life, to find my place in the world. But all I knew then was that with each clacking mile, I was traveling farther west than I'd ever been. Galesburg, Burlington, Ottumwa, Omaha. I recorded each stop in my journal, feeling lighter at each station. I didn't understand the significance of the trip then, how it represented my last journey as a child, or how this separation was the first in my life made on my own terms. I knew only that I needed to get away from the ashy snow, the tests and grades, and my scattered family.

I wanted to see the California of the movies. I wanted the palm trees of my Florida youth. I wanted to smell the Pacific Ocean, walk barefoot on the beach, feel the sun on my shoulders and let it burn the tops of my feet. In a hurry to grow up, I wanted to start my life *then*. I wanted to become a fashion model, volunteer as a Big Sister, and learn to scuba dive. I hoped that I would find my future husband in California, that I would have my babies there. But first, like we said then, I needed to find myself. And I prayed she was waiting for me in sunny California.

On the last day of 1977, I celebrated New Year's Eve at a ritzy restaurant in Omaha with Dad and his current girlfriend. I disliked Jennie immediately, judged her by her dyed auburn hair, pancake makeup, and high-pitched voice sloshy from several scotches. Chasing away any silence, she chattered about their last motorcycle trip to a vacation cabin in southern Missouri. Earlier, Dad had shown me the helmets with two-way radios they used while riding side by side on the highway, and I had felt a covetous sting from the intimacy they implied.

He and I were trying to renegotiate our relationship. In some ways I felt grown up, almost a peer, but inside I was still his little girl. I hated this woman butting into my time with him, especially since she was hanging on his arm as if she'd drown if she let go.

I didn't want to have to share him for New Year's Eve. *He's my father and I've known him a lot longer than you have,* I wanted to scream.

"Happy New Year!" Jennie proclaimed at dinner, clinking her champagne glass onto my father's. "Seventy-eight will be great!" She laughed at her rhyming prediction as if it had been profound, and my father beamed at her. I decided she was stupid. Across the cloth-covered table from me, they held hands while Jennie stared, as if seeing me for the first time, as if trying to get me in focus.

"Why do you call him 'Dad'?" she finally asked.

Her question jolted me. Did she think twenty-year-olds were too old to call their fathers Dad? Or did she assume that because I was his stepdaughter I called him Tom? I wanted to shout at her but instead gave her a patronizing scowl.

"Because he's my father," I said.

"Oh," she said and, finally, shut up.

Another night Dad took me out to dinner alone, and he and I talked about our family coming together and breaking apart. "When I met you kids," he said as we picked at our desserts, "I was blown away. I fell in love with you and Mike instantly." He stared hard, checking to make sure he had my complete attention. "I loved your mother, of course, but I knew I had to have you kids in my life."

I was speechless, dumb with surprise. Over the years, he had often told me he loved me, and he was still generous with physical affection, but this news stunned me. I hadn't known I meant that much to him; I'd always felt as if I'd come along with the package. Seeing my tears, he scooted around on the booth's seat and wrapped his arm around me, pulling me to his side. I lay my head on his shoulder and, embarrassed, brushed tears away. Then, self-conscious, I checked to see if anyone in the restaurant had witnessed what I saw as a pathetic public display of emotion. I couldn't yet see the moment as one in which I'd finally revealed my vulnerability, unmasked my true feelings, my love for him. Instead, that night, I had something to prove. I quickly straightened and scooted away. I didn't want him to think I needed him. I couldn't give him that satisfaction.

On the Omaha Amtrak platform, three days after I'd arrived and a little after one in the morning, Dad and I paced while we waited for the California Zephyr, stomping our feet to keep warm. It was middle-of-the-night-Midwest-winter cold, and I did not have a proper coat, just a lined raincoat I'd bought for the mild California climate. A minute before my train was due, he stopped pacing, turned toward me, and grasped my elbow.

"I know I wasn't always the best father," he said.

I stared at him. I'd never heard him acknowledge a mistake or weakness, and when I realized that he was perhaps afraid of losing me, I felt a rush of power. Could it be that he needed me more than I needed him?

"That's true," I said, smiling. "You haven't been." I'd never been this brazen with him. There was so much I could have said. *Why did you leave us?* But the train's headlight appeared from the east. "Thanks for saying that," I said, and then pointed into the dark. "It's almost here."

I hugged him hastily, boarded the train, and waved good-bye through the window. He stayed on the platform until I couldn't see him any more.

Thirty-six hours later, the train scaled the summit of the Sierra Nevada mountains, and as we neared Truckee, the snow's depth thrilled me. It reached rooftops and pulled at branches of giant evergreens, tugging their weighty arms toward the earth. Gradually, farther down the mountain, the ground morphed from blinding white to the deep ochre of wet dirt, then to gleaming grassy hills and, finally, to the long verdant valley.

I arrived in San Francisco that January during a record-breaking rainy season. I got a job at a stationery store downtown, and on weekends read paperback bestsellers on my studio's sofa bed while the rain slashed at the window. On a cassette player with foam rubber headphones, I listened to the Eagles, Linda Ronstadt, and Marvin Gaye. Over and over, I played songs like Barbra Streisand's "Evergreen" that pulled me back to a longing for where I'd been and what I'd left. I wrote to my friends back at college, to my boyfriend, to Cyrus and Ursula and the kids in Kentucky, to my pen pals, and to Grandma Rose. When I read their letters, I sat at my tiny kitchen table wondering why the hell I'd left, if I'd made a mistake, if I should just go back home. But while Indiana still felt like my home state, I didn't feel connected to a house there. I had a bedroom in my mother's new house but felt no pull to return to it. The stronger yearning was to make a new home. Every few days, I telephoned Mom collect from a leaky phone booth across the street and returned to my apartment to wait for the next day to begin.

She visited that spring and rented us a car so we could stroll through Muir Woods with umbrellas and window-shop and walk the beaches in Carmel and Monterey. When it was time for her to return home, we walked from my apartment to the bus that would take her to the airport. Inside the shelter, we waited in silence. When the bus appeared, she turned to embrace me, and we held each other tightly. "You're the light of my life," she said, choking up.

I couldn't speak. As we pulled apart and she turned to climb the steps of the bus, I stood just outside the shelter in the drizzle, my tears streaming as fast as the rain. I no longer felt like a brave soldier but a lost soul.

By summer the rain had stopped, the ocean turned from gray to blue, and I moved into an apartment in the Haight-Ashbury District, celebrating my twenty-first birthday at a discotheque with new friends. On weekends I slogged up and raced down the city's asphalt hills on my used ten-speed bicycle, pedaling across the brick-colored Golden Gate Bridge to Sausalito, whizzing past houseboats and harbor seals, wheeling my bike onto the ferry to cross the bay and get back home. San Francisco was alive, and she wrapped me in her foggy embrace.

But there was also a darker side to this place. In November, Jim Jones, an Indiana transplant, forced a mass suicide of his Bay Area followers at Jonestown, in Guyana. Two weeks later, at San Francisco City Hall, Dan White shot and killed Mayor George Moscone and Supervisor Harvey Milk. I questioned why I'd come to California and what had drawn me to a place so different from the Midwest.

Like many young adults, I may have been searching for my roots in an idealized place. I had chosen this spot for its particular mystique and had bought the myth of the easy California life. I'd expected the floury beaches of Florida; I didn't know that the coast of northern California was often foggy, the sand buff-colored and coarse, the water icy. While sunsets burned the sky over the water in the fall, most beach walks required a sweatshirt year round. The first palm tree I'd spotted from the train had symbolized the state; silhouetted palms always stood in the foreground of California sunset postcards. But I would soon discover that it was the southern part of the state that looked like the Florida I had known as a child. Northern California had more evergreens than palms. Even the stereotype of young, blond surfers with tanned chests was shattered. Northern California surfers wore full wetsuits so they wouldn't die of hypothermia while waiting for waves. They also weren't all blond, of course, and at least half of them were old enough to be my father.

Despite this inauspicious beginning, I believed that in California I would find my true home. A temperate place, a place far away from the family I both needed and didn't need, the place where I would give birth, where I would put down roots. The place where I could finally stop fighting gravity.

NINE

Daddy's Girl

Eight years later, in the summer of 1986, I arrived at Stazione Roma, where my stepfather and his new girlfriend, a twenty-two-year-old American clarinet player, were waiting for me. After his brief marriage to Jennie, Dad had moved to Italy. He and Stephanie had lived together in Perugia for about a year, but he hadn't mentioned her until I told him I was coming to visit.

Stephanie's jeans slunk below her jutting hips, and her long, streaked hair hung in two clumps that swung like pendulums as she and Dad walked toward me, their arms around each other's waists. He'd just turned fifty, and I'd snickered years before when he'd bought a blow-dryer and begun primping in front of the mirror. Now he wore jeans, loafers, and a brown leather jacket. Stephanie was seven years younger than I, could have been his daughter, should not have been his lover, I thought, and as they approached, and she hooked a finger through one of his belt loops, I wanted to push her onto the rails.

"Hello, my Kithi," he said when we met up. The lines in his face had deepened since I'd seen him last, and the flesh under his cheekbones sagged, giving him gaunt jowls. He seemed shorter. "Hi, Dad," I whispered, leaning over to embrace him. I no longer called him Ditti, even when he slipped back into calling me Kithi. It felt too intimate when I was struggling with our relationship, struggling with how much distance there was and how much closeness I wanted.

We spent the day in Rome sightseeing and stopping at sidewalk cafés for pasta and gelato and then boarded a train for Perugia. As Stephanie dozed with her head on Dad's shoulder, I stared out the window at passing vineyards, terraced olive groves, and ancient, fairy-tale, hilltop towns, remembering the last time I'd seen him.

It had been two years earlier, during a stopover in San Francisco, and we had met at the St. Francis Hotel for a drink. Living on my own, and still hungry for his approval, I couldn't wait to show him my new adult life. I had moved to Fremont, a town on the southeast side of San Francisco Bay, and was working as a residence counselor at the California School for the Deaf. I'd become fluent in sign language, I had begun a master's program in school psychology, I had my own credit card. I lived with my boyfriend Peter in his condo, and I was playing stepmother to his five-year-old daughter for part of each week. The three of us had come to feel like a family, and Peter and I had talked about marrying. I wanted my father to recognize all of this. I wanted him to know who I was.

When we settled into the bar at the St. Francis, I, still hopelessly naïve, wanted him to say, "Look at you! Taking care of yourself, working, going to school, mothering. You were brave to come out here by yourself; I'm proud of you."

But instead he talked about his conducting gigs in Europe, his writing an opera, his recording with the Oslo Symphony. Then, when I ordered my favorite drink, a coffee amaretto, he chuckled and smiled at the cocktail waitress as if they had a private joke and I was the out-of-town country hick.

"A coffee amaretto? Before dinner? Don't you want a real drink?"

I locked eyes with the waitress. "A coffee amaretto, please."

When he didn't sputter an objection, or order for me, I let my shoulders drop and met his gaze. I prepared for a disapproving shrug, or a jabbing comment, but instead he was quiet, the power hissing out of him like a deflating balloon. I remembered a Christmas when I was a child and I'd given him a shirt I'd picked out by myself. I'd chosen a large shirt, and when he opened it and held it up next to him, we both knew it was too big. It was then that I realized for the first time that he was a medium-sized man, not the giant I'd thought he was.

During my visit to Perugia, two years after that coffee amaretto, Stephanie called him Tom, and I felt like a little girl calling him Dad. I had never called him or my mother by their first names, and to others I had always called him "my father" or "Dad." Even though he missed my driving test, my high school graduation, my move to college, I had always thought of him as my father. I just didn't know what to call him anymore.

My struggle went deeper than a need to sound adult and to be taken seriously, though. Grappling with how to address Cyrus and Tom, I was also trying to figure out which one was my father. Whether I had one father or two. What if you have two fathers but feel as if you have none?

Or, if you never knew your father, never met him at all, can you grieve something you never lost? I think of my own children and their absent father, the sperm donor. Our experiences, while overlapping in some ways, have been entirely different. They have no memories, fuzzy or clear, of their biological father. They did not know and then lose him. They have not had two fathers present and absent in a variety of ways over their lives; they have always been fatherless.

Although I don't remember it, I must have grieved the loss of my Daddy when I was a little girl. I must have missed the man who had walked me around the Indiana University campus in my stroller while humming classical music and pushed me on a swing at the park. As a teenager, I assumed the persona of a fatherless girl—a girl who had been abandoned by not one but two fathers. Later, when I was a little older, I convinced myself that I didn't need a father, thank you anyway, and I pushed them both away.

I sometimes question what children need a father for. It can't be just for wrestling on the floor until someone gets a rug burn, or for tickling until somebody throws up, or for watching *Star Wars* movies until everyone's eyes glaze over. Of course, I know it's more than stereotypically male activities that children need. They need someone of either gender to feed them, acknowledge them, celebrate them. They need guides to lead them through early life, model human behavior. Parenting literature tells us that children usually model their behavior on the parent of the same sex. But I believe others can stand in for a father—mothers, uncles, teachers and coaches—and provide the mirror into which children can watch themselves grow. I may sound defensive when I try to rationalize all of this, and maybe that's what I need to do to reconcile my decision to have made my children in the manner I did. But boys (and girls) have grown up without fathers since accidents and wars first took them away. Children raised by single mothers, widows, and grandmothers not only survive but flourish. The literature now says so, and, if you look closely, you will find these fatherless children all around you.

TEN

Origins

People who hear my Italian surname before they meet me are often surprised at the blue-eyed, five-foot-ten blonde with size eleven shoes in front of them.

"What nationality are you?" a professor once asked me in college. "You sure don't look Italian." She paused. "Are you Swiss, or German?"

Sometimes, when I couldn't rally the energy to talk about the three generations of adoptions and the tangled roots of my family tree, I have lied. *Yes, right, from northern Italy.* I feel both a perverse pleasure and a wave of shame at my deceit. For a long time, I felt there was something wrong with me for not looking Italian. I took the blame for not meeting people's expectations.

But that time, I told my professor the truth. "No, I was adopted by my stepfather and changed my name."

"What was your original name?" she asked, still trying to stick a label on my physical features, so I made sense, so I had a beginning, a place from which I originated. I'd questioned this, too. I'm fair, with ashy smudges under my eyes inherited from my mother and grandmother. On the news one night, I watched an interview with a refugee from Yugoslavia. Studying her narrow, pale face and long, sharp nose was like looking into a mirror.

"What's 'Manfred'?" my professor asked when I told her Cyrus's surname, the name I was given at birth. "Is it German?"

I paused for a few seconds. "I have no idea," I said, not yet aware how her questions were kindling my curiosity again, reigniting the desire to fill in the missing half of my family tree. "I never asked him."

A few months after my trip to Italy, just before Christmas 1986, I traveled to Cyrus's house again. A sprig of mistletoe hung from the large doorway, and the mantel was decorated with fragrant pine boughs and red ribbon. One evening, I approached the furry bear on wheels that my brother, Mike, and I used to ride. I ran my hand over it. I found the cord hidden under its belly but didn't pull it, didn't want to trigger the feral howl in the quiet house. Instead, I stood back and imagined the antique parked in my living room, my future children playing on it.

I crossed the room, settled into the couch, and opened a novel. The frost had sketched an intricate design on the living room windowpanes, and soon I abandoned my book to scratch at the snowflake art. The old house groaned and ticked as it settled deeper into its foundation.

Over the years, Mike and I had visited our father's house several times together, sharing the driving from Indianapolis a couple of times. Once, we'd taken the younger kids to the Baskin-Robbins in town, where I'd run into a college kid who spotted my P.O.W. bracelet and told me he attended class with Charles Shelton's daughter. When we returned home to Indianapolis from that trip I wrote to Lea Ann Shelton.

Her response had touched me. *Thank you for wearing my father's bracelet*, she wrote. *His plane was shot down on his thirty-third birthday, when I was twelve. I never saw him again*. Her handwriting was large and loopy, and she wrote on stenographers' paper with ragged edges on top. *I loved my father so much*, she said. *And I wish I could have known him better.*

Mike had moved to California a year after I had, and for this visit we had flown together from San Francisco for Sarah's wedding. That December, Sarah was only twenty-two, too young to be getting married, I thought. At twenty-nine, and the eldest of my father's five children, it should have been me walking down the aisle, grasping our father's elbow.

Across the living room, a spindly tree decorated with homemade ornaments tilted a good fifteen degrees to the left. Staring at that dopey, off-center Christmas tree, I noted its scanty branches, the gifts underneath, and, more importantly, the absence of certain gifts. None of the packages wrapped in glittery paper were for Mike or me. And we'd placed none there. Our families didn't exchange gifts. I could not remember receiving gifts from my father, Cyrus, when we had been a family, but he must have given his little girl a doll or a book or a plastic nurse's kit; we had shared three Christmases and birthdays. I don't remember if he sent us birthday cards and gifts after our family broke apart, but I would bet he had.

It's strange to me that I remember branches lacking substance, and the absence of gifts. Even now I focus on trees—eucalyptus, banyan, avocado, magnolia, catalpa, even a coat tree that shed Dad's belongings when he gradually left us—when I describe a place. For me, trees provide a crucial element of setting. They are rooted in place; they provide shelter, sometimes sustenance. They don't get up and walk away.

Cyrus entered the living room and began to pace, his long arms swinging back and forth as if executing a Tai Chi movement. "Don't let me disturb you," he said, pretending to ignore me. He still spoke with only a trace of a Kentucky accent, one he could turn off and on. During my visits I'd heard him affect a Southern drawl when he needed it, calling "How-do!" from his porch swing as neighbors ambled by.

My own accent is flexible, too; it can float on a sluggish Southern current or stiffen up into a Northern ice floe. I can mimic many dialects, but, when at ease, I tend to relax into a smoother way of speaking, rounding the edges of words, omitting consonants, talkin' easy, like someone who doesn't know any better, who never learned how to pronounce words precisely. My voice has been influenced by a hodgepodge of regions. I can slide into a nasal Indiana drawl and then flip over to the sharp sounds of a California professional.

"Can I ask you something?" I said, partly to get him to quit pacing and partly to take advantage of this moment alone with him.

He joined me on the couch, crossed his legs, and swung the top one back and forth. "Shoot."

I faced him. "I'm curious about your family—your parents—their medical history especially." I had been reunited with Grandma Manfred when I found Cyrus, and had again visited her chilly apartment in the senior center, framed photos and knickknacks crowding her small space. I had had a few brief visits with the woman who, despite her pronounced lisp, could talk my ear off, but I'd never met Cyrus's father. No one had ever spoken of him, and I'd always assumed he'd died young. These were my blood kin, I thought then, and I wanted to know about them.

"Every time I fill out a form in a doctor's office," I said, "I check off the diseases from Mom's side. Your side I always leave blank. I don't know much about your parents." I paused. I was curious about how long people lived, what they died of, whether there was a genetic condition I should know about.

"Sure thing." He rose from the couch, left the room, and jogged upstairs. I hoped that Cyrus had stories about our kin to pass on, that finally I could graft his branches of our family tree onto the one I'd drawn, filling in those bare spots that had taunted me for so many years.

He returned carrying a single piece of paper. "You might like to have this," he said, sitting again and unfolding it across his lap. He straightened the page slowly. It was his family tree, only five names sketched out in pencil. Above his name were his parents'. Above his mother's name were her parents' names, but the spaces on top of his father's name were blank. It was the shortest family tree I'd ever seen, a scrawny sketch of a family. Compared with Mom's tree, which reached back to England on her father's side and to Holland on her mother's, this one was pitiful.

"You don't know your father's parents?" I asked, scanning the sheet, trying not to sound derisive. I wanted to tread carefully, too, so he wouldn't cut me off, change the subject, or just turn quiet.

"My father left us when I was just a lad; I believe I was about four," he said, hugging his arms around his chest. "He packed a suitcase one day and just walked out the door. My mother and I went to live with her parents." Cyrus swung his foot in a wide arc. "I believe they raised me up just fine."

Instead of hooting in amazement, I hid my surprise. I didn't want him to close up, so I fought the urge to shriek something inappropriate like, *Holy shit! What is it with men leaving in this family? What a coincidence!*

It could have been more than coincidence, I thought then. It could have been an unconscious repetition, his leaving his children at the same age he had been left by his father. In graduate school, I'd studied family repetitions over generations, learned about patterns of alcoholism, divorce, adoption. I longed to ask Cyrus more, but I didn't know how.

"I can't help you much with the medical history," he said, getting up again to roam. "Because I was adopted. I may have mentioned that to you sometime."

"Adopted?" I shook my head. Again I wanted to shout something improper. *Why the hell am I just learning this?* But I fought that impulse, too. "No, I didn't know that," I said, feeling disappointment creep in. It looked like I'd have a missing branch on my family tree forever. Adoption, with all of its secrets, meant I would be thwarted before I'd even begun.

Cyrus had birth parents, his people, out there somewhere, maybe even half-sisters and -brothers. I might have another set of grandparents and a slew of kin. But I knew about sealed adoption records, inaccessible birth certificates. Back then young women "visited their aunts" out of state for several months and then returned, mysteriously changed. I believed I would never find this lost family through all the red tape and road blocks I was sure to encounter.

"I've been pretty dang healthy, and you kids, too, so I reckon' we come from strong stock. Just wish we *owned* some strong stock," he said. I wondered whether his wisecracks plugged up any holes where pain threatened to escape. I wondered what he felt about any of this. He was up again, bouncing on his feet between the Christmas tree and the wall where his cello case stood.

"I have an adoption paper around here somewhere. If I can put my hands on it, I'll send it to you."

"Thanks, I'd like to see it." I said. "Have you ever tried to find your birth parents?"

"Oh, no." His eyes found mine and locked on them for a moment. With his fingers, he combed a shock of hair back from his face. "No, I never thought of doing that." Swinging his arms again, he danced out of the room.

The next morning, I came downstairs after he had left on his early morning walk and found a note on the breakfast table, his jagged scrawl covering a yellow Post-it stuck on a paper folded in thirds.

Thought you might like to have a look at this, he'd scribbled. I picked an apple from the bowl on the table, took a bite, and unfolded the paper. I scanned the document from the Circuit Court of St. Louis.

"In the matter of Jimmie Earl Foster. November 21, 1933." I laughed, thrilled with the information. His birth mother had named him Jimmie Earl. Drafted on a pica typewriter, foggy letters overlapped in spots and suffered wide gaps in others. I set down the apple and smoothed the paper on the table.

His adoptive mother, my grandmother Hazel Cyrus Manfred,

had attended the hearing, but an attorney had represented his adoptive father, William Manfred. Why didn't his adoptive father go to court? Possibly, since it was during the Depression, he was looking for work; or if he was working, he couldn't afford the day off. Or even more likely, since he would leave them when Cyrus was four, it was something else.

My eyes locked onto another name on the page, and I abandoned my questions about Cyrus's father. "The court further finds that Mavis Foster is the mother of said child and is a single and unmarried woman and that she has given her written consent...for transferring the custody of her said child into the Children's Home Society of Missouri."

Mavis Foster. His birth mother had been named. I'd expected her name to have been blackened out. Adoptions, particularly during that era, were closed and shrouded in secrecy, even from family members. They were shameful burdens for birth mothers and their families since they usually signified unwed pregnancies. Adoptive parents, too, often believed that keeping secrets from adoptees was better than admitting the truth. How had Cyrus gotten this document? Maybe he'd found it in his adoptive mother's boxes when he helped her move, had never told her what he knew. It was beginning to feel as if we were conspiring in something illicit.

Finishing the apple, I perused the page again, slower this time. Mavis. An unusual name; it sounded Southern. And what nationality was Foster?

What a gift this knowledge was. But it was a teaser, too. My Grandmother Mavis, a young woman, a teenager maybe, had handed over her newborn either to a social worker or directly to Hazel and William. She might have been sobbing, holding him close, the baby screaming. Or she might have elected not to see him after his birth, instead signing papers without touching him. I didn't understand how Cyrus could have ignored this all these years. Or why he didn't want to know the woman who had given birth to him. Or why I knew no one as driven toward reunions as I.

With the court document, a private detective would be able to find her. Or, I thought, given my lust for genealogy, I might be able to find her myself. I loved detective work, loved the dusty smell of libraries, the exhilarating potential of records offices. I was a school psychologist now, and I solved mysteries every day. I discovered clues that my testing uncovered and followed them to deduce a child's disability. Earlier, I'd been one of those freaks who *liked* writing research papers in high school and college, knew they taught me more than any of the tests I'd crammed for. For the job of finding Mavis Foster, I was the one.

When he returned from his walk, Cyrus found me on the front porch, slowly rocking the swing forward and back with the toe of one shoe. The morning was nippy, the sun muted, but my wool sweater kept me protected from the chill. He joined me on the swing, pushing off the floor half a beat after I did, causing a lopsided, jarring ride.

"Jimmie Earl?" I said. "That was your name before you were adopted?"

"I reckon so," he said, chuckling and exaggerating his drawl. "A good ol' Southern name. My parents gave me my mother's maiden name, Cyrus, to replace Jimmie Earl."

"Since we have her last name," I said, "I might be able to look your birth mother up. I might be able to find her. It sure would be interesting to know what happened to her."

"I've been pretty content so far. My mother, and my grandparents, did a fine job raising me, I believe."

"You don't want to look for her?"

"Oh, no."

"I might be able to find her," I said again, afraid to ask directly for his permission, afraid he would give me a definitive no.

Cyrus stared quietly at the empty street. "I don't know that I'm ready for that yet," he said, his voice so soft I almost couldn't hear him.

By showing me his adoption record, though, he'd unwittingly handed me a challenge, and it nudged my compulsive nature. I was about to turn thirty, Cyrus was fifty-seven, and I figured that Mavis—if she were still alive—would be at least seventy, perhaps nearing eighty. I wanted to see what she looked like, what she'd done with her life, and what kind of person she was. I wanted to know if I looked like her when she was younger, shared mannerisms of hers. I wanted to know if she waved at people within speaking distance, too. I would visit her in the summers and rock on her porch swing while lightning bugs flickered across the lawn and crickets chirped their evensong. I wanted to be the one who found her.

By reuniting Mavis with her son and introducing her to her five grandchildren, I could bring joy into her life near its end. Perhaps, back in 1930, she had nestled him to her breast after his birth, kissed his silky skin, inhaled his newborn scent. I envisioned her weeping silently on his birthday each year, keeping the secret from her husband, her other children, silently praying to see him again some day. I wondered if at some point she had tried to find her Jimmie Earl.

Or she might have pushed it all away and pretended it had never happened. It would be selfish, this search. If I did find her and she refused to speak with us, Cyrus might be rejected all over again. I didn't want to do that, but a familiar urge propelled me anyway. Despite the risk of opening Pandora's box, I needed to find her. I felt as if I were sixteen and on my way to meet Cyrus again. I began to imagine the next reunion. There was no question. I would search for her.

"Mavis must be healthy because we all are, and that's all we need to know," Cyrus said over the phone a couple of weeks after my visit. It was hard to believe that he didn't want to know more. And, now that he'd had time to contemplate what he'd told me in Kentucky, was he telling me to not look for her? He had saved that court document, the only connection to his birth, all those years. All that time had passed and he hadn't searched for his birth mother. It was beyond my comprehension, this tendency to leave well enough alone.

Outside the back door of my apartment in San Leandro, the scent of imminent rain merged with a hint of jasmine. The sun was fighting its way through inky clouds, and in my wild, winter garden, waist-high weeds threatened to choke the prickly pear cactus, giant poinsettia, and the rosebushes I'd planted. I loved my first garden, my own space. On clear days, looking northwest beneath a tangle of power lines, a sliver of the San Francisco skyline was visible from my yard. Today, though, only shrouded, naked maple trees stood against a conflicted sky.

"I don't want to hurt my mother," Cyrus said, "by looking for this Mavis person."

This Mavis person. I was surprised that this was how he referred to the woman who had given birth to him. *This Cyrus person* was how I could have referred to him before we reunited. He had never known Mavis; his mother was another woman. I didn't remember Cyrus; my father was another man.

I had only recently begun calling him Cyrus. Earlier, unsure how to address him, I practiced saying his name by talking about him with others. "I'll ask Cyrus," I'd say. Finally, I tried it out on him. "Um, Cyrus, would you please pass the salad?" He had answered as if it were perfectly natural for his daughter to call him by his first name, but it still seemed wrong.

"I'm curious whether I've got any half-brothers and half-sisters out there," he said on the phone. "But I'm not planning to look for them."

I struggled to find words, unable to admit my disappointment. I wanted him to give me the unrestrained permission I sought. I wanted him to share my dizzy excitement. But I could not make myself ask him, and I was confused about his mixed messages. Was I supposed to guess what he wanted from his cryptic clues? He might have thought that I wouldn't take it any further, but that was just proof that he no longer knew his tenacious-as-a-barnacle firstborn child, didn't know that once handed a mission, she stuck with it. I would show him what I was capable of, and I believed someday he would come to appreciate my gesture. With my typical optimism, I thought finding Mavis might repair our fractured relationship, might help me feel like his daughter again.

The following week, I hiked with a friend on a path next to the San Francisco Bay. Our dogs ran ahead of us, chasing scents and each other. From the Golden Gate Bridge to the hills in the east, the wind had scrubbed the sky clean. The air crackled, and the ground beneath us was spongy from recent rains.

"I don't know if I should look for her," I said. "What if she has Alzheimer's or some other hereditary disease? That kind of news would be like looking into a crystal ball; no wonder Cyrus doesn't want to know."

Janice pulled a tennis ball from her pocket and threw it for the dogs. "She could be in jail. Or a mental hospital."

"Hey, that's really helpful. Makes me want to run right out and find her."

"You'll never know for sure if you don't try." Janice didn't mess around with ambivalence.

"If I did find her," I said, "it might dredge up painful stuff for her. It's possible she kept Cyrus's birth a secret and never told anyone about him. I could mess up her life." I whistled for the dogs. "But you know the thing that scares me the most?" I waited for Janice's gaze. "That I might kill her with the shock of my telephone call."

"I doubt that," Janice said. "And anyway, she might already be dead."

I took a moment to consider this again. "I don't know if he'd be disappointed or relieved about that."

Ever since he'd shared his reservations with me, I'd wondered what Cyrus had meant about not hurting his adoptive mother. She was ninety-eight, for God's sake, and living in a retirement home a mile from his house. Cyrus visited Grandma Manfred a couple of times a week, sneaking in a beer for her to sip out of a glass while they talked baseball.

I wanted to tell him she didn't have to know if we didn't tell her, but I hated the idea of more secrets. My half-sister, Sarah, had told me recently that she used to flip through our grandmother's photo album when she was a little girl, puzzling over snapshots of two older, towheaded kids. "I questioned who you guys were, but I got the runaround for years," she said. "I don't remember exactly when I found out about you and Mike. I guess when we finally got together."

That missed opportunity made me want even more to break my family's stranglehold of secrecy. I knew my search would not be simple. I would be looking for a grandparent, not a birth parent, trying to dig up fifty-year-old records, following a cold trail. And I'd be going against Cyrus's wishes.

"I feel like I have to search but that I shouldn't," I said to Janice. "It's like a wicked itch that won't go away."

"A burr against your butt, huh?"

"Something like that."

"A bee in your bonnet."

"Yeah," I said. "Got my knickers in a twist."

We laughed, and I continued. "I've told myself that I shouldn't be so driven, and that I should just let it go, but I can't, so I'm stuck. I don't know what to do, go ahead or call it off."

"I think you should just go find her already," Janice said. She waved the tennis ball in front of the dogs and hurled it into the water. I stared off toward the hills, painted with houses and all sorts of trees.

PART II

ELEVEN

Receiving

Inside the vast assembly hall of the Veterans Building in downtown Berkeley, my friend Pam and I negotiated a hundred folding chairs, a regiment of parallel lines forming a grid across the wooden floor like a giant game of musical chairs. The room smelled like boiled vegetables and patchouli oil, and it vibrated with voices engaged in soft conversations. We had come to the psychic fair that Saturday afternoon for a reading, a ten-minute glimpse into our past lives, and it felt like we were shopping at a Kmart of psychics.

"I guess we're supposed to be drawn to someone, huh?" Pam said, raising her eyebrows.

"This is serious now." I shook a finger at her while grinning. It was anything but serious. We were on an adventure.

Pam taught deaf and hard-of-hearing students at Tilden School, where I worked as a school psychologist a couple of days a week. Forty-one and single—it was rumored that she was a lesbian—Pam had loose curls framing her face and round, startled-looking eyes the color of mahogany. She kept an inhaler in the back pocket of her cords, puffing on it regularly to keep the deep, racking coughs of her asthma at bay.

At first I interpreted her quiet nature as snobbishness, but I soon realized I was mistaken. In many ways she was my opposite, a soft-spoken woman of few words, but we shared a deep shyness, mine masked by nervous chattiness. We also shared humor, hers a dry wit, mine more silly and impulsive. At twenty-nine, I was twelve years younger than she. I was also a psychologist, trained in the sciences, appreciative of facts and data, and skeptical about that which cannot be proved. I did not believe in UFOs or ghosts. And I was way too sensible for psychic phenomena.

When Pam and I met at the psychic fair in January 1987, we had been exchanging books for several weeks, discussing them on our lunch break in the teacher's lounge or on a bench on the playground, forming our own private book club. In college, Pam had majored in English and history, and on visits to her cozy Berkeley house, I'd perused the tall bookcases filled with novels and poetry. Not reading great literature now though, instead we were exchanging Shirley MacLaine's reincarnation memoirs, Jane Roberts's *Seth* books on psychic channeling and ESP, and anything we could find about past lives, astral projection, and communicating through dreams, phenomena we'd come to call "woo-woo." We were not gullible, we reminded each other, rolling our eyes to show we hadn't been truly converted. But we were still fascinated, something drawing us both into the past, to the possibility that we had lived before.

I needed a new friend. Peter had been my lover and best friend for five years, but although I'd loved being a stepmom, we'd never figured out how to negotiate the intrusions of his ex-wife and balance our private time with his daughter's schedule. Our conflicts had become angry fights that ate away at our tender feelings. After I moved out, he and I spoke on the phone a few times, but the break had been complete. I had cried for months during evenings alone in my apartment. I would dream about him for years.

At the fair, most of the psychics were engaged, so Pam and I wandered the aisles formed between the lines of chairs facing each other. I hadn't known what to expect, what a room full of psychics would look like, but these were typical Berkeleyites, dressed in anything from bright Indian fabrics to blue jeans and flannel shirts.

We approached a young man with a short haircut, waiting to read for someone. I headed toward him, but before I reached him he leaned back in his chair and yawned loudly. Pam and I exchanged glances and I fought to keep from laughing as we passed him. "That wasn't too inspiring, was it?" I whispered.

I wanted to scope the place out, get a feel for how one might find the right psychic, but just as we passed one psychic and her customer, the customer stood and walked away, leaving her chair vacant. I was eager for my turn, and this psychic felt right. Her two long brown braids beginning to show gray suggested experience, and I sensed a down-to-earth quality that appealed to me. I plopped down in the chair across from her, and Pam continued on to find her own psychic.

I handed the woman five dollars and, not knowing what to say, simply smiled and waited. She tucked the bill into the pocket of her ankle-length denim skirt. "What would you like to know?" she asked.

I hadn't prepared a question. "I'm not sure. The standard beginner's reading, I guess," I said, diffusing tension with laughter. "Is there such a thing?"

The woman smiled and I relaxed. At least she wasn't bored with me. "Sure," she said. She closed her eyes and stilled her body. "I'm just getting ready to receive."

Receive. Like a television being switched on. I studied her face for a moment, even though I feared she'd open her eyes and catch me at it. Tiny lines radiated from around her mouth and eyes, and she looked perfectly at peace. Her eyelids didn't twitch like mine did when I forced myself to relax. Her breathing became slow and deep, like an accordion inhaling and exhaling. I glanced around the room, distracted by the buzzing of voices bouncing off the walls.

"You have deep hurts," she said.

I whipped my head back. Her eyes were still closed.

"But you are resilient. Your soul is old and on a journey toward peace."

What the hell does that mean? I thought, then panicked for a second, praying she couldn't read my mind.

"You have lived many times, and your mission is similar each time. Would you like to hear more? We have time to explore one or two lives now."

She began to tell me about two of my past lives—one in Renaissance Italy, another in an eighteenth-century village in Africa. She said that I was a poetic soul and that I was working very hard in each incarnation. I liked that; it fit how I saw myself. But *what* was I working on, I wanted to know.

I probably wanted a psychic to help me understand not past lives, and not even my future, but the past of my current life: my childhood, my family and all of its divisions. I wanted to know what it all meant and how it would all turn out. *Look what I've gone through,* I wanted to tell someone. *Will I be okay now? Will someone love me and stay with me? Am I worthy?*

"You are grasping for things just out of reach," she said, and I flashed on wanting to have a baby. I was approaching thirty. I'd toyed with the idea of having a child alone, adopting or finding a sperm bank, but it scared me; I didn't know if I could raise a child by myself. The psychic was right. About men and babies, about the missing members of my family, and about knowing what I wanted. It *did* feel as if I were grasping for something just out of reach.

I found myself latching on to those parts of her spiel and immediately discarding the rest. I liked the stories about my striving toward goodness, and I coveted the optimism for my future that I heard in her voice. But the stories, although intriguing, were so universal they could have applied to most anyone, like horoscopes in magazines. I began to feel foolish for spending my time and money on something so frivolous. When Pam and I met up at the exit, we were both somber. "What was yours like?" I asked.

"Interesting," she said. "Kind of silly, though."

"Mine too." And for a change, I had nothing else to say.

I felt like a high school girl around Pam, restless and eager for our next meeting, when we could embrace in greeting and parting. When she brushed my arm in conversation, a warm blush traveled across my skin. Some mornings she left a miniature bouquet of pink Cecil Bruner roses tied with a rubber band on my desk before I got to work. We exchanged Hallmark friendship cards and talked on the phone late at night, drunk with sleepiness and promise. "Good night, sweet friend," she said, and inside my chest something shifted. But even in my journal I was afraid of admitting my feelings. *We're just friends*, I wrote.

Growing up in Indianapolis, I had known only one openly gay person, a florist (yes, a florist) who rented the apartment above our garage, sharing it with his wooly mammoth-like St. Bernard and an occasional boyfriend. I don't remember conversations about homosexuality in our house, but the unspoken message had been that our tenant was a good person, a welcome addition to the social circle. He brought us extra arrangements of flowers from time to time and one year decorated our home with fragrant winter blooms for a Symphony Yule Tour.

In retrospect, it was extraordinary of my parents to have rented to him in the early seventies given that there were "children in the house," given the conservative social surge of the time and place, and that they might have been criticized for it. Being creative, and somewhat fringe, members of society themselves, may have contributed to my parents' acceptance. Some of the musicians they entertained in our home on the northern (i.e., white and middle-class) side of town were from other countries, some were people of color, and, although I wouldn't have known it then, a few undoubtedly were gay.

From media and peers, though, by my late twenties I'd learned that homosexuality was aberrant at minimum, like getting cooties from someone in grade school, and possibly something even more serious, like leprosy, which required shunning. The year before I moved to San Francisco, Anita Bryant had begun her Save Our Children campaign to fight an antidiscrimination ordinance in Florida. I don't remember boycotting orange juice, but I knew she was a bigot and I did enjoy seeing her get a pie in the face on television. When Grandma Rose heard I was moving to San Francisco, she cited a news magazine article referring to the city as the "Sodom of America." I'd had to look up the word "Sodom," and although I didn't understand all of its connotations, I'd taken her words as a grim warning.

When I'd moved to San Francisco almost a decade earlier, the owner of the office supply store where I first worked was an older gay man, and the manager, a lesbian. I hadn't known any lesbians before, and she both intrigued and frightened me. Once, when she reached in front of me to collect extra bills from the cash register, her bare arm brushed against mine and I'd recoiled, stepping back so we wouldn't touch again.

Except for one other straight woman, the sales clerks were all young gay men who wore creased khakis and Izod sports shirts over their muscular chests and biceps. In certain sections of town, gay men walked with their hands in their boyfriends' pockets, an intimacy that had surprised me. When they kissed in public, I was both fascinated and appalled. Some of them flaunted it, in part because people like me were trying to send them back into the closet with our moth-eaten morality, and in part because they were not ashamed—a novel realization for me. San Francisco was a brave new world for me when I had arrived. I wore a beige London Fog raincoat with its belt tightly cinched and rode on the outside of the cable car, my waist-length blonde hair blowing behind me. I was so straight, so naïve. I *was* Mary Ann Singleton of Armistead Maupin's *Tales of the City*.

That February, almost ten years after moving to San Francisco, and a few weeks after the psychic fair, Pam and I met after work for dinner at the 4th Street Bar and Grill, a seafood restaurant near the Berkeley Marina. The young trees outside the restaurant sparkled with white lights wound around their winter-bared branches. Inside, warm scents of spices and colognes intermingled. Seated at one of the tables next to the windows, we smiled at each other as if it were impossible to stop.

"This is nice," she said, her curls shimmering in the candlelight like an aura. I tuned out the people on either side of us as we talked, gradually aware of the flip-flopping, tingling sensations in my stomach and the rushing heat connecting my face, gut, and groin—something I'd felt only with men before.

"Hey, let's send a message in our dreams tonight," I said. "Just one image or one word, want to?" There was an even stronger charge between us tonight, and I was sure we could communicate this way, too.

"I'll send it," she said, her stare boring into my eyes, "and you concentrate on receiving it."

"And tomorrow at work I'll tell you what word or image I get." I met her intense gaze and felt giddy. I was eager to get to bed, to carry out our experiment, so I could be with her in my sleep, too.

When we parted outside the restaurant three hours later, we held our embrace longer and tighter than I had with other female friends. This was different from friendship; I didn't want the evening to end, didn't want to say goodnight to her. But I didn't know what I meant to her, or whether she behaved this way with all her other straight female friends. I even began to question whether she was gay. Lesbians had boyish haircuts, wore clunky boots, and didn't shave their legs. Pam didn't fit the stereotype.

At home, I fantasized about kissing her and tried to imagine what it would be like to make love with a woman, how it would work, how it would feel. But this was not in my Life Plan, and I didn't know how to understand my feelings. Was I enjoying a temporary diversion? Was I experimenting, resisting expectations? Expectations of others as well as those of my own. I had always assumed I would marry a man and have babies. I didn't want a relationship I'd have to keep secret. Time was running short, I was almost thirty, and I needed to find my life's mate. I wanted those babies. This—falling in love with a woman—was not supposed to happen.

At seven o'clock the next morning, Pam's 1970 VW bug buzzed to a stop in front of my San Leandro apartment. She had never dropped in like this, and my apartment was not even on her way to work.

"Did you get my dream message?" she asked when I opened the door and saw her standing there next to the calla lilies. Tiny wings inside my chest fluttered. I'd gone to sleep the night before desperate to receive her words, but it wasn't words that had appeared to me. Instead, I'd dreamed about swimming, finding her underwater and kissing her, the two of us hidden from the rest of the world beneath the mirror-like ceiling above us.

"No, I didn't get it," I said. "I really tried. What did you send?"

She smiled, shook her head slightly. "You try sending me something tonight, okay?" Pacing my tiny kitchen while I sliced tomatoes for my lunch, she said nothing for several moments. "What's happening here, with us, I mean?" she said finally, smiling with her mouth and frowning with her eyes.

"I have no idea."

"I wasn't looking for this—falling in love with you."

My stomach flipped over. "Me neither."

I placed the paring knife in the sink and wiped my hands on a kitchen towel, trying to steady them. As she passed me, I reached out and rested a hand on her shoulder. She spun to face me, and I leaned down to kiss her, shocking myself with my audacity. It was a gentle kiss; we joined tentatively at first, then more passionately, releasing the tension built over the weeks. When I brushed her cheek with my fingers, its softness amazed me.

"Wow!" she whispered after we stepped apart.

I clasped my hands behind my back to keep them from trembling.

"What are we going to do now?"

She shook her head, kissed me softly again, and left for work.

I'm not attracted to women, I wrote to my friend Nancy in Indiana, the friend who in high school had known me as boy-crazy, who had taken me to get the pregnancy test in college. Now that we lived on opposite coasts, we wrote each other occasional letters and telephoned on birthdays and with big news, like her recent pregnancy. *But I'm falling in love with this person,* I wrote. Instead of mailing the letter, though, I hid it in my journal.

For the next few months I was torn. On weekends, Pam and I walked our dogs together on the Berkeley campus, ate dinner in town, and held hands in the dark watching art films at the UC Theater. We sat kissing in one of our cars before parting for the night.

The excitement, novelty, and the temptation to act out, to radically part with what was expected of me, fought with my need to keep things unencumbered and safe. *I just want a normal, happy home life and family,* I wrote in my journal. Normal. But normal was changing. I'd become friends with the gay men at the stationery store, had been called a "fag hag" one night outside a disco by a carload of boys probably from the suburbs. I was no longer afraid of a lesbian brushing against me, but I still couldn't share this with my family and friends. My Indiana friends did not openly disdain gays and lesbians, but we had shared an unacknowledged sense of superiority, even relief, that we were not "that way."

As my friendship with Pam deepened, I wanted to believe, *needed* to believe, that my parents thought life was more interesting, more harmonious, when differences were embraced rather than dodged. But it was one thing to rent an apartment to a gay florist, another to learn your daughter was kissing another woman, was contemplating making love with her.

Even after kissing Pam, I didn't feel gay, and I didn't think being gay happened like this, so immediately. Everything I'd read suggested that people suspected they were gay at least by adolescence, and that was not my experience. I couldn't explain what was happening to me. I also couldn't understand what was wrong with something that felt this good, this right, how it could be wrong to love someone. Eventually, I even began to feel slightly *superior* to heterosexuals, in a free-spirited-nudist-hippie-Esalen kind of way. *Look what I'm experiencing,* I thought. *I bet you aren't as enlightened as I am.* But I was still confused. I had no answers. I didn't feel disgusted or ashamed, only sad that I couldn't share with anyone what was happening to me.

After several weeks' titillation, kissing, and tentative touching, one evening I took Pam's hand and led her to my bedroom. Clothed, we lay next to each other on my bed, and with fingers, lips, and tongues explored skin hidden under shirts and slowly unzipped jeans.

I stopped dating men. Every Friday evening, I loaded my laundry basket and my dog into my Nissan Sentra and drove the ten miles to Pam's house in Berkeley for the weekend. We were in what we called Phase One of our relationship: In love and hot for each other. But when people at work asked about my love life, I shrugged and laughed. Sometimes I invented boyfriends, conjuring up men I'd dated in the past. While I was more in love than I'd ever been and wanted nothing more than to be with Pam seven days a week instead of two, inside I was a mess. I had a huge secret, and I hated keeping it. I asked my mother to call me on Thursday evenings instead of Saturdays, making up something about a ceramics class so I wouldn't have to tell her why I wasn't home on the weekends.

On Sunday evenings, I reluctantly packed up my clean laundry, led my dog to the car, and returned to my apartment. On the days that I worked at her school, we behaved with collegial reserve. Telling the truth could have caused us irreparable harm, we feared. Although it was hard to imagine, I believed my family might disown me, and I'd read about gay teachers being fired, even in the late eighties, even in California. I had many friends and a strong sense of community in my adopted state, but this secret disconnected me from my circle. I began to grind my teeth in my sleep, and I shouldn't have been surprised by the return of the dream that had chased me since college.

In the dream, I can't find my way back to the dormitory after classes. I wander outside, my breath quickening; I can't locate the right building. Then I'm inside a dorm, roaming its halls looking for my room. The building is usually a tower, often the halls are circular, and I trudge around and around looking for a door that looks familiar. I climb the stairs to try another floor, but I never find my room.

TWELVE

Wedding Gown Closet

At my grandparents' house one summer when I was a teenager, Mom pulled her ivory wedding gown from the closet of her childhood bedroom. She placed the oversized white box onto her dressing table and pulled back tissue paper before lifting out the satiny gown. I took it from her and, holding it in front of me, studied my reflection in the floor-length mirror. The dress looked ridiculous with my braids flopping across its bust and dirty sneakers poking out from below its hem, but it looked as if it might fit. Posing in the mirror, I imagined wearing it on my own wedding day. I loved the idea of tradition, a mother's wedding dress becoming her daughter's.

On a fogless morning that May of 1987, Pam and I climbed our favorite trail in Point Lobos State Park near Monterey. Clumps of cotton ball clouds hovered over the horizon, and the sun made the Pacific Ocean glitter. Resting at a lookout, we gazed at the boulders below, covered with guano like a dusting of snow and sprinkled with cormorants and dozing sea lions. The water swirled and waves battered the boulders, sending spray up almost as high as we were. We fed off the warm scent of the Monterey pine trees, the cool, briny breeze, and the baked mulch of the path. Scuba divers emerged dripping seawater from the cove, its surface still and glassy, kelp fields undulating in time to the surf's rhythm.

I'd been scuba diving at Point Lobos with my dive buddies many times and loved hanging suspended in the underwater kelp forests, sandwiched between the surge and sandy bottom. I'd laughed into my regulator as harbor seals shot past in games of tag, their dappled flanks blurred in flight. Underwater I felt weightless, my joints loosening their grips on my bones. I was an astronaut floating untethered. Underwater I was free.

On the ridge, Pam and I found a smooth boulder thirty feet from the trail and negotiated the worn, narrow path through the ice plant leading to it. We wanted a scenic spot for our private commitment ceremony that day, a place where the two of us would exchange vows and rings without witnesses. In 1987, lesbian and gay couples were just beginning to celebrate unions in churches and temples, but it wasn't common practice yet. We couldn't imagine our families celebrating our union, and we didn't want anything marring our joy. We had told no one of our plans.

We wanted privacy when we kissed or held hands on our boulder next to the ocean. I feared hikers' faces wrinkled in disgust as they passed on the trail. Although unlikely here, in the Bay Area I sometimes feared a gang, wool hats covering their faces, following us after a late movie and beating us with baseball bats. *Teach you lezzies a lesson.* Even in peaceful settings like this, images from news stories rose up, frightening me. It was the era of Jesse Helms and Jerry Falwell. The Moral Majority. Representative Barney Frank had just come out publicly. Matthew Shepard's murder was still a decade in the future.

We settled onto the huge granite rock and pulled velveteen pouches from our jeans pockets. With the whoosh of the ocean as background music, I spilled a gold band with black jade inlay onto my palm and then slid it onto the ring finger of Pam's right hand.

We had both decided to wear our ring on a finger other than the typical wedding ring finger. That way we could wear the token of our union and at the same time be able to disguise our relationship when necessary. After scanning the trail for hikers, I leaned over and kissed her.

A tern swept overhead, heading toward the cove. Pam squeezed her ring's mate onto the middle finger of my left hand. I buffed the ring on my jeans and held it above my head, raised to the sun so the gold glimmered.

We kissed again, keeping our eyes open to watch for hikers, and then laughed at what seemed like our game of espionage. We clasped hands and sat facing the ocean, enjoying the pungent breeze, keeping a lookout for whales migrating north. A minute later, voices crashed into our reverie, and the four capped heads of hikers bobbed into view. We loosened our grasp and gently dropped hands.

On the drive home, I reminded Pam of the agreement we'd made earlier. "I'll give up the wedding for you," I said, "but not the babies."

"I know," she said, nodding. "We better get started or people are going to assume I'm their grandmother."

For months, I'd spent weekends with Pam in her little 1920s stucco house, and near the end of the school year, I began bringing my belongings to Berkeley, one Nissan Sentra load at a time. When the school year ended, I moved the rest.

That summer, my mother and I took a trip together visiting lush farms in New Zealand, exploring a few cities in Australia, and scuba diving from a boat on the Great Barrier Reef. Near the beginning of our trip, on a country road on New Zealand's north island, Mom pulled our rental car into the parking lot of a large yellow Tudor, a roadside restaurant where we'd agreed to stop for lunch. Bare ivy vines clung to a trellis and wound along scalloped eaves. On the screened porch, which wrapped around three sides of the house, patio furniture sat stacked for winter, covered with olive-colored tarps.

Pam's airmail envelopes had awaited me at each of the bed-and-breakfast inns, and I could no longer hide my pleasure at reading the love letters inside. I couldn't sneak one into my pocket to read later without Mom noticing, nor could I open them in front of her without blushing and smiling like a fool. I hated the lie implicit in my silence, so I chose to tell her in New Zealand because we were stuck with each other halfway around the world. She couldn't walk out on me. And we'd have three weeks to sort it all out.

The winter July sky was a blue washed canvas, and a cold draft accompanied us into the restaurant. We had just bought heavy wool sweaters in Rotorua, and I kept mine on as we sat down inside the restaurant and ordered soup and bread.

"I have to tell you something," I said as the wind pushed against the window next to our table. My heart rammed my ribs, and I hugged myself, trying to stop my body from shaking. "This is hard, but I need to say it."

Mom's lips pressed together and the lines around her eyes deepened. I turned my gaze to my hands spread open on the table. I didn't look at her; I was afraid to see her mouth freeze in shock.

"I don't know the best way to say this, but Pam isn't just a friend." I paused and took another breath, lining up the flatware on either side of my plate so each piece pointed straight up. "We're sweethearts."

What a silly word I'd chosen. I realized as soon as I uttered it that it was an absurdly outdated word. But I couldn't bring myself to use the word "lover"; that word sounded more sexualized, and I believed I needed to temper this for my mother.

Mom's eyebrows shot up, wrinkling her forehead in a tangle of lines. I read her surprise but wasn't sure what else she was feeling.

"I'm really happy," I said, wiping tears away. I pushed out a cough-like laugh.

She was quiet. I wanted her to say, "I still love you. You'll always be my sweet girl."

My mother cleared her throat. "I don't think we need to tell Grandma about this," she said softly. The air left me so fast it felt as if I'd been socked in the gut. Then, before I could numb it, the pain shot from my chest to my fingers. I fought to keep the feelings off my face. This was what I'd learned from her, one of our family's rules. Feelings were not for sharing, so I wouldn't show my surprise, my disappointment, or my tingling-in-my-heels sadness. I believed I'd disappointed her or worse, since she was too ashamed to tell her mother, the grandmother to whom I was closest.

Mom stared out the window, face pinched. I thought I had heard resignation in her soft and sad voice. Maybe she had already known.

"If you have any questions, you can ask me," I said, trying to free the dam in my throat.

"No." She looked stage-struck, as if staring into bright lights. "No, I don't think I do."

Finally, I risked more. "Do you still love me?" The words had to fight their way past the dam. I laughed aloud at the ridiculousness of my question. Even though she rarely said so, I knew my mother loved me.

Her face registered horror at the implication. "Of course I do." The hurt was unmistakable in her voice, and her eyes filled with tears that didn't spill. How could I have doubted it, was the implication. We finished our lunches in silence, and soon climbed back into the rental car to continue our trip.

I wrote to Pam from Australia. *It was the most difficult conversation I've ever had,* I told her, but the relief I finally felt at not having to hold on to the secret anymore justified the disappointment and pain. Pam had not yet come out to her parents, a conservative, Episcopalian couple married for nearly fifty years. She hadn't yet come out to anyone in her family, even though she had lived with a "roommate" for twelve years, had purchased a cabin in the mountains with her, and had grieved their breakup, telling her parents it had felt like a divorce. But she'd never told them she was a lesbian. And they'd never asked.

Sweet Love, she wrote in her next letter, which I would find waiting in Sydney. *I'm so proud of you.*

For the rest of the trip, Mom and I behaved as if I'd never told her. Although over the next few years she would clip articles about gay marriage from the *New York Times* for me, we never mentioned that conversation again. And even though Grandma Rose stayed with Pam and me in Berkeley one Christmas before she died, I never considered challenging my mother's request. Although I could have asked Mom after some time had passed whether she still felt the same way, it didn't occur to me, so great was my own shame. I still regret that I never told my grandmother that Pam was the love of my life, but maybe, in some way, she knew.

Back home again, I wrote to Dad in Italy, first telling him that, because of budget cuts, I'd been laid off from my job in Oakland and had taken a school psychology job in Modesto, a town in the valley an hour's drive away, in a region more conservative than the Bay Area. I told him of my plans to begin a doctoral program in clinical psychology the following year, and that I'd bought another used car after the one he'd given me five years earlier had lost its clutch on the Altamont Pass on the way home from work. Finally, near the end of the letter, I told him what I needed to. *I've fallen in love with a wonderful woman named Pam. She's the best person I've ever known, and I couldn't be happier.*

I had pulled away from him in the past few years, ignored some of his letters, skipped sending him a birthday card once, and I wouldn't have been surprised if he had made me wait for a reply. But his return letter arrived ten days later, him asking if I would need any help with tuition, and then surprising me first with the news that his sister, my Aunt Joan, had recently come out too, and was living with her female partner in a house they'd bought in St. Louis. Then he responded to my news. *My sweet angel,* he wrote, *the most important thing is that you feel free and happy, and that you know I love you more than ever.*

If there was anything I could count on with Dad, it was that he would always surprise me, that he would say or do what I least expected.

"It gives me hope," I said to Pam after I read his letter. I was still hungry for his approval. "Maybe he and I can be friends now." She put her arms around me and pulled me close, her head nestled against my collarbone. "I hope so, sweets," she said.

"This sure wasn't in my life plan," I said to Pam one night at dinner. I was still unsettled by the way I had strayed off my carefully plotted course. Pam and I were still buying each other monthly anniversary cards, calling each other Sweet Love, spending hours in bed exploring each other's bodies. Falling in love with her had fulfilled me, excited me, but it still confused me.

I read everything I could find in the library about how sexual orientation develops. Most anecdotal evidence was consistent: from a young age, gay men and lesbians had some inkling of being different. For most, falling in love with someone from the same gender did not come as a surprise but felt as if something finally fit.

Not me. As a child, I sat on my bedroom rug orchestrating elaborate weddings for my Barbie doll, staging my own future ceremony, directing the action and dressing her in glimmering gowns and those ubiquitous spiky heels, borrowing my brother's G.I. Joe doll to accompany her down the aisle. If I'd had a couple of Ken dolls, I might have used them to represent my two fathers, with Barbie/me gliding down the aisle of a church lightly grasping, with her plastic opposable thumbs, the elbows of both men. Later, as a teenager, I feared I would offend one of my fathers if I didn't ask him to give me away—an expression I find highly ironic now given how things have played out—so I'd always planned to ask them both.

It was a scenario that for years I believed I might enact later, in real life, until I finally understood I would not have a traditional wedding ceremony. Growing up, I had had crushes on boys in school and infatuations with male rock stars and movie stars. I'd bought teen magazines and covered my bedroom walls with posters of longhaired, smooth-faced boys with sharp jaws and baby blue eyes. I loved Shaun Cassidy from the Partridge Family and Davy Jones of the Monkees.

Even after I moved in with Pam, I still had sexual fantasies about men, had pleasurable memories of sex with men, and when I looked at women, most didn't turn me on. The exception was an occasional butch lesbian with a boy haircut, a female version of the boys and men to whom I'd been attracted.

Years later a friend would ask me, "Do you think sexual abuse makes women lesbians?" I would tell him that I'd once had a theory that girls who went to all-girls' schools or summer camps would turn out to be gay, but that I laughed at that naïveté now. It was much more complex and multifaceted than simple exposure. I would tell him how author Dorothy Allison responded when asked the question about sexual abuse. "Oh, I doubt it," she said. "If it did, there would be so many more."

That fall, I found a support group at the Pacific Center in Berkeley, just south of the university and housed in a restored Victorian painted two shades of purple. If I went to a coming-out group, I believed it would speed up the process and I could begin to acknowledge my "inner lesbian," understand my heretofore denied sexual orientation and finally accept it.

During one of the first meetings at the Pacific Center, I introduced myself and told my story. "I don't feel gay," I said. "I just fell in love with this person."

Several of the women in the group smiled. "We call women like you 'dyklings,'" someone said. Others nodded, as if they'd been there. Dykling. I liked the term; it was clever and irreverent and it might explain what was happening to me: I just hadn't evolved into a full-fledged dyke yet.

Many years later, while writing a psychological report in my office in an elementary school in Oakland, I would receive a phone call from a lover with whom I hadn't spoken in many years. Gene and I had dated briefly after I'd broken up with Peter and before I'd fallen in love with Pam. He was calling from the East Coast, where he'd moved for graduate school; his wife was pregnant with their first child. After a few minutes of catching up, he got to the point. "You broke my heart," he said. I sighed. It had been fifteen years. I wondered if a therapist had suggested he track me down, to sluice this unresolved grief he'd carried so long.

At the time, I knew my thoughts were mean and pompous, but I didn't recognize my hypocrisy. Look in the mirror, I could have told myself. Who are you to judge someone for getting stuck on people in the past?

After I apologized for breaking his heart, he asked me if I'd married and I told him about Pam.

"Did *I* cause that?" he said, and I laughed before I realized he was serious.

"God, no," I said. "There were a few men after you." I gave him the line that was becoming rote: I'd just fallen in love with a person who happened to be a woman.

Over time, I have contemplated my attraction to Pam, the timing of my finding her, my decision to commit to her, raise kids with her. Had Gene been right? Did he or someone else cause what he believed was my "tumble" from heterosexuality? Or was it father loss that doomed my relationships with men? Did I see men as weak because two generations of men in my family had left children behind? Perhaps I had learned not to trust men because of the frailty of my relationships with my fathers, who were so transitory in my life, so unreliable from a child's point of view, that I had generalized this notion to life partners. Or maybe because my mother's two marriages had ended in divorce, I feared following on her path. It may have felt more secure to be with a woman.

Or maybe that's all bunk, and it's just the way my karma was spiraling this go-round; the goddess of love, sex, and parenthood was bored one day and decided to move my player piece to the other side of the game board. Or maybe, at twenty-nine, I needed something different. I needed to try another kind of ice cream because I was just tired of the same old chocolate chip.

I believe that sexual orientation is biologically determined. In ten or twenty years we'll have located the gene or combination of genetic markers that influence sexual attraction. Someone will prove that those heat-seeking pheromones can be hetero-, homo-, and bisexual. That could explain why I've been attracted to men over the years, and even more so as I approach fifty. Midlife hormonal regression to heterosexuality for perpetuation of the species. Or maybe I'm a straight woman who has simply lived for almost twenty years with the person she loved the most. I still sometimes feel as if I've never been a legitimate member of the LGBT Club but that I've been pretending to be someone I'm not, my internal voice chanting *imposter, imposter.*

Now that the club is sometimes broadened to LGBTQ, the Q for "questioning"—and usually referring to youth or those in the process of coming out—I wonder if someone can spend years of their life questioning their orientation.

Maybe someday I'll learn how it is that I spent thirty years on the heterosexual side of the seesaw and then switched sides, without falling on my ass. Or the better image might be me standing in the middle of the seesaw, straddling the center bolt, moving my weight back and forth. While the bisexual character in the movie *Torch Song Trilogy* alternated between genders on a monthly or yearly basis, maybe I'm one who spends decades on each side.

What some call a choice—whether to follow the heterosexual

or homosexual or bisexual path—didn't feel like a choice for me, nor did it feel like I was following biological inclinations. It did seem like a predetermined path, though, a spiritual blueprint. Fate. Karma. Or is what I'm describing simply gender-blind romantic love? I might have said to myself, *Loving Pam, making love with Pam, wanting to live with her for the rest of my life is wrong, must be wrong, because society says it is.* I might have convinced myself that I needed to have that Barbie doll wedding, slip on my mother's wedding dress, dance with both of my fathers at my wedding reception, and open stacks of gift boxes—the size crystal tureens come in—wrapped in silver paper. Because it's what people would expect. But of course I didn't. The pull toward bliss was too great.

THIRTEEN

Seeking

In September 1988, the month I began the doctoral program at the Wright Institute in Berkeley, I came across Cyrus's adoption record in a stack of papers on my desk. On the copy he'd finally sent me, he'd stuck a Post-it on which he'd scribbled, "Do what you wish." I'd ignored it for over a year, but finding it again roused the familiar longing to know where my other grandmother was. I had convinced myself that although he didn't realize it yet, Cyrus wanted to know what had become of her, too. And I believed Mavis Foster was waiting for me to find her.

I typed a letter on the computer I'd bought for graduate school and printed enough copies to send to every Foster in the St. Louis and East St. Louis phone book, hoping that Mavis had stayed near the adoption agency after relinquishing my father. *I'm researching my family tree*, I wrote, not telling the whole truth but not exactly lying either, *and I'm trying to contact Mavis Foster, born around 1910.*

Next I wrote to the Children's Home Society in St. Louis. *For medical and genealogical reasons*, I wrote, *I'm requesting information about my paternal grandmother. I'm hoping you might have records you can share with me.* I signed the letter, *Kathy Manfred Briccetti,* slipping in the surname I had given up twenty years earlier, when Tom Briccetti had adopted me.

Half of the return postcards I'd enclosed in the dozen Foster letters arrived in my box within days of each other. Flipping each one over, I scanned the handwritten responses, hoping for "Yes, that's me!" or "We're related!" But no one had heard of Mavis Foster. *Not our people*, someone had written. *No kin to us. Good luck with your search*, another said.

Years later, I would watch a documentary about public schools in East St. Louis and realize that most of the town's residents were African American. I can laugh at my ignorance now, but I felt a flash of embarrassment when I realized that I'd written to black families in search of my roots. What must they have thought, hearing from a woman named Kathy Briccetti who wanted to find a blood link? On the other hand, my blunder also made me consider another potential connection, not the type I had ever hoped to claim. Some early Fosters may have been slave owners, and we might have been related somehow through that shameful route.

From the adoption agency, I received a speedy reply. *At the present time, Missouri law only provides for the release of information from adoption records to adoptive parents, adult adoptees, and birth parents under certain circumstances. The law does not provide for the release of information to children of adoptees.*

I met Pam at the door after work and showed her the letter. "How dare they deny me access to my family!" She read over my shoulder as I ranted. "I already know her name; why can't they just give me the rest?"

"I'm sorry, sweets. Can you ask Cyrus if he wants to request the information?" She always remained unruffled while I reacted with indignation. I wasn't sure if I liked that. Sometimes I wanted her to get angry along with me. "He won't do it. The last time I asked, he said he wasn't ready. I wish I could just do it myself. Maybe I'll sneak into the adoption agency, hunt for Mavis's file, and steal it. I have a right to this information. She was my grandmother!"

Pam nodded and went to the kitchen, leaving me to fume alone. I could see she didn't share my fiery disappointment. I wanted my life partner to do more than mumble sympathies; I wanted her to rally with me, tell me I was doing the right thing. I wanted her to offer to sneak into the agency with me, distract the social worker, maybe lure her from her desk, giving me time to scan the information in Mavis's file, letting me memorize an address and look for other names, like that of Cyrus's birth father.

But it was not to be, and I returned to my desk, straightening the piles of papers on top of it. When I finished, I moved on to the desk drawers. The paper clips needed sorting.

At work, traveling between two elementary schools, a middle school, and a high school, I was still in the closet. Ten years earlier, in 1978, the year I arrived in California, the Briggs Initiative threatened to bar gays and lesbians from working as public school teachers. It hadn't passed, in part because, of all people, former governor Ronald Reagan spoke out against it, an act that had probably served to fire up the gay community even more. But now, a decade later, not much had changed. The climate still felt threatening, and I believed my job was at risk if I told the truth.

I felt vulnerable on a personal level, too. Old friends had known me as a straight woman, and I found it difficult to divulge anything that would change their perception, make them think less of me. I'd made friends at the new schools to which I'd been assigned, but balked at telling them about my lover. Since they had no preconceptions, it should have been easier to come out to them. But I was still not comfortable with my new persona, and I couldn't risk my connections with others. This closet I inhabited was huge, a walk-in redolent of cedar and mothballs, holding old wool coats on wooden hangers and every pair of shoes I'd ever owned, from sneakers and sandals to hiking boots. It was a closet into which I'd retreated because of the world's view toward homosexuality, but it was also a closet of my own making, a place where shame had driven me.

I finally ventured out of the closet as I began graduate school. It was like starting a new life. At the Wright Institute in Berkeley, I found tolerance rather than homophobia. Although in some psychiatric circles, homosexuality was still believed to be caused by dysfunctional relationships with one's parents, and only a few mavericks were intrepid enough to suggest the possibility of a genetic link, it was at least no longer considered a form of psychopathology and had been removed from the American Psychiatric Association's diagnostic manual two years earlier. It would not have been politically correct to disdain the handful of gay students and the two or three openly gay faculty members at the school, so it looked as if I'd found a haven. Instead of changing the subject, or pretending I had a boyfriend, as soon as I could work it into the conversation, I told my fellow students, "I'm living with my lover, Pam." Here I was almost proud of my new status, silently daring anyone to behave like a bigot.

The world outside was a different story, though. Ronald Reagan was now at the end of his second presidential term, during which he'd long ignored the AIDS epidemic. Only the bravest lesbians walked around holding hands in public, even in Berkeley. On television, Roseanne wouldn't cause a ruckus by kissing Mariel Hemingway until 1994, and Ellen Degeneres wouldn't come out on her sitcom, ruining her ratings in the process, for almost another decade.

That summer of 1988, Pam and I had been coming home from the movies, walking at a clip because it was later than we liked to be out at night downtown, when we passed a darkened store's doorway and a man spit the words "Fuckin' lezzies." When we were a block away and my heart had settled, I thought, *How could he tell?* He had been dusky with dirt and grease, his words had spewed out sloppy, and he'd smelled of unwashed hair and exhaled hootch. And yet how had he recognized in a glance who we were to each other as we passed him that night? We were not holding hands, we did not have masculine haircuts, we did not walk with particular heaviness or wear work boots. I didn't understand what had given us away. Our jeans and fleece jackets, our purposeful strides, our synchronized gaits? Perhaps we walked a little too close to each other. Or perhaps it was just a lucky guess. Maybe he shouted those words at all women parading by.

Don't you realize what town you're in? I wanted to ask him when I was two blocks away, when I could breathe again. *This is Berkeley, you know, Bezerkeley, and here in Berkeley you don't spit out that word, or the others. Fag. Queer. Butch. Dyke. I don't call you a fucking homeless squatter alky or call the cops to run you out of town. So don't call me a fuckin' lezzie.*

I loved the T-shirt I once saw on a woman that read, "My lover is a lesbian." I was comfortable with people knowing the truth about me at grad school, but still I could not use the "L word" to describe myself. Calling myself a lesbian would have felt akin to calling myself an Italian. Sure, I was sleeping with a woman, and yes, I did have an Italian surname, but neither characteristic defined me truthfully. So I hedged. "My lover is a woman," I said to other students, hoping this would make the news more palatable and prevent the subtle rejection I still feared no matter what word I used.

Although I wasn't aware of it at the time, the coming-out process amplified my need to search for belonging within my family of origin. Uprooted from the comfort of familiar and socially accepted relationships made me even more fervent about searching for my place. I still waited for the return postcard from Missouri that would lead me there.

Doctoral students at my graduate school were required to participate in individual psychotherapy in order to experience therapy from the client's perspective. At first I resisted, fretting over the expense and believing it would be a waste of time since I believed I had no problems to work out. "Why don't you use it to learn more about yourself?" a friend suggested.

I met with a psychologist in town for about six months, and I used part of the time to question my sexual orientation and part of it to explore relationships in the present and with my family of origin.

"You have qualities of an adult child of an alcoholic," the psychologist said after we'd been meeting for two or three months.

I bristled. "But I didn't grow up with an alcoholic parent," I said. "There was no abuse in my family, and we weren't nearly as messed up as the families I see at work."

"I think you've taken on the role of the responsible child," she said. "The perfectionist, self-sufficient high achiever." I remembered how my family had teased me about what my summer camp counselor heard me mutter in my sleep when I was twelve years old. "I'm so good," I'd announced from the top bunk in the middle of the night.

The therapist was partly right. As a teenager, my brother, Mike, had turned from Golden Boy to Wild Child, acting out the tension in the family and distracting us from what wasn't being talked about. I knew I'd been the Good Girl from early on, but although I can see now why she would liken me to a child of an alcoholic, the therapist wasn't seeing the whole picture. She didn't know about the missing branches on my family tree or how they had affected me. There is another way of understanding why I tried so hard to be perfect, wanted to control whatever I could in order to prevent bad things from happening, and why I needed more approval than others. What the therapist didn't know was that I also shared many personality characteristics of an adoptee.

Finding books on the psychology of adoption comforted me. I needed to know I wasn't a freak, or that at least there were other freaks like me. In Betty Jean Lifton's *Lost and Found: The Adoption Experience*, I found my personality profile. My lifelong worries—anxiety at goodbyes, stronger than usual need to fit in, and deep sadness at exclusion—were right there on the page. I had found my people.

Although I'm not a typical adoptee since I was not relinquished as an infant and did not lose both birth parents, I share with adoptees a loss over which we had no control. So, control becomes an issue for many of us. Some adoptees over-control and order their lives precisely to try to prevent anything bad from happening again, and some become overwhelmed in many situations, don't like to make decisions, and tend to defer to those who are more assertive. Some can become a combination of the two extremes—over-controlling on the one hand and deferring on the other—struggling to find middle ground. That's me. Control freak. I need to know everything, and I'm wounded when left out. But I can also become paralyzed at simple choices. Which cereal to buy. What to wear to a party.

Reading about adoptees and their myriad personality quirks brought me immense relief. I needed to be part of a group in order to feel less odd, less outside the norm. It validated my drive to connect, my need to belong. Not only do I need to belong to a group, I need to belong to a group of people that need to belong. It's an eerie feeling, like an Escher drawing, this spiraling in on myself.

In my second year of graduate school, I began working as an intern therapist at a family therapy agency in an old Victorian house in Alameda. I loved the intensity of feelings boiling over, the power I had to contain those feelings, make sense of them and recognize the patterns that rendered families stuck. It was gratifying to find the reasons behind one child's acting out and another's withdrawal. I had become a Professional Helper, my adult incarnation of Good Girl. I helped families repair old wounds to keep them together, and helped couples separate while protecting their children. It was sometimes deceptively simple, pointing out how an individual's actions have an effect on the whole system, the family, and how parents' relationships almost always affect how children behave.

Two deaths in 1990 intensified my need to find Mavis Foster. When I was halfway through graduate school, both my mother's mother and my stepfather's mother died within six months of each other. First, in the spring, just a few months before her ninety-fifth birthday, Grandma Rose, my lifelong pen pal, slumped over in her wing chair in her Minnesota condominium. I had last visited her the year before, when I'd come to help after her hip surgery. She had been my favorite grandmother, the only grandmother I'd known since birth and the only grandmother I knew who was related to me by blood.

Mom didn't want a memorial service for her mother but a celebration of her life, and, at first, I agreed. When we arrived at Grandma Rose's church, we were met with the resonant, soulful sounds of a viola—one of Mom's closest friends warming up—and I couldn't hold back tears any longer. Mom could have her celebration, but I was there to grieve my grandmother's death.

My mother was raised under a dogma that valued stoicism: Don't cry. Be strong. Everything will be all right. Feelings are not for public display. But, as I've learned, denied feelings inevitably emerge from the muck to revisit us. Mine have morphed into self-soothing rituals, like cleaning out the junk drawer in the kitchen and lining up the shoes in the entryway. Organizing the shelves in the garden shed is my Xanax.

In late summer, Grandma Briccetti's car was hit by a drunk driver. On my thirty-third birthday, I flew to New York for her memorial service. There, I was overwhelmed with memories, from swinging high on my new grandparents' tire swing hanging from their massive oak, to the large, joyous Briccetti family reunions we all gathered for at their huge house on a hill in Somers. "It was not her time to die," Dad said, choking up during his eulogy at her Catholic church. This rare display of vulnerability touched me, and I felt close to him again.

After returning home, somehow I ended up with a copy of the page in her will on which she had bequeathed gifts to her four grandchildren. To each of her biological grandchildren, the children of her younger son, she left $10,000. To Mike and me, her eldest son's adopted children, she gave $5,000.

After reading this, I pulled the vacuum cleaner out of the closet and dragged it through the house, assaulting the rugs. My other grandmother, my mother's mother, Grandma Rose, had had five grandchildren, and two of my cousins were not related to her by blood, one being my uncle's stepson and the other having been adopted as an infant. When Grandma gave one cousin her old Plymouth because she couldn't drive any longer, she gave the rest of us equivalent amounts of money. This was how I believed it was supposed to be done.

I understand now that Grandma Briccetti may have made her bequest unequal because our cousins were younger and not yet established in their adult careers. But at the time it felt like we'd all had price tags stuck on us, our value announced, our ranking in her heart revealed. I knew that my Briccetti cousins had been her first grandbabies, that her Italian blood ran in them, while we gangly towheads had been presented to her not as infants but as young children, the progeny of another man, not her son.

I remain absolutely convinced today that she loved me; I have saved tender letters from her and a photo of the two of us on a beach in California, our arms around each other's waists, me more than a foot taller than she, her face beaming up at me. But back then, her gift was bittersweet. The money, more than I'd ever been given, was a thrill, yet the disparity stung, and it too nudged me to search for Mavis, my other blood grandmother.

A few months later, in early 1991, I wrote again to the adoption agency in St. Louis, pleading for information about my father's birth mother. I had grown up with a biological grandmother and a step-grandmother, and I had met Cyrus's adoptive mother, already giving me one more grandmother than most people get. But still I wasn't satisfied. *Both of my grandmothers died this year*, I wrote, hoping to garner enough sympathy so that someone would bend the rules. This time I received a longer reply, but the records were still off-limits to me.

I called Cyrus. "You can request non-identifying information about your birth mother," I said, my voice too loud and reverberating through the phone line.

"What kind of information?" he asked, his soft voice making mine sound all the louder in comparison, like unexpected laughter in a hushed library.

"If your file still exists, we can get a physical description of your birth parents, their nationality, religion, and medical history." I paused to let him take this in. His adoptive mother was 102 years old, hanging on in the retirement home, and I hoped he wouldn't use the fear of offending her as an excuse again. "And, it says here, if you want, you can petition the court to begin an identifying search for your birth parents." I didn't mention that this would cost $120 and would require authorization from the court, consent of his adoptive parents, and consent of his birth parents, if locatable. I had laughed when I'd read the last. That was the whole point, I wanted to remind the social worker: the locatability of his birth parents.

If I could just get my hands on the non-identifying information, I knew I could find Mavis Foster. If only he would do this much for me. I waited for his response.

"I'm just not ready to write that letter," he said finally, a note of remorse playing in his voice.

Damn.

"All right," I said. "Talk to you soon." I hung up quickly so he wouldn't hear my voice wobbling. I wish I could have simply said, "This is important to me. How can we get this for me and still protect your feelings?" But I was still the girl who didn't want to make people angry, the girl who let others' feelings trump her own. It was as if I had one foot on the gunwale of a rowboat and the other on shore. To get what I wanted, I would need to climb in, push off, and row.

But I didn't. I stayed on shore. That night I slid the letter from the adoption agency into a large manila envelope, added Cyrus's adoption paper and the returned postcards from the St. Louis Fosters, and wrote in large letters across the front: MAVIS FOSTER. I placed it on a closet shelf and turned out the light. Although I didn't know when I'd get it out again, I knew I would eventually return to that envelope. And, of course, I did. But at the time I had no idea how radically, in the intervening years, my life would change again.

FOURTEEN

The Baby Bank

"This has got to be the strangest thing—" I whispered as Pam and I eased onto a Naugahyde loveseat the hue and texture of a lemon rind. It whooshed under our weight, and, like kids, we laughed at the sound. In one corner of the private room, a low bookcase held a pile of worn *National Geographics*, a pink plastic tub holding children's ABC blocks, and a Raggedy Ann doll flopped on her side, legs crossed at the socks, prim and proper.

The windowless room was deep in a labyrinth of hallways in the Sperm Bank of California, an office building in the heart of Pill Hill, Oakland's medical quarter. For us, the building was an oasis, a safe island in the center of a world that in 1992 did not yet fathom, much less accept, what we were doing. Even in California. Although cryobanks had been selling the goods to infertile heterosexual couples since the nineteen forties, the Oakland sperm bank had been founded only ten years earlier and was one of the few clinics in the country providing semen to single women. Nowhere in the brochure, though, did it mention that the clinic catered to straight *and* lesbian single women, as well as to lesbian couples. We'd heard about that through the local lesbian grapevine.

Outside the clinic, the wind whipped down the street, but once past the heavy, opaque glass door, the only sound came from a fax machine whirring down a hall. I felt insulated there, both from the cool outside temperature and the chilly attitudes of the outside world. For a time, we were safe from judgment, safe from fear.

When I look back on this scene, the trepidation I felt then surfaces briefly. My gut tenses, and I have to remind myself to take a couple of deep breaths. Although same-sex marriage is in the news regularly now, and gay couples are having babies via all sorts of methods, it was a different era at the end of the twentieth century.

In the late spring of 1992, when we arrived at the sperm bank, the "Gayby Boom" was about to explode in the Bay Area and around the country. We were trailblazers, not at the front of the pack but near it. We'd met a few lesbian couples at the sperm bank's monthly support group, but we had no role models for our family and few books telling us how to do what we were doing. Because Berkeley was one of the most liberal and tolerant cities in the country with its antidiscrimination laws and protections for the disabled, and since San Francisco, the gay mecca, was just across the bay, I held out hope that the area would feel like home for our family. Still, though, I feared what it would be like each time we told the truth to someone outside our nest. I struggled with whether we should try to pass as heterosexual women and if we would be tempted to lie to outsiders in order to protect our child. *Pam and I are roommates*, I imagined saying, years before Don't Ask, Don't Tell.

Cyrus was the last person I had told about Pam. My half-sister Sarah had married and divorced, and my half-brother Cody had fathered a son with a woman he had not married. Still, I feared that telling Cyrus the truth about my relationship with Pam would cause a new rupture between us. I imagined him simply not answering my letter or writing sporadically and then not at all.

But I needed to tell him. The truth was becoming the litmus test for my relationships. It would answer the question How secure was our bond? Two years after my commitment ceremony with Pam, and three years before our trip to the sperm bank, I wrote him. He did not make me wait long.

"*We're glad you're happy—*" he wrote immediately in his familiar scrawl. "*You mean a lot to us—your Kentucky kin.*"

I was relieved and disappointed at the same time. On the surface he had accepted my news. For that I was grateful. But I wanted more. I wanted pure joy. When my friends announced their engagements, people threw them parties; when they married, they threw them even bigger parties. But when I announced that I had found my life's love, reactions were muted. I felt like Cinderella; no one ever expected my foot to fit into that slipper.

Pam and I were guilty, though, of perpetuating a charade by pretending to be roommates. Other times, paradoxically, I resented that we were perceived as such. It was a contradiction that had played out in Pam's family as well.

Her parents had joined us at our cabin in the Sierra Nevada mountains the summer before she and I visited the sperm bank. Far off the highway, in redwood and giant sequoia country, the cabin was our place of respite. Quiet and scented with pine needles and duff, it was the place where we left the world behind. We spent lazy days reading and hiking with our dogs. In winter, we built fires in the wood-burning stove and made love in front of it.

When her parents had visited us at the cabin during previous summers, we'd taken off our matching rings and hidden them away, once again playing our "we're just roommates" roles. But this time, because we were tired of hiding, tired of lying, we gave up the façade. The rings, coupled with our sharing a queen-sized bed, gave her mother the final clues.

"My mother wants to talk to me," Pam whispered in the kitchen the morning after they'd arrived.

"Okay, but why are we whispering?" I wanted to laugh because my family drove us to do the same thing. But her expression was grave.

"Go with my father to get the Cadillac filled up or something. Give me a little time with my mother." Her edgy voice surprised me. "Please."

Her father drove slowly a couple of miles down the mountain to the gas station. He and I made small talk, and he filled up the car's tank. "I've never seen Pammy happier," he said on the way back up the mountain. "I think you're good for her."

I couldn't believe what I was hearing. He was a conservative man with traditional values. He had retired from a job in the defense industry and enjoyed fishing and church activities. He and Pam's mother voted Republican, so we steered clear of politics during visits with them. But it sounded as if he understood my relationship with his daughter and that he was accepting me. Although they were not a physically affectionate family, it felt as if he'd opened his arms and pulled me into an embrace.

But back at the cabin the air was acerbic. Pam's mother was tossing things into suitcases and muttering. "We can't stay here. We have to leave."

"What happened?" I asked Pam, out of earshot on the deck. Her father had gone in to his wife.

"My mom asked me if I was gay, and I told her yes." Pam's hands shook slightly and she folded them under her arms. "She's freaking out. She says she's going to consider me their 'handicapped child.'"

She laughed, but I knew she was about to cry. I put my arms around her waist. "She might feel betrayed after all these years you haven't told her the truth. She'll calm down after she gets home."

"Why did I tell her?"

"Our kids. We can't make them keep secrets; we're not going to do that to them."

Pam's parents didn't leave early after all, but the next three days were strained, all of us trying to pretend nothing was wrong. As soon as they pulled out of the driveway, Pam went into the bedroom, lay on our bed, and fell asleep. Back home, we waited to hear from them. They still phoned regularly, but after each call Pam looked drained and sad.

"It's a relief not to be hiding it from them," she said, "but it hurts, too. Daddy acts like nothing's changed, but I know my mother can't accept it."

Pam and I had come to the sperm bank because we wanted a donor who had relinquished his paternal rights, who could never take our child away from us. We had briefly considered asking Pam's brother to be our sperm donor, but it felt too strange for our children to be the cousins *and* half-siblings of his three children. And we'd been tempted to ask our unmarried, straight friend, Jack, for a huge favor but came to realize we didn't want to co-parent with a third adult. We didn't want to share our child, or worse, lose our child to a man when he married and convinced a judge he was the better parent. We wanted an anonymous donor who would release his identity when our child reached eighteen. And we were not alone. Eighty percent of the sperm bank's clients requested identity-release donors. However, only sixty percent of donors were willing to be identified.

"No way will I keep my child's beginnings from him or her," I'd told Pam earlier. "My family has enough missing people on the family tree." I didn't want my children to be frustrated someday by secrets, closed records, and dead ends.

Now, after almost a year of charting my daily basal temperature and examining the fluctuating viscosity of my cervical mucus, I knew when my body was ripe, receptive. When I menstruated next, we would call in our order, and two weeks later we would carry home a vial of frozen semen in our six-pack cooler full of dry ice. But first, we had to choose the father of our child.

"Are you sure you want to do this?" I asked, eyeing the tower of folders on the low table in front of us. The creases in Pam's forehead deepened and she gave a tiny shrug. When she caught me looking at her, she found my hand and squeezed it.

Privately, I was questioning my judgment, and I longed for reassurance that we were not making a huge mistake. I was thirty-four and, with characteristic impatience, believed that time was running out. I was writing a doctoral dissertation while working as a psychology intern at a San Francisco hospital's psychiatry clinic, pushing myself to finish the degree on time so we could start inseminating as soon as I was free of school obligations. "You have your life mapped out on the head of a pin," a friend said when I told him my plan to give birth during my summer break the following year.

"If we have a boy," I had asked Pam before our trip to the sperm bank, "how do we teach him to pee standing up, to shave?"

She laughed. "We'll figure it out."

"What about wet dreams?" I asked. "How do we explain that?"

She shrugged.

What concerned me more than guiding a boy through puberty, though, was the possibility that someday my child would hold me responsible for the way I made him or her. "Are we being selfish?" I'd asked Pam. "Making kids this way, without a father?"

"Two mothers can do just as good a job as a mother and father," she said.

"And if we have a girl?" I asked. "What will it be like for her to grow up without a father?" I hadn't let myself think about my own experience; I needed to believe that since I had turned out just fine, thank you, my daughter would end up even healthier since I'd be an educated mother and I'd know what she needed to compensate for the lack of a father. Part of me felt wise, but I also knew that I was too close to the situation, and that this closeness made me biased, defensive.

Pam said something soothing, but I couldn't shake the feeling that I was being selfish because I wanted to experience being pregnant, giving birth, raising my biological babies. I thought of my children someday asking, "Where did I come from? *Who* did I come from?" and I feared they might hate me when I could not give them an answer.

Even if they didn't suffer from being fatherless, I wondered whether my children would be subjected to people's harsh judgments, whether insensitive people would tell them they were created unnaturally, that since they were not "love children" produced by a man and a woman, they were unworthy.

But I argued with myself. Is a three-minute fuck in the back seat of a car a better way to make a baby? What about a man who forces his wife to have sex? Is that "normal"?

Pam handed me half the stack of file folders and flipped open one from her pile. "Come on, Ms. Virgo," she said. "We're paying by the hour."

"Excuse me?" I asked. "Look who's talking, Ms. Virgo."

Our similarities—efficiency, goal-directedness, and sense of fairness—were partly what had attracted me to her. We still negotiated things like who would wash the dishes. "I'll do them tonight, love," I'd say. "No, you did them last night," she'd say. "Let me."

I opened to the first page of a donor's chart. I was our self-appointed secretary, jotting notes about each sperm donor—his education, resume, medical history, how much alcohol and which drugs he'd used, or at least those to which he had admitted using. The records would also give us his hobbies, eyesight, exposure to toxic chemicals, and the causes of his grandparents' deaths. From these notes we'd choose the father of our child. Because the demand was higher than the supply, though, we would need to list several donors in order of preference. We had been warned that if our number one guy's deposits hadn't cleared quarantine yet, we'd have to settle for our second or third or maybe even fourth choice.

"Good God," I said, reading from a chart. "This guy weighs 220 pounds and he's five-nine."

Pam glanced over her reading glasses and scrunched up her nose.

"I guess he could be a body builder." I lowered my voice. "Or do you think they use fat guys?" I did a quick check of the room, searching for a video camera in a corner near the ceiling or a little sliding window with tiny double doors, the kind you slip your urine sample into. I imagined the staff listening in and laughing at us, or finding us unworthy recipients of the precious goods and sending us away.

"Mother had breast cancer," I said. "Reject pile." My mother had a mastectomy when she was fifty-two, and I did the recommended monthly breast exams every Monday morning in the shower. I didn't want to stack the deck against my daughter by giving her two grandmothers who'd had breast cancer. As if I possessed that God-like power, or control over any of this. This genetic prioritizing we were doing seemed wrong, but I was afraid of scary diseases, Coke-bottle eyeglasses on toddlers, imperfection.

The ancestry list of each donor was interesting, and it didn't matter if our donor's family immigrated from Ireland, Greece, or Russia, but we had decided not to cross races. Our children would be challenged enough having two mothers. Why add the struggles of an interracial family? Besides, I had a secret bias for tall, fit men and wanted to make blond, blue-eyed babies who looked like me; however, I kept this from Pam, my physical opposite. She was almost a half-foot shorter than me. Her jeans were size six and so were her feet.

"Is this weird for you?" I asked her. "Our kids won't look like you. They'll be a mixture of me and someone we've never seen. Or they'll look more like the donor than me and seem like little strangers."

"I really don't mind," she said, tapping the folder on her thigh. "It's just not as important to me as it is to you."

Pam didn't share my desire for pregnancy and childbirth but did want to share mothering with me. She'd also agreed to my ideas about what our children would call us. "I've always wanted to be called Mommy," I'd said. This may have been the final vestige of the heterosexual parenting fantasy I was unwilling to relinquish. I would give up the wedding but not the kids, nor being called what I'd called my mother when I was a child. "Is it all right if they call you Mama?"

I reached for the next folder in the pile. "This is ridiculous; I *slept* with guys I didn't know this much about," I said, laughing. "If I were doing this the regular way, I doubt I would interview the man, subject him to blood tests, semen analyses, and a study of two generations of his family's medical history." I slapped the folder down on Pam's pile. "I don't think we want this guy. His vision's 20/200."

At home, we'd found humor in the pamphlet from the sperm bank that had come in the mail: *What is semen?* But arriving at the sperm bank to make the choice, things seemed more serious. We were paying $30 an hour to read the donors' files. The vials went for $75 and $108 a pop, according to size, and most inseminees took home a couple of vials at a time in order to better their chances. We could recite the three most important factors in semen analysis: sperm motility, count, and shape. We knew that donors had undergone an eight-month medical screening and testing for sexually transmitted diseases, including HIV. We knew that they were checked again six months before their semen left the building. We also knew that, despite all the tests and waiting periods, the sperm bank could not guarantee the semen to be free of disease-causing organisms.

We lapsed into silent reading again, tuning out murmurs in the hall. I wondered whether sperm donors and prospective parents ever met here, eyes lingering over each other, wondering, are you the one?

"Only a high school education," I said, flipping a folder closed. "I'd rather go with the Ph.D. in physics; he's also got a master's in nuclear engineering."

"Lemme see that." Pam snatched the file from me. "High school education. Kathy, he's only eighteen years old! How could he have any more education?"

"An eighteen-year-old?" I took back the folder. "I could be his mother."

We both snickered. It was anxious "what the hell are we doing here" snickering.

Thousands of babies had been conceived so far with what has been called artificial insemination, but I hated this term. "Artificial" implied the negative, something not genuine, something false and unnatural. It implied that what we were doing was creepy, like a basement laboratory experiment. I appreciated the recent, less judgmental term "alternative insemination," and, finally, I found in the sperm bank's brochure the term I liked best: donor insemination.

Three hundred thousand children had been conceived this way since World War II, so could it be that bad? Yes, it could, according to a group of donor offspring who in the 1980s organized a self-help group and developed a pamphlet. In *101 Things to Consider Before Choosing Artificial Insemination*, an adult looked back: "Never did I worry about being a bastard. No, what upset my whole sense of being was that nobody knew my 'real' father. It was as though half of me did not exist. My mother clearly felt a sense of shame, for I was sworn to secrecy. It has haunted me every day of my life."

How could I, with my history, deny my own child a father, setting him or her up for lifelong confusion, insecurity, and haunting shame? I convinced myself I was not like the parents depicted in the pamphlet, people more concerned with how they appeared to others than with what their kids needed. I believed the writer quoted in the pamphlet was overreacting. Things were different when their parents had made them. Infertility carried greater stigma then, and many parents led children to believe they were being raised by their biological fathers. It was these secrets, I convinced myself, and the feelings of betrayal when the truth finally emerged, that caused their pain. I soothed myself with the promise that we would not lie to our child. I knew the dangers of family secrets, and I would not make the same mistakes.

Even if we did everything right—told the truth, didn't get uptight and pass our anxieties to our kids—I still worried that conceiving them this way, and raising them without a father, would screw them up. I didn't know if Pam would be an equal partner in our parenting or whether she'd lack the quality that would allow her to truly attach to our child. Maybe, like some heterosexual mothers, I'd be possessive of our baby and insist on doing things my way, take over the parenting. And she'd let me.

Each morning, when my eyes were still fighting the light, I groped for the thermometer on my nightstand and slipped it under my tongue. I was afraid of falling back to sleep and biting off the end, spilling slivers of glass in my mouth. Every evening before bed, I plotted my daily basal temperature to a tenth of a degree on a graph, zealous about the orderliness and predictability of the charts I'd been keeping for nearly a year. If I had placed my monthly graphs together side by side in a line, they would have resembled the leitmotif from a symphony score: da da da dee da dum. Da da da dee da dum. I ovulated to a precise clock, on the fourteenth day. If those sperm were healthy, and we could awaken them from their long nap and prod them back into service, we might get lucky on the first try.

At home in Berkeley a month after our sperm bank visit, her hands in grass-stained garden gloves to protect her from the dry ice, Pam rummaged through our six-pack cooler. Its lid, once red but now sun-faded to salmon, lay overturned on our bedroom rug. Her movements were slow, as if she were in awe of the ghostly vapor and potent cold.

The donor we'd ended up with had been our fifth choice. Instead of the physics Ph.D., the jazz musician working as a doorman, the honors graduate in economics working as a waiter, or the introverted political scientist, all of whose samples were unavailable that month, we got the twenty-five-year-old former Air Force sergeant who managed an electronics store. Even though we'd chosen him, I felt like we'd been relegated to the bargain basement. The man had spelled a word wrong on his questionnaire; how could I put his sperm into my body? How could we be sure that he'd been honest when filling out the medical section or whether he'd "forgotten" to mention a few details, like the crazy uncle locked up in the attic, the cousin with a Hummel Doll fetish? Would he, knowingly or unknowingly, pass on something to my baby? A flicker of nausea spun from my gut to my head and then disappeared.

Still, I didn't want to wait one more month. I knew of women who had inseminated for a year or two before getting pregnant. I wanted to get started, and if this bank withdrawal didn't take, we'd try again with somebody else's deposit. I told myself that we didn't need the sperm of an extraordinary donor. I hoped only that our donor would contribute healthy genes, giving Pam and me the job of making our baby smart.

"It's not here," Pam said, placing the largest chunks of dry ice on the cooler lid and digging a little deeper. The disappointment in her voice mirrored my fragile feelings. Although it was a balmy June evening, I felt a chill sitting in my nightshirt at the end of our bed, my feet swinging over the edge like a child's. It looked like we'd miss our chance to make a baby that month. By the time we got to the sperm bank the next day and then returned home, it would be too late. The egg would have popped out and made its journey alone.

All the anticipation, the surreal experience of ordering semen, bringing our cooler home, waiting for the right day, had tenderized my emotions, pounded them pulpy. I wanted a baby so badly I'd ignored the strangeness of our method and plowed ahead. Perhaps the missing sperm was a sign that we should abandon our crazy plan. Instead, I could find a man in a bar for a one-night stand. Or we could adopt one of the many children awaiting a home. Or we could forget about kids altogether and enjoy summers of traveling. I longed to stop riding these frenzied waves of feelings—cresting anxiety, roiling anticipation, deep hope.

"Here it is," Pam said, and I flinched as if startled by a Jack-in-the-box. She pulled a Ziploc sandwich bag to the surface of the milky icebergs. Inside lay a tiny plastic vial, the size of the department store perfume samples I collected in junior high. She held up the frost-coated tube filled halfway with a dropperful of frozen white liquid. On its side, written across the length, ran a code in fine-tip permanent marker: #042-75; 5 c.c.; 8/4/91. She removed the garden gloves and tucked the vial under her arm like a duck in its nest settling over her egg.

"That ought to do the trick," I laughed, and motioned for her to join me on the bed. "That should bring them back to life."

I didn't tell her I feared the stuff might hurt me somehow, that I imagined a tiny alien coming out of me in forty weeks. I fluttered the insemination instructions against my bouncing legs, which refused to keep still.

"Are we doing the right thing?" I asked, my voice wobbling. "We don't know this guy."

We did know that he was just over six feet with sandy brown hair, blue eyes, and good vision. But we'd never seen a photograph, never heard his voice. He was not three-dimensional to us but a faceless cardboard cutout. "Talk about a leap of faith," I'd told Pam when we'd gone through the charts at the sperm bank. Was he gorgeous like a model, striking in some way, or plain-looking, homely even? Did the sperm bank staff ever reject a guy, telling him sorry, you're too ugly to be a donor? I'm embarrassed now to admit my superficiality. At the time, I speculated on what features this stranger would bestow on our child, whether our child would look like him or me. I guess it wasn't much different, though, than my checking out the faces and physiques of men I had dated for their potential genetic contribution to our future children.

"I wish I knew what kind of person he is," I said. "Would we like him? He could have lied on his questionnaire; he could be a drug addict—"

"That would have shown up on the blood and urine tests."

"—or a serial killer." I took a breath. "Or a closet Republican."

"Ha ha," she said, not laughing.

"Why do you think he donated his sperm? I mean the real reason, more than the money. They have to go through all those medical tests, then fill the cup at the sperm bank a bunch of times." My legs no longer belonged to me; they were swinging on their own.

Pam inspected the vial, tipping it. "How do we tell if it's thawed out? I think it's still frozen in the middle." She stuck it under her other arm and took the instruction sheet from me.

"Do you think we'll ever meet him?" I asked.

"Depends on our kid," she said, reading the insemination steps to herself for the fourth time. "Anyway, don't you think you're jumping the gun? We need to get this to work first."

When Pam tipped the vial again, the semen rolled gently back and forth, coating the sides. Our precious sample was ready. She twisted off the miniature cap and gently placed the slim syringe, blunt without a needle, inside the vial, then pulled back the plunger in slow motion. She looked as if she were working with a volatile substance, and I snickered.

"I don't want to kill any of them," she said. "Do *you* want to do it?"

"I'm sorry," I said, shaking my head. "You're doing fine."

When all of the liquid was withdrawn, the rubber tip of the syringe briefly stuck to the bottom, making a soft sucking sound.

"Okay," she whispered. "I got it. Are you ready?"

I lay back on the bed, propped my hips on several pillows, and lifted my nightshirt to my waist. With warm fingers, Pam gingerly inserted the cool plastic tube, narrower than a tampon, and slowly engaged the plunger, releasing the newly roused swimmers on their upstream journey to the entrance of my womb—the land of Os. The irony was not lost on me at the time, that after years of paying for birth control to keep that opening impenetrable, I was now paying big bucks to sow seed in my fertile tunnel. I had put out the vaginal welcome mat.

I wondered how many trips to the sperm bank, how many months or years, it would take to get me pregnant, and whether the gods would mess with me. *So* now *you want to get pregnant. At thirty-five? You had your chance before. Now you'll just have to wait and see if your turn comes around again.*

Pam placed the spent syringe on the table and eased herself onto the bed. She lay next to me nuzzling her head until it rested on my shoulder. "We did it," she said.

"Yeah, we did." Unexpectedly I began to cry—a jumble of emotions finally releasing. "This isn't how I thought I would make my babies, though." I hadn't needed scented candles or sitar music, but maybe we should have put massage oil on the list, or exchanged our not-exactly-sexy nightshirts for something slinky from Victoria's Secret. "It's so clinical," I said.

"I know, sweet love," Pam said. With her thumbs she traced the trail my tears had made.

I had relinquished my Barbie doll wedding fantasies and had never imagined this particular scenario. I was still trying to understand how my life had taken this turn, still wondered whether it was a detour, if one day I'd wake up and realize my mistake.

Following the directions from the sperm bank, I swiveled my hips and swung my legs onto the wall, letting gravity help in the Miracle of Conception. There was some debate at the time about whether or not an orgasm following insemination would increase our odds, so we'd come to bed early in order to check that off the list, too.

I finished my half-hour spider pose and settled into bed. Pam's soft fingers searched for my belly under my nightshirt, and finding it, she stroked in a light circle between my jutting hipbones. Her touch descended, I reciprocated, and, afterwards, we fell asleep nestled in the middle of our bed, my legs cradled in the soft, warm curves of hers.

FIFTEEN

The Lesbian Birth

A warm May breeze floated through the open window as I climbed into bed and wrapped myself around my giant body pillow. I began to read another chapter in *What to Expect When You're Expecting*, still seeking advice, still feeling guilty for not giving up bagels and pasta like the book commanded. It had taken three trips from the sperm bank with a frozen vial packed into dry ice. Now, my basketball belly stretched to its limit, my pajama pants rested far below my navel. Every few minutes I stopped reading to pull up my shirt and watch the baby turn my abdomen into rolling earthquake country. These quiet times were my favorite part of the pregnancy: feeling the baby push against my spine, and then watching for knee or elbow to jut out, making mounds that gently undulated or jabbed like a boxer.

My due date was three weeks away. Pam and I had already chosen two names, a boy's and a girl's, and after our first childbirth preparation class, we'd packed a bag and set it by the front door.

Earlier that day, I'd felt persistent, deep aches in my lower back and groin, slightly more severe than menstrual cramps. They had waned, and now, eager for sleep, I adjusted the pillow between my knees, scooted a bath towel underneath me, and welcomed the dark.

Ten minutes later, still floating toward sleep, I both heard and felt a muffled pop inside me, like a submerged balloon breaking. A gush of water warmed my thighs, and I reached down to pull the towel between my legs. Although it wasn't time for this baby to come, I wasn't surprised or particularly concerned. A baby coming three weeks early was not at terrible risk. I did still worry some about difficult labor, or birth trauma, but my mother had had short and relatively easy labors, and I hoped I would carry on that tradition.

I had wanted those final three weeks to rest, to cling to my last days of childless freedoms, but we were ready, and I felt a sweet thrill. The baby's room waited with a borrowed crib already assembled, new curtains that Pam had sewn from a bold animal print, newborn clothing folded neatly in drawers under a changing table. A wicker bassinet sat on its stand next to our bed. All we had to do was call the diaper service to start delivering.

I didn't wake Pam, who, suffering from a head cold and fever, slept next to me in a version of Child's Pose, to trick her asthma from settling in her vulnerable lungs. Instead I climbed out of bed and roamed the quiet house. Within thirty minutes, pulsing aches in my lower back wrapped around my belly like shoots of a climbing vine, squeezing rhythmically.

After two hours the sensation had changed, and it felt as if a wide belt was being cinched tighter and tighter around my abdomen. Waves of fatigue were making me vulnerable to loneliness, and I roused Pam. "Tonight?" she said. "We haven't finished the class!" She curled over, coughing. We were halfway through the childbirth preparation class, and I had learned only one method of breathing, the one used during early labor. None of that mattered, though. I was focused on the pulsing constrictions around my belly that were coming six minutes apart. At first I resented her ability to sleep through this event. But I knew I'd need her later. Better that one of us was rested. "It's not time yet," I said. "Go back to sleep."

At five o'clock, seven hours after my water had broken, rose-white light began to blossom over the hills to the east. When the obstetrician returned my call, her voice was deep from interrupted dreams, and I was afraid she'd tell me to call back in three hours. I couldn't do this for three more hours.

"Why don't you mosey on down to the hospital and get settled in," she said. "I'll meet you there in a bit." They can hear it in your voice, I'd learned, the desperation that tells them when you finally need to head to the hospital. I cried silently with relief and shook Pam awake again.

Twenty minutes later, after ordering Pam to charge through red lights on the empty Berkeley streets, I walked into Alta Bates Hospital alone while she parked. In the lobby, I refused a wheelchair from the security guard, instead walked in large circles, stopping to cradle my sides and breathe deliberately when each contraction began. Like a cocoon, my own small world had closed in around me, buffering stimuli from outside. I was in another zone, one that included only my baby and me. This, having a baby, was what I had always wanted. I felt an unexpected tranquility.

Upstairs, I climbed onto a labor bed. A nurse snapped on a pair of gloves, preparing to check my cervix. Her frizzy, brick red curls were pulled back in a bun, and a mask covered the lower half of her face, so I focused on her deep-water blue eyes. I was so relieved to be there, to be in her hands, that I sank back into the pillows.

"How lovely," she said, nodding at Pam who was shouldering my overnight bag and wiping her nose with a tissue. "You brought your mother with you." I groaned but not from pain. *She would have given birth to me at age twelve*, I wanted to say. I remembered a nurse practitioner in a clinic years before who, after querying about birth control and learning that my partner was a woman, had handled me roughly during my gynecological exam.

I knew we were not the first lesbians for this labor and delivery department. Our neighbors, true lesbian-mom pioneers, had had a baby ten years earlier at this hospital. They'd told us about the faces crowded at their labor room door, witnessing The Lesbian Birth. But when we'd arrived, the labor and delivery department didn't have my medical chart since we were showing up in May and not in June as expected. The nurse had already called me by another patient's name, reading it off the wrong chart.

I fought a moment of panic. We should have brought our Affidavit of Domestic Partnership. Why had we not packed it in the bag we'd set by the door three weeks earlier? And we could have used a copy of the Power of Attorney, the document we'd added to my medical chart in case something happened to me during the delivery—the chart that was still locked up in the obstetrician's office.

"No, this is my partner," I said. I had not invited my mother to attend the birth of her first grandchild. When I'd told her that Pam and I wanted a week to become acquainted with our baby, our new family, I'd heard the hurt in her voice. It may have been a mistake, but at the time Pam and I assumed our families were uncomfortable sharing this event with us, and we feared their feelings about our relationship might dampen our joy. We believed we needed to protect ourselves and our new baby. Perhaps we weren't seeing past the fences we had built.

The nurse lowered her head at her blunder. "Oh, sorry," she said, sounding truly contrite. "This'll just be a second. Then I'll take you on a tour of the floor, show you where the juice is, and let you hop into the shower." I desperately wanted to stand under scalding water, let it numb my back, soothe my constricting abdomen, ease my anxiety.

The nurse was quiet as she checked my cervix, but then her voice jerked alive. "Oh, my goodness, you're nine centimeters; you're not going anywhere." Things began to speed up then. Trays of instruments were rolled in with a clatter. The room filled with gowned figures. Pam held my hand and swabbed at my forehead with a damp towel, and I breathed deeply, focusing so intently on a blister on the far wall that I began to lose track of everything else. The obstetrician arrived fifteen minutes later, quickly changed into scrubs, and after half an hour of my pushing through contractions and breathing with the only method I had learned, our baby's head emerged.

Once his wide shoulders were free, the nurse showed Pam where to grasp under his arms to ease him out. The two of them lay him face up on my belly, head tucked in the valley between my breasts, springy legs unfolding over my abdomen. I cradled his jaw and caressed his temples with my thumbs. "Hi there," I whispered to the crown of his damp, baby-bird head. He was deliciously perfect. Whole and pink and breathing and living outside of me. I was overwhelmed with relief that labor was over, that he was in my hands. "I'm glad you're here," I whispered.

The nurse clamped the umbilical cord in two places and handed Pam shears to sever it. Then, because he was three weeks early, a pediatrician snatched him from my belly and placed him howling and red in a bassinet under a fierce light to inspect him.

"Is he a little blue?" I asked the room.

"The girls come out pink and the boys blue," our red-haired nurse answered, playfulness in her voice. I smiled, but it was all I could muster. I collapsed back on the bed, not taking my eyes off my baby. Eyes squeezed shut, he was still howling.

"Full-term," the pediatrician proclaimed. "Eight and a half pounds. Perfectly healthy." He smiled like a proud grandfather as he handed my swaddled son to me. Finally, holding my baby snug in my arms, I closed my eyes, a delirious grin on my face.

Tidying the room, our nurse murmured to someone. "We should have videotaped that one, to show how it *can* be." I was proud, but mostly grateful that the labor had been short and that I had sunk into a breathing rhythm so exactly matching my baby's descent that the contractions were bearable. I knew it had been out of my control, that I'd been graced with a relatively easy labor, but I still soaked up her praise and relished her acceptance of us. We had not only been accepted but smiled upon. Unexpectedly, ironically, we'd become examples of how it *could* be.

When the obstetrician finished sewing the tears in my perineum, I held my baby to my breast, where he began to suckle. Pam balanced on the edge of the narrow bed, an arm resting on the pillows above my head. "Nice job, love," she said. I was heavy with lost sleep and spinning with adrenaline. Instead of a Kodak moment of blissful bonding, though, I was only exhausted, my speech slurring from fatigue. "He's really here, isn't he?" I cradled him with one arm as he nursed, and Pam wrapped an arm around me. Then, with two fingers, she caressed his cheek below the tiny blue and pink hospital cap. "Hello, Benjamin," she whispered. "Welcome to the world, sweet boy."

Pam called her parents after Benjamin's birth and repeated what I'd said to my mother, "You're a grandmother." But her mother surprised her. "I don't feel like a grandmother this time," she'd said. Pam's voice cracked when she told me this, and I shook my head in sympathy.

When Pam brought Benjamin and me home from the hospital the next day, we found balloons and a banner hanging over our front steps. "Welcome Home Baby Benjamin!" My friend Barbara and her two kids had signed the banner, and the kids had drawn pictures of babies, bottles, and rattles. Pam busied herself with unbuckling Ben from his car seat, and I carried my overnight bag up the steps, stopping to study the banner up close. "Where's the camera?" I asked, tears rising. "We have to get a photo; I don't want to forget this."

A week later, my mother arrived from Indiana. Inside our front door, she dropped her suitcase and headed straight for the bassinet in the front window where Benjamin slept. Her eyes filled with tears, and she turned to embrace me. "Can I hold him?" she asked, finally letting me go. "Please, can I hold him?"

Holding back my own tears, I lifted my son and placed him in her arms.

SIXTEEN

First Link

One evening in early winter, Pam and I relaxed on our couch, reading at opposite ends, toes touching like a pair of bookends. Benjamin crept on the rug, mouthing toys in his path, while cedar logs spit and crackled in the fireplace.

"I've been thinking of Mavis having her baby," I said, watching Ben scoot toward us. "Since she traveled to St. Louis to have Cyrus, I bet she was born somewhere in Missouri."

I often pictured her still living somewhere in the Midwest, but every time I drove past the senior apartments near the grocery store, I fantasized about her living here—four blocks from our house. We could have passed each other in the vegetable aisle at Andronico's. I could have walked right past my biological grandmother as she squeezed tomatoes or sniffed melons and not even have known it.

"I'm sure you're going to find out," Pam said, returning to the newspaper. But she wasn't smiling, and I knew that she still didn't understand what this meant to me. How I needed to fill the holes in my family's history, find the missing persons, and bring us all back together. It was yet another way that I felt like an oddity—the fact that nobody else understood what I wanted. Benjamin reached the couch and lifted his arms to be picked up. He squealed when

I hoisted him into my lap. "Bed time for you, Ben-Ben," I said, standing and then leaning over so he could reach Pam. "Give Mama a kiss. Night-night, Mama."

Rocking and singing him to sleep in the quiet dark, it finally occurred to me what I could do. I should have thought of it before; I'd done it so many times with my genealogy research. It was simple: I would order a copy of Mavis Foster's birth certificate from the Department of Health in Jefferson City. Her birth certificate would give me her birthplace. Then I'd look up Fosters in that town, and these people would without a doubt lead me to her. It's possible that she had never moved, was still there, in case her child ever came looking for her.

After moving Ben to his crib, I dug through the stack of papers on the shelf in my closet, pulled out the MAVIS FOSTER envelope, and found Cyrus's adoption record again. Guessing that my grandmother had been a teenager in 1930, I requested a birth certificate that had been filed between 1910 and 1915. I scribbled out a check for ten dollars to the State of Missouri, claimed genealogy as my motive, and placed the envelope in our mailbox.

That night another version of my recurring college dream visited me. In this one, I approach the student mailboxes in my dormitory, but because I've been away and haven't checked my mailbox in so long, I've forgotten its combination. Peering through the tiny mailbox window, I see that my box is full of letters. I recognize my Grandma Rose's pink stationery and my Norwegian pen pal's blue tissue paper airmail envelope, and I approach the counter to ask the student clerk to look up my combination. I have to wait while she does this, and I'm impatient. I've seen things in my box that, although I've been neglecting them, I must read right away.

It had been more than fifteen years since I'd lived in the college dorm, and I thought I'd left that clunker of a dream behind, but it was back, rattling me again. For me, letters were my connection to the world, to those who loved me. They fought off loneliness. But inside that annoying, recurring dream with all its obvious symbolism, I'm thwarted. I can't access my mailbox. I'm stuck, pining for something just out of reach.

Eleven days after mailing the request for Mavis's birth certificate, I settled Benjamin in his Johnny Jump Up—a bungee cord seat hung from the doorjamb—and pulled the mail from our box. I had the radio tuned to the classical station and a spirited march filled the living room. I flipped through the stack of mail until I reached an envelope from the State of Missouri. I joined Ben in the doorway, nudging his jumpy swing with my foot. "Look at this, Ben-Ben. Look what Mommy got."

I ripped open the official-looking envelope, pulled out a photocopy of a birth certificate, and shrieked. Ben spun around in his seat and stopped bouncing.

"Mavis Frankie Foster," I read out loud to my audience of one, his eyebrows cresting in curious waves. "Born May 24, 1914, in Fairdealing, Missouri." My audience bounced with enthusiasm. "What a funny name for a town."

My grandmother's name was printed with a thick calligraphy pen as if it were intended to look fancy or formal. But the scrawl looked childlike, as if someone, barely literate, all those years ago had tried to make it look official. I brushed my fingers over the raised seal on her birth certificate, a mandala of ridges erupting on the slick paper. Now I had a place and her parents' names. I could find her.

I grabbed a pencil from the bookshelf behind me and jotted dates lightly on the back of the birth certificate. She'd be turning eighty in a few months, if she was still alive. She had celebrated her sixteenth birthday in May 1930, a month before she gave birth to my father.

Who had gotten her pregnant at fifteen? A boyfriend? Or had it been rape? Incest? I wanted to know whether her parents had helped her or had kicked her out of the house when they learned about her pregnancy. Had someone accompanied her to St. Louis to deliver her baby, or had she traveled alone? Did she go by train? Car? Greyhound bus?

I lugged the oversized world atlas from our bookshelf and blew off the fuzzy layer of dust coating its top edge. Kneeling on the living room rug, I leaned over the book, searching the Missouri page for the town of Fairdealing. A web of scarlet lines spread over the blue-green wash of the mountainous region—threads of roadways crisscrossing the state in a tangle.

The dot was so tiny it took me several minutes to locate it. A hamlet-sized town, Fairdealing sat in the southeast of the state, just north of the Arkansas border. I traced the route from Fairdealing to St. Louis, two hundred miles or so to the north.

I knew then that I would go to Missouri and find her birthplace. Find *her*.

Benjamin squealed, spinning in his Johnny Jump Up. "This is your great-grandmother's birth certificate!" I said, pushing his seat like a swing and making him smile. "You might get to meet her someday."

I wanted a reunion. I wanted to present my baby to my grandmother. I wanted a photograph of Cyrus and me embracing her, with Benjamin in her lap—four generations of blood kin. I pined for a family reunion picnic under a stand of weeping willows on a southern Missouri farm with children playing tag through mowed fields. I imagined a long table covered with checkered cotton tablecloths and dozens of platters and bowls of food, and saw myself chatting with my new relatives as they passed my baby among themselves. We'd sip iced tea with fresh mint sprigs, and the farmhouse door would flap against its frame with all the foot traffic.

At first, I didn't know whether to tell Cyrus about the birth certificate or to hold off until I finally located her. He might have been upset that I'd requested it. He might have preferred not to know. But it was his mother's birth certificate, the closest we'd come to her yet. It was a gamble. If he was pleased at my news, it might bring us a little closer; if he was upset, we could lose ground.

I decided he should see it. Once he did, he would forgive me for proceeding with the search. Pushing Ben in his stroller, I walked to the copy store, and on the way home I slipped the copy of my grandmother's birth certificate into an envelope and dropped it into a mailbox.

When Pam returned from work, I rushed to show her. "That's great, Kath," she said, her tone contradicting her words.

"You don't care about any of this, do you?" I asked, suddenly angry. "You don't understand. Your family has no adoption, no divorce, no people up and leaving. You don't know what it feels like to lose your father, grow up with another father, and lose him, too." I was surprised by the accusatory tone in my voice, but it didn't stop me. "You don't have a clue what this means to me."

"I'm sorry," she said. "You're right. I just don't get it." She took the birth certificate from me. "But it's cool," she said. "I'm glad you got what you wanted." She reached out to embrace me but, still angry, I shrugged her off. I picked up a sponge and began scrubbing the counters.

Three days later Cyrus called, rustling through papers on his end. "Well, hecky, gosh darn. Yes, indeed, I found Fairdealing on my triple-A map," he said, his voice rising with anticipation. "I must have gone through there on the way to my high school reunion in Oklahoma a couple of years ago. I like to go the back roads; they're so much prettier. That's green country and rolling hills down there."

I let out a silent breath. He had surprised me again. When I'd first told him I wanted to have a baby, he'd tried to dissuade me. "You don't need a child to be complete," he'd said. But after Benjamin's birth, the cards and packages from Kentucky began arriving. "Welcome to the family," Melissa had written. And from Cyrus, "We're so happy to get photos of the fine lad. They're up on the refrigerator so we can see him every day."

But today we were talking about his birth mother. "She was a young girl when she was impregnated," he said, sounding relieved, as if a teenage mother was so much better than some of the other scenarios we both had considered but had never admitted to each other. My relief melded with his.

"Yeah," I said. "And she'd be almost eighty now."

I'd already rehearsed in my mind many times what I'd say to my grandmother when one day I called her and she picked up the phone.

I'm researching my family tree and I think we're related, I'd say. I wouldn't blurt out everything at once, but would dole it out gradually. I needed a gentle, roundabout way to say, *Did you have a baby in 1930? I think you're my grandmother!* I thought it might be safer to find a relative, a sister or brother, to break the news to her, sit next to her on the couch, ready to catch her if she slumped over.

"I wonder if it'll freak her out if we find her," I said.

"Indeed," Cyrus said, "it might freak her out, and might freak out you and me, too." His voice had lost its jauntiness.

So that was the reason he hadn't wanted to search for her, his own fear of how it would be to find her. I had suspected as much, but chose to go ahead anyway.

"With her birth certificate I know I can find her, alive or dead," I said.

"Okay," he said. "No hurry, though."

I heard the reticence in his tone but took his words as the permission I needed anyway. The next day, I sent for Mavis's death certificate. A week later, I received a reply. There was no death certificate on file for Mavis Foster in Missouri. She could still be alive. Or she might have died in another state, or out of the country. Or she could have died in Missouri, in the same town where she was born, her death certificate filed under her married name.

I had requested records of Mavis's parents from the State Historical Society of Missouri and soon after received a copy of the front page of the *Prospect News*, the Fairdealing newspaper. On it I found an obituary for Mavis's mother. That year, 1918, an influenza epidemic had killed over 20 million Americans—more than died in battle in both World Wars, Korea, and Vietnam combined. It appeared that my great-grandmother, forty years old, had been one of its victims. I read the last sentence twice. *Two of Mr. Foster's boys are sick with fever, one of them seriously.* My God, he just lost his wife and had two sick kids. And, I quickly calculated, Mavis had been four years old when she lost her mother, the same age Cyrus had been when he lost his adoptive father, the same age I had been when I lost Cyrus.

SEVENTEEN

Adoption Trilogy

In St. Petersburg, Florida, in 1967, the year I turned ten, I was adopted by my stepfather. On that day, I buckled the skinny straps of my new patent leather shoes while Michael sprinted back and forth past my bedroom door. He wore the same suit he'd worn to Mom's wedding to Tom Briccetti the year before. Now the pant legs were too short, and the sleeves of his dress shirt exposed his narrow wrists. His hair was white-blond like mine, but the cowlick above his forehead, left longer than the rest of his crew cut, had rebelled against our new father's water-and-comb treatment. We had no air conditioning, and the dew of Florida humidity clung to every surface.

"It's Spaghetti Day, Spaghetti Day," Michael sang as he sped by again. He still had difficulty pronouncing Briccetti, which would be our new name after that day. "The two c's sound like 'ch'," Mom had taught me. Earlier, I'd sat at the kitchen table with a piece of lined notebook paper and practiced spelling the long name over and over, in case the judge quizzed me.

I hadn't seen my father, Cyrus, since before Mom's wedding, and I was losing his last name today; I would no longer be Kathy Manfred. At least I wouldn't be called "Fred-man" any more at school. I didn't understand, though, the deeper ramifications of changing my name, how it represented leaving my father behind, how it would alter my identity.

"What will we have to do in court?" I asked Mom. She stood behind me buttoning my favorite dress, the one with lace around the collar.

"Probably nothing. We're just going so the judge can sign the adoption papers. You get a new father today." Her tone was the one she used when trying to convince me that I would enjoy eating the liver draped with onions on my dinner plate.

I wondered if we'd be sworn in on a Bible, if we'd see any holstered guns on deputies, if we'd join robbers or murderers standing before the judge.

"He might ask you a couple of questions."

What questions? I wanted to know, but Mr. Briccetti was already tooting the horn and Mom was shooing us out the door.

In the car, I thought about the man who would become my stepfather that day, so unlike my fair, lanky father with his hushed voice and tentative kisses. I was still getting to know Mr. Briccetti, as we called him until that day, that mile marker of a day, when Mom said we should switch to "Dad." He was a man who grabbed Michael and me in bear hugs and pinched our cheeks. He made us all laugh with his huge repertoire of jokes, and he added terms of endearment to his proclamations: "Look at this, sweetie" or "Pass the bread, honey-bunny."

Inside the Florida family court building, the chilly air raised bumps on my bare arms and legs. A bailiff, his holstered gun prominent on his hip, directed us to the judge's chambers, a large, luminous room with modern office furniture and floor-to-ceiling windows with a view of silky heat mirages on parking lot asphalt. The four of us settled into swivel seats at one end of a vast conference table, and I spun my chair around twice before Mom reached over and placed a hand on my knee. The judge entered—I remember him as a giant with neatly parted hair, a starchy suit, and skinny tie—and he shook hands first with Mom and Mr. Briccetti, then Michael and me. He sat, rolled his chair into position at the head of the table, and looked us over.

"So, why do you want to be adopted?" he asked, smiling and glancing from Michael to me. Perhaps his question was addressed to me because I was the eldest, or maybe it was because Michael's expression said *Please don't make me talk.* I peeked at Mom, who leaned forward and then back as if she wanted to coach me but knew it was too late. Most of her cherry-colored lipstick had rubbed off, but her glossy hair was perfectly combed. I didn't answer. The judge raised his eyebrows, his smile fading.

Thinking about this now, I'm appalled that a judge would put this question to a child, would force her to answer a question when he himself didn't understand its implications: the loyalties she would be forced to betray, the hidden grief over the loss of her father. That day I wasn't sure I *wanted* to be adopted because I didn't know what it would do to summer visits with my Daddy, his wife, and their little daughter, but I had the foreboding sense that I would not see them again. I was beginning to forget his scent and, without photos of him, I was beginning to forget his face. If I wanted to be adopted, did that mean I would have to pretend my father, Cyrus Manfred, no longer existed?

Although I balked at the weight of the judge's question, the brief taste of power also made me giddy with possibility. I could have said, "Now that I think about it, I *don't* want to be adopted." If I had, I could have stopped the strange game in the middle, even changed its outcome.

But I knew I needed to give the right answer. I couldn't risk making the adults angry, and the pressure pushed at my chest.

"Because we love him?"

The adults sighed in unison, like a spent but faithful church choir, their faces settling into satisfied smiles. The judge arranged the adoption papers on the table and handed his shiny gold and black pen to my mother, then to Mr. Briccetti.

We have no photographs of that day, but I remember the four of us skipping down the court steps holding hands, acting curiously euphoric, like a family in a television commercial. I didn't understand why we were supposed to be so happy. It's this confusion that I remember more than whatever else I was feeling that day. I imagine I became carried away in my parents' excitement, but I undoubtedly resisted it, too, wondering what it all meant, what was expected of me, what I was *supposed* to feel.

In the winter of 1993, almost thirty years after my own adoption, Pam, Benjamin, and I passed through metal detectors in the lobby of the Alameda County Superior Court. Pam's anxiety was palpable; her rutted forehead and wind-scattered curls made me want to draw her into my arms, reassure her. Balancing seven-month-old Ben on a hip, she stepped into the elevator and I followed—our plum-colored backpack filled with mini rice crackers, extra diapers, a camera, and an envelope of legal papers slung over my shoulder.

The Oakland courthouse, a granite wedding cake with terra cotta icing, overlooked Lake Merritt. Despite a chalky December sky, the lake was a bucolic tease in the center of Oakland. We had come to court for a rare event then: a woman adopting a baby boy, thus upping his number of legal mothers to two. A same-sex, second-parent adoption. We were still a decade ahead of the 2004 gay marriage extravaganza that would take place across the bay in San Francisco, when gay parents would charge out of closets—men in tuxedos cradling infants, women in matching wedding gowns with toddlers on their hips, and scores of working parents pulling kids out of school to rush to City Hall. Although these marriages eventually would be nullified by the courts, the attention paid them would nudge the country another baby step closer to acceptance of families like ours.

At the courthouse in 1993, though, we were forging new ground, and my feelings swirled in a mucky jumble. As the elevator made its climb, I imagined something going wrong, being rebuked, getting sent away without our adoption decree. The day after I'd given birth to Benjamin, a hospital administrator watched me fill in the draft of his birth certificate. Looking over her glasses, she saw me scratch out the word "father" and write in "mother" and add Pam's name. Home alone six weeks later, though, I tore open the envelope from the State of California, pulled out my son's birth certificate, and read the sole word typed in the space under "father": *Withheld.* I felt like a teenage mother of an illegitimate child. As if I'd both done wrong and had been wronged. I was angry at a society I believed had reproached me unjustly. I wanted our trip to family court to begin to rectify that.

The three of us left the elevator and made our way down the hall. Neither the State of California nor the county's Department of Social Services had approved Pam's adoption of Ben. Our lawyer had warned us that in our county only two judges had ever overruled the Social Services policy and granted adoptions by homosexuals. In neighboring counties there were none. Some states were testing the process, but in most it was still against the law.

It was Pam who had released the awakened sperm into me and thirty-seven weeks later, holding our baby under his slippery arms, pulled him out of me. Even though she had cut through his umbilical cord, even though she had cooked and pureed and frozen organic vegetables in ice cube trays and pushed our baby in his doorway swing so I could eat dinner, the State had deemed our family unsanctioned, morally lacking, illegitimate. "Children need both a mother and a father" we'd heard over and over in the media, or they risked personality disorders, and "sexual deviance" of their own. I didn't believe most of it, but did worry we might make an effeminate boy or a super-feminist girl, children who would have trouble fitting in with the rest of the world. There was no data yet, no long-term studies of children of gay and lesbian parents like those that would come later and prove the frightened, conservative pundits wrong. There was only hype and horror stories.

Mary Louise, the Alameda County child welfare worker who had overseen our adoption home study, was a married woman with teenage children. She wore skirts and stockings and makeup and looked as if she lived through the tunnel, past the line delineating the liberal Bay Area from more conservative territory. We worried that she'd feel uneasy in our home, that she'd write a negative report about us simply because lesbians gave her the creeps. Before she arrived, we cleaned our house as if we feared it could be repossessed on her whim.

We'd begun the adoption process halfway through the pregnancy. Mary Louise had visited in order to interview us, inspect our home, and collect the thick questionnaires that Pam had filled out, intrusive queries about drug use and psychiatric history. She had come again after Ben was born, inspecting his room, waking him from a nap because she had to lay eyes on him. "Had to make sure he wasn't bruised and emaciated," I'd grumbled to Pam afterward.

On her final trip to our house, a month before the court date, she sat in our living room shuffling through papers on her clipboard. Pam held six-month-old Ben on her lap, planting razzing kisses on his bare soles from time to time. He laughed at this, and I hoped this made us look good. "So, how'd we do?" Pam asked near the end of the visit, the strain evident in her voice. "Did we pass?"

Mary Louise placed her clipboard in her briefcase, stretching out the moment, as if we were filming a made-for-television special. "You guys are great," she said, and it took me a few seconds to take in the compliment. "You've got a beautiful home, and this baby is obviously well cared for." As if on cue, Ben cooed, a poster baby for second-parent adoption. I didn't dare look at Pam or we both would have laughed.

"I have to warn you, though," Mary Louise said. She placed her briefcase at her feet and looked at each of us in turn. "It doesn't matter what I say. The department's policy is to deny these adoptions. I'm sorry."

Our lawyer had forwarded Mary Louise's report to us a week

before the court date. It extolled Pam's suitability as a parent and supported our desire to "legalize a relationship that already exists." But as she had warned us, she was bound by policy. Her report ended with a summary. Pam and I stood in the dining room, the day's mail strewn across the table, Pam reading over my shoulder.

> In this worker's opinion, the petitioner's suitability to adopt the minor is not in question. She has lived with him and has been committed to him since his birth. Both women obviously love this child and share the responsibilities for his care and development.
>
> Despite the fact that the petitioner and the natural mother are not married, they have formed with the minor what is a viable family unit. They now want the adoption granted in order to give the minor the protection and support of two committed parents. They believe, and this worker concurs, that the minor can benefit from the security that this adoption will provide and that his best interests will be served by the granting of this petition.
>
> However, the Agency and State policy recommends denial of same-sex adoptions because the child does not benefit from a legal marriage. The undersigned worker, while viewing the petitioner as eminently qualified to adopt, will abide by that policy.
>
> RECOMMENDATION: The Social Services Agency of Alameda County recommends that the petition of Pamela Harris-Craig for the adoption of Benjamin Craig be denied.

"Damn it," I said, flapping the paper in front of Pam. "We paid two thousand dollars to the county for this?" I wanted to rip it up. Even though we'd been warned, I hadn't expected to feel such a wound from seeing the words in print.

Pam took the paper from me and smoothed it out on the table. "We knew it was coming. State policy."

"It still pisses me off. She knows what we're like. She knows we're good parents, that we're just two women who had a baby together. She knows that Ben is loved, that he has that beautiful room with the curtains *you made*—" I gestured toward Ben's room, where he was napping.

"I know—"

"Why can't someone say, 'Just a minute here, let's do the right thing for once? We need to break the rules because the rules are wrong.'" I resented the state scrutinizing our adoption simply because we were a same-sex couple. That Pam had to be fingerprinted in order to adopt Ben, and that we had to ask our friends and colleagues and neighbors for letters of reference vouching for her character. When a married woman used the sperm bank to inseminate, her husband didn't have to go through anything like this; the state considered the kid his own. But because we weren't married—and of course we couldn't legally *get* married—Pam was treated like a suspected criminal needing fingerprinting and background checks. The State didn't screen gun buyers as scrupulously as it did gay parents.

"It isn't fair," I said, feeling completely justified in my complaining. "The double standard sucks." As I think about this now, I'd bet that my stepfather didn't have to leap through so many bureaucratic hoops, that his marriage certificate was all that was necessary to adopt us.

"She said more than likely the judge would overrule it." Pam's tone was flat; she was unperturbed, paradoxical given that it was *her* legal relationship with Ben that was at stake. Pam often countered my anger by staying composed, unmoved. Her calm, steady temperament during my spells of emotional tumult would sometimes make me want to pinch her. *React, damn it!*

Only two judges in our county routinely overruled Social Services, and if we didn't get one of them, our adoption would be denied and we would be left no recourse. "*If* we get the right judge," I reminded Pam. "And not some homophobic dinosaur."

"We will," she said, reaching up to massage my shoulders. "Don't worry."

I shrugged off her touch. "'Don't worry'? That's pretty naïve, Pam." I left the room, coddling my anger.

* * *

We had used a donor who had relinquished his ties to our child by giving his semen to the sperm bank instead of directly to us, but I still worried that if we didn't complete this adoption, a judge might—in a legal fluke—take my child from me and give him to the donor and his wife simply because my partner was a woman. There was precedent for this; I'd read news stories about more than one divorced woman who'd fallen in love with another woman and consequently lost custody of her children. The legal system was too schizy for me to trust it.

"We need to ensure your rights," I'd said earlier. "We don't want the donor, or a judge who doesn't know any better, taking Ben away from you." A lesbian couple in another state was fighting over custody of their six-year-old, also a product of a trip to the sperm bank. Because the nonbiological mother had not adopted, in the eyes of the court she had no rights, and she'd been denied even visitation with the child she'd raised since birth.

But I hadn't admitted my deeper fear, the possibility of our breaking up someday, and what might happen to Ben if we did. One of the couples in our lesbian moms' playgroup had already separated and now shuttled their eighteen-month-old between two houses. I had not admitted that part of me wanted to skip this adoption and hold on to legal custody of Ben. I could imagine a time when I might want him to myself, and this frightened me, my potential for behaving badly. I was afraid of the power of repetition over generations. Because my Grandmother Mavis, Cyrus, and I had each lost a parent at age four, I feared this mysterious force would somehow conquer one more generation. I encouraged Ben's adoption, because even if Pam and I no longer wanted to live together someday, she would never have to give up her child. And, even more importantly, *he* would not lose her.

Entering the Oakland courtroom, Pam, Ben, and I paused at the doorway, succumbing to its reverential hush. The room was plain, boxy with an unadorned, absurdly high ceiling that siphoned off voices. A row of windows placed high on the wall broke the vastness of the mahogany paneling. No one stared at the lake or daydreamed out windows in this courtroom.

As we settled into the hardwood theater-style seats in the gallery, Pam removed Ben's jacket and I handed him a rice cracker. I tried to fuss with his socks, but she beat me to it, pulling them up over his chubby legs. She had dressed him that morning in blue overalls with a small teddy bear appliqué on the center of the chest. A large red heart filled the center of the bear. It was an outfit he'd worn several times before, and I didn't think about its significance until later. When I looked at photos taken that day, though, I wonder whether Pam chose that piece of clothing deliberately, or whether it had been an unconscious act, and she had been sending the judge a subliminal message: I love my Moms (and they love me).

Pam smoothed Ben's hair at the temples and kissed his cheek. He gummed his rice cracker and babbled with pleasure. I wanted to reach over and squeeze Pam's hand but resisted, thinking of the drunk we'd passed on our way home from the movies years before. Pam and I had never spoken about it, but we limited our displays of affection to home. There, with our curtains drawn, we embraced, kissed, caressed.

The light from outside the courtroom, eking in from the windows above, was winter-weak. Other families wandered in through the double doors, equally burdened with baby paraphernalia and legal papers, and found seats around us. Across the aisle, a Caucasian woman and man, both with graying highlights, took turns chasing an Asian toddler in a lacy, rose-colored dress around the spectators' seats. In the row in front of us, a woman with skin a shade lighter than the mahogany walls adjusted an ebony-skinned boy's necktie while a fair-skinned blond man, his hair in dreadlocks, tapped his fingers in a restless rhythm on the boy's shoulder.

Ben squawked, joining the other babies in an infant opera. Parents shushed their children, but the noise mounted, and the room began to sound more like a daycare center than a courtroom. We were the only lesbian couple waiting with a baby, and Pam hovered over Ben, on high-maintenance-mother mode. "More crackers?" she asked.

"Do you want Mama to get your bottle?" A meltdown would not have looked good at that moment. It seemed we'd tacitly agreed that she'd carry him into the courtroom that morning, that she'd take care of him during this event. Like in a job interview, we'd show whoever was watching what a good parent she was.

I forced myself to sit still, resisted leaping up and pacing. I bounced my knee as if Ben was on it and wiped my palms on my slacks. Maybe the judge, the one on whose calendar our lawyer had found us a spot, had called in sick and the substitute judge would refuse to see us. Or he would usher us in only to scowl, lecture us on the necessity—the right—of a child to have a mother and a father. Because she was expensive, we'd asked our lawyer not to accompany us to court. All the paperwork had been filed, and we were gambling that this would be an uncomplicated formality. "It will probably go your way," she'd said when we discussed it. "But you never know." Maybe she should have been there in case something went wrong.

I pulled the sheaf of papers from the backpack and pretended to study the one on top, the order terminating the sperm donor's parental rights—one of the documents necessary for this adoption to proceed. I studied it even though I already knew every word on it and how many ways it said that my child was fatherless.

1. BENJAMIN ROSS CRAIG has no presumed father under California Civil Code section 7004 (a).

2. BENJAMIN ROSS CRAIG having been conceived through artificial insemination by donor, the sperm donation having been made through a licensed physician, has no legal father pursuant to California Civil Code 7005 (b).

3. No man has formally or informally claimed to be the father of this child.

It didn't occur to me that day, but I wonder now what my father Cyrus had to sign to relinquish us, clearing the way for Tom Briccetti to adopt us, a practice more common then than now. I'm sure that story is a sad one, and I will probably never ask him to tell it. I'm beginning now to recognize more differences than similarities between the two adoptions in which I was a part.

The clerk's voice rang clear in the cavernous room. "Benjamin Ross Craig. Katherine Briccetti-Craig. Pamela Harris-Craig." It was the first time I'd heard our family name spoken in public. Pam and I had only begun using our hyphenated names a year earlier, adding a surname we'd found on both of our family trees to our fathers' surnames. Not only was it Pam's mother's maiden name, Craig was also the middle name of her brother and mine. It was my father Cyrus's middle name, too. His adoptive mother's maiden name had been passed on to him and then to my brother. In court that day, hearing our names with their common denominator was strange and comforting and a source of pride at the same time. I wanted the world to know that the three of us shared a name. I wanted to stand up and shout that even though there was no father we were still a family.

We gathered our belongings from the seats around us. The adoption process was beginning to feel more like a commitment ceremony than when Pam and I exchanged rings seven years earlier, perched on the boulder overlooking the glistening Pacific Ocean. It would prove more binding than registering with the City of Berkeley, and later with the State of California, as domestic partners. Like in divorce, those contracts could be nullified. Not so with adoption. Ben's adoption decree would tie me to Pam forever, because no matter what happened in our lives, whether we stayed together or drifted apart, we would always have this child binding us together.

We followed the clerk, in her bold floral dress, past the judge's vacant bench into a hall leading to his chambers, Pam carrying Ben chest-to-chest, I trailing with the gear, the family's Sherpa. As the birth mother, I had already signed papers allowing Pam to adopt my biological child without giving up my parental rights. After today, if everything went our way, no one would be able to take our child away from her. Not my family, not the court, not me. *If* this judge overruled the Department of Social Services and granted our adoption.

In his chambers, bespectacled Judge Morimoto, wearing a white starched shirt with rolled-up sleeves and an off-center tie, reached across his cluttered desk to shake our hands. He had a wide, round face, and I searched it for a clue as to how this would go. When Pam leaned forward, Ben tilted toward the judge, who took that opportunity to stroke our baby's marshmallow cheek with thick fingertips. "Say hi," Pam told Ben, and she waved his chubby hand at the judge. Ben stared at the man, mouth open, not blinking. Given the distractions—children to watch in the courtroom, this unfamiliar man making eyes at him—he had not fussed once that morning. And for a minute I, too, was distracted. I glanced out the judge's window at the lake where a crew team scuttled across the water with smooth, dash-like strokes.

"Tuesday mornings I do the adoptions." He stared at us above his thick glasses, and I still couldn't read his expression. Standing next to him, his clerk arranged papers on his desk; because she stood so close, it looked for a second as if the judge had a second pair of hands. "It's the best part of my job," he added, smiling, and a whisper of calm settled inside my chest.

I glanced at the decree of adoption our lawyer had optimistically prepared. And as Judge Morimoto signed his name to it, I read a few of the upside-down words. *IT IS THEREFORE ORDERED, ADJUDGED, AND DECREED that the petition for adoption is granted.*

It was finally over. An anchor inside me released. I tossed away ballast, my body becoming lighter. And I felt something else: the pure satisfaction of a victor.

The judge looked up. "Congratulations," he said, scooping up the papers and straightening them against the desktop before handing them to his clerk. I checked Pam's face and, for the first time that morning, she smiled at me.

"We're legal, little boy," she said, brushing her lips over Ben's wispy hair. I put my arms around the two of them and squeezed, smashing us together. When I kissed Ben's cheek, he squealed and kicked his legs.

A minute later, Judge Morimoto took his black robe from a coat rack in the corner, slipped it over his shirtsleeves, and met us in front of his wall of legal volumes. His clerk snatched our camera and, as the four of us positioned ourselves, Ben wriggled in Pam's arms, ready to get down. "It's okay, big boy," she whispered to him. "We're almost done." We flanked the judge, who spoke to Ben in a voice used with babies. "Say 'Happy Adoption Day' for the camera." Ben babbled, imitating the judge's intonation. From behind the desk, the clerk framed us through the lens and released the shutter.

EIGHTEEN

Acceptance

Near the end of my second pregnancy, in the spring of 1995, I trudged up the school's wide staircase, grasping the railing both to support my bulky body and heave my heaviness against the pull of gravity. We had used the same sperm donor again, and an ovulation predictor kit had given us an advantage this time. We'd nailed it on the first try. I had worked part-time through this pregnancy, and that day I had just finished testing a third-grader and was headed for my last appointment of the day, a meeting with a parent in the library. When this was over, I could pick up Ben from his family daycare, take him home, and fall onto the couch while Pam cooked dinner.

Pam and I had come out to only three or four of the teachers at the elementary school where she taught a class of deaf children and I evaluated special education students. Only our closest friends knew the truth about our relationship. Even though I was pregnant again and we wanted to be forthcoming about our growing family, we feared how the deeply religious teachers and staff members at the school would react. We still imagined losing friends, colleagues shunning us, and the school district finding a way to fire us.

I'd survived coming out to my family, but Pam's mother's

difficulty accepting us had been painful for Pam and disturbing to me. Her mother didn't seem to understand what we were doing. "Will he inherit from you?" she had asked Pam after Ben's birth. "Yes, Mother," Pam answered. "I'm legally adopting him."

Ben's first summer, Pam's parents had visited us again at our cabin so they could meet him, their fourth grandchild, the first not related to them by blood. They'd driven up in a new Lexus that time, and Pam met them on the gravel driveway while I stood on the deck with Benjamin in my arms. "Here come your grandparents, Ben-Ben," I'd whispered, hopeful yet guarded. "Are we ready for this?"

Pam and her father grabbed suitcases, and her mother approached me, her car pillow under her arm, purse over the other. When she reached me, she set her purse on the railing, handed me her pillow, and thrust out her arms. "Give me that baby," she said, cradling him and kissing the top of his head.

Later, she told us only that the priest at their church had counseled her. "He helped me see things differently" was all she said, and Pam and I sent silent thanks to this stranger who had helped her accept our relationship, our family. Over the years, both Pam's parents would carry photographs of Ben and Daniel in their wallets alongside those of their other grandchildren. "We are so proud of you," they would tell the boys when they did typical kid things like play soccer on a team or get a good report card. "And your moms," Pam's mother would say, "we're proud of them, too. They're doing a great job with you."

When I opened the door to the school's library, I immediately backed out again. Instead of a parent waiting to talk to me, the principal and most of the teachers and instructional aides sat around the tables chatting. Across the room, Pam laughed with another teacher. It looked like a staff meeting, but something was off. The mood was too jocular, and I'd glimpsed helium balloons and a pile of gifts on a table near the door. I peeked in again. "Surprise!" the group shouted and burst into applause. My eyes filled as I took it all in, but someone whisked me to the head of the table, sat me down, and presented me with a piece of chocolate cake.

"Oh, my goodness," I said, taking in all of the smiling faces. "This is unreal. What a total surprise." I looked at Pam. "And you knew about this?" She nodded and the room echoed with laughter.

At home, Pam carried two shopping bags of gifts into the house while I unlatched Ben's seatbelt and helped him out of the car.

"I can't believe how generous everyone was," she said when we got inside. No one working at our school made much money, but everyone had brought something for our baby. Even the church ladies, as we had flippantly called some of the staff, had given us stuffed animals, books, and tiny clothes.

"I'm blown away," I said.

"We're definitely 'out' now," Pam said. "They've known about us for a long time. We're the ones who've been in the dark, not them."

"Yeah, we put ourselves in the closet, didn't we?" I lowered my moose-like body onto the rug with Ben even though it would take a good minute to get back up. "I feel kind of stupid for not giving people enough credit. It's all right with them, I guess."

"I don't know about that, but if they don't approve, they still accept us."

It was liberating, no longer keeping secrets at work about my life. Although I carried forty extra pregnancy pounds, I felt lighter. I could now go about my day without fretting about who would ask about my husband or who might whisper behind my back as I lumbered down the hall, my belly preceding the rest of me by quite a distance.

After Daniel was born in the spring of 1995, a student nurse stepped into my hospital room, a clipboard pressed to her chest. She acknowledged

Pam with a nod and then turned to me. "May I ask you a few questions before you go home?" She kept her eyes on her clipboard.

When I agreed, she proceeded through her checklist, and at the end of the interview, posed her final question. "What birth control will you use now?" she said, glancing up. I so badly wanted to laugh, just howl with exhausted pleasure at her expense, but I resisted, and she flushed deeply when she realized her gaffe. "Oh, sorry," she said, dropping the clipboard to her side. "I guess that's a stupid question." She left, apologizing again, and closed the door behind her. Pam caught my eye and we moaned with mean delight.

We named our second son Daniel Thomas Craig, the middle name for Pam's brother's son, and as an ambivalent gesture to my stepfather, Tom Briccetti. *Great name!* he wrote after I sent him the birth announcement, and I, still seeking redemption, was happy to have earned another checkmark on the Good Daughter scale.

On a clear fall day a year and a half later, the four of us drove into San Francisco with Ben's preschool buddy, James. Our mission: the dinosaur exhibit at the museum in Golden Gate Park. In the back seat of our '90 Toyota wagon, the preschoolers sang rhymes about dinosaur poop as we barreled across the Bay Bridge into a thick shroud of fog. From his car seat up front next to Pam, eighteen-month-old Daniel made motor razzing sounds at each truck and motorcycle we passed.

We emerged from the Treasure Island tunnel, and a lull in the chatter of the three-year-olds lent a moment of calm. The fog was floating back toward the ocean for its daily intermission, and the spear point of the Transamerica Pyramid jabbed clear through into the blue. If the clouds retreated far enough we might picnic at the children's playground after the exhibit. Just as I began to drift farther into my own thoughts, James broke the silence.

"So, Benjamin, do you have a dad?"

Pam and I locked eyes in the rearview mirror. She raised her eyebrows, and I widened my eyes to say *Oh boy, here it is; this is big, this is important, what do we do now*? We'd talked about what to say to our children when this moment came, but it all left me.

None of Ben's friends had asked about our family yet. They knew I was Ben's mommy and Pam was his mama, but I worried James was about to say something that would hurt Ben's feelings.

I shot a glance at my son. I wanted to jump in and answer for him, take care of this for him, make sure he felt all right about it. But I took a deliberate breath and waited to see how he would handle it.

"No, I have two women." His voice was buoyant, unencumbered. I stifled my laugh. And I guessed by the look in her eyes that Pam was doing the same.

"Oh," James said. "But you have to have a dad."

"No, I have two moms." Ben sounded less sure, as if there were suddenly something wrong. I ached for him, but didn't want to interfere. Plus, I was curious how he understood all of this.

James was silent for a minute, but he wasn't finished. His little forehead was scrunched up with three-year-old thinking. "Did your dad die, Benjamin?"

"No."

Silence.

"Yeah, he must have died, cuz you don't have one."

Benjamin looked up, his expression saying *What do I say here*?

I couldn't hold back any longer. "Do you want me to help explain it to James?"

Ben's eyebrows returned to their proper place on his face. "Yes."

I didn't want to screw it up, make too much of it, create an aura of anxiety instead of nonchalance. In terms of tone, I aimed for blasé.

"James, do you know how you have a sister and Benjamin has a brother?"

"Yeah."

"You know how some families have cats and some have dogs?"

"My cat's name is Bella."

Ben jumped in. "Our dog is Chesie!"

In the front seat Daniel echoed, "Sessie!"

"Some families have a mom and a dad; some have two moms or two dads, and some might have just a mom or a dad." I remembered the previous Mother's Day when Mom had joined us for dinner and my brother Mike had appeared at our door with three bouquets of flowers. "For all the mothers here," he'd said, beaming. With James, I didn't go into all the possible configurations. Grandparents. Foster families. The sperm bank and adoption stories could wait for later.

What would James say next? Had I told him what he wanted to know, or was he not buying it? Had I said enough? Too much?

"Oh," James whispered. Deep in thought, he gazed out the window at the San Francisco skyline. We were closing in on the exit to the park. "I hope I get to see a brontosaurus," he said. "That's my favorite. The brontosaurus."

Talking with preschoolers about our family was easier than coming out to strangers. I had yet to try that, and knew it needed to be soon. We would no longer try to pass as heterosexual, lie by omission, or avoid answering questions about our relationships. I was ready to battle the legacies of my family of origin.

Totland Park was only a few blocks from our house, and the boys and I played there several mornings a week. One foggy day later that fall, a couple of moms and dads, a half-dozen nannies, and a gaggle of toddlers were at the park dressed in sweaters against the chill. I pulled eighteen-month-old Daniel out of a swing, and he plopped down in the sand to play with a bucket and shovel. Ben rode scooter toys on the pathways, and I found a spot on a bench where I could take a load off while keeping an eye on my kids within the park's fenced yard.

"How old is your son?" the woman next to me asked, knocking me out of my exhausted-mother reverie. She was gesturing toward Ben, who had just pedaled past us on a souped-up toy race car.

"He's three and a half," I said.

"Oh, he's so big!"

My defensive mother radar pinged with the fear that instead of being impressed with his advanced development, she found him freakish. We watched as Ben abandoned the race car and climbed up the slide, his burly, sturdy body more like a kindergartner's than a preschooler's, and I readied myself for what would come next, as it always did.

"Is your husband tall?"

My face grew warm. I had never answered this question directly to a stranger before but had become adept at leading conversations off in another direction. Or sometimes I simply dodged pronouns, answering questions as if Pam were my husband. If someone asked what my husband did for a living, I didn't say, "He teaches," but just, "Teaches." This way I wasn't really lying.

But that day in Totland Park with my boys, I decided to tell the truth, test it out on this woman I might never see again. We lived in Berkeley, after all, and if I couldn't come out to other parents here, where could I? And what did I really fear, that she would leap to her feet and run off screaming, "Eeeeew! A lesbian mother!"?

Pam and I had promised each other we wouldn't keep secrets from our kids, nor force them to keep secrets about our family, even if we were still apprehensive. We wanted them to know the truth about how they came to be and that we were not ashamed of how we made them, even though I was still struggling with shame that day. I wanted to show my boys how to talk about their family, how to answer questions about their absent father. And, right then, I needed the practice.

I answered the other mother, speaking too quickly like I do when I'm nervous, my words running together in a piled up heap. "I don't have a husband, my partner is a woman, and we used a donor from the sperm bank to get pregnant. My partner adopted both of our boys."

There. It was out. I felt something close to relief but my heart was still wild. I looked over at the other mother and waited. There was a five beat pause followed by a long, "Oh…" and then, "Wow!"

I couldn't gauge her reaction. I didn't know if her "Wow!" was an enthusiastic wow or a disapproving wow. I promptly filled the silence.

"We don't know who the donor is, but we know a lot about him. And we used the same donor for both of our kids." I gestured toward Daniel toddling by. "And, yes, the donor is a big guy," I said, finally answering her question.

"Wow," she said again. "Have you seen a picture of him?"

"No, but we have a description. And we know how tall his parents and grandparents and sisters and brothers are, and we have all their medical histories."

As I told her all this, I thought again how strange it was to know all these facts but still not really know what the guy looked like. I didn't tell her how I often speculated about the shape of his nose, chin, and eyes and wondered whether the boys looked more like him or me.

"Someday we might get to meet him," I said. I worried she found *me* freakish now.

"What do you mean?" She rose from the bench to push her daughter on the swing. I followed, keeping an eye on my children, now playing together in the sand.

I told her about the sperm bank's identity release program, how we could look up the donor when the kids were eighteen. "That's important to me," I said. "My father was adopted, and I don't know anything about half of my ancestry."

"That's amazing," she said. She began picking up sand toys and getting ready to leave. I didn't know if she was eager to get away from me or if she was just heading home for lunch and nap time.

Ben called for me, crying because Daniel had just pounded him on the head with a plastic shovel. My adult conversation was over for the day; the other mom and I waved good-bye to each other over our shoulders. As usual, I had only told part of our story. I wanted to say *Wait a minute, there's more*. And *It's great*. But I was relieved, finally, at having accomplished this much. And I was proud for having at last told a stranger the truth. I had passed a test of my own.

I couldn't wait to tell Pam about the encounter, to write about it, authenticate it. The boys and I ambled home from Totland Park, stopping to stow our sweaters in the stroller basket because the sun had, for the time being, chased away the ever shifting fog.

NINETEEN

Loss Revisited

From across the restaurant table, Cyrus studied me. His head wobbled, from nerves or a degenerative disease, I wasn't sure, but he'd ordered a beer as soon as we'd sat down, saying it would calm him. I had invited him to lunch—the only time we would spend alone during his visit to California. He'd joined us for dinner at our house in Berkeley, but he and I hadn't had any time to shoot the breeze yet, like we had at his house during my visits. It seemed, though, no matter where we parked ourselves, California or Kentucky, we didn't have much to say to each other. Alone together, we often stared out over each other's shoulders.

Setting up our lunch date, I had suggested Japanese. He wanted a burrito. Somehow we ended up at the Chinese restaurant near my brother's, where Cyrus was staying because our house in Berkeley was too full and I was too busy. He had come on an impulse—a cheap senior airfare—but it was Mother's Day weekend, and I feared his visit would interfere with our celebrating with Mom, who had moved to California when Daniel was a year old, no longer willing to live so far from Mike and me and her two grandsons.

"You're so pretty," Cyrus said from across the table.

I sputtered a denial and lowered my eyes to the tightly folded hands in my lap. I was a thirty-nine-year-old mother of a two-year-old and a four-year-old, with a saggy belly, storm gray half moons under her eyes, and shallow tributaries sprouting around her lips. I didn't know what to say. I felt like someone who hadn't studied for the test but showed up to take it anyway.

We were pretending to be father and daughter, but in truth, too much time had passed. There was too much distance wedged between us, and the lost time had become a chasm neither of us knew how to cross. After twenty years of getting to know him, my father was still a stranger, and I still felt unmoored around him.

When we'd greeted each other earlier that day, he'd pecked me on the cheek, his bristly chin scraping my jaw. "I love you, honey," he'd said, and then, thank God, didn't wait for a response but began filling the space with words.

I love you, too was caught somewhere in my throat, and I couldn't bring it to the surface.

I didn't *know* him. And if I ever felt like I was beginning to know him during our visits, even beginning to feel affection for him, we would part again, go another couple of years without seeing each other, trying to keep our relationship alive with letters and infrequent phone calls. I had no doubt that we had bonded when I was a baby, but in adulthood we'd suffered from too much apartness.

We'd had our reunions over the years since I'd found him—me, Mike, and sometimes even Mom getting together for brief visits with the Kentucky family. But Cyrus had missed all the milestones in my life between the day we'd been separated and my Wright Institute graduation in Berkeley in 1992. After that commencement ceremony, I presented Mom, Mike, and Cyrus with T-shirts with the inscription "PHinisheD," like one I'd bought myself. We each pulled the shirts over our fancy clothes, and Pam gathered us for a series of clowning photographs, capturing the four of us in disparate colors—florescent pink, deep sea blue, pine green, and parakeet yellow—catching us with goofy grins or in mid-laugh. For the photographs, we'd draped our arms around each other's shoulders, our poses implying a certain intimacy. But I felt dishonest in front of the camera that day, as if I were an actor playing a role. And I was jarred by what felt like a lie: a grown woman flanked by her mother, father, and brother. Her first family, a family that existed only for an instant three decades earlier, the photographs giving the illusion they'd been together all along.

Over spicy prawns and chow mein, Cyrus asked me about my work and then, as I began to answer, cut me off with his own chatter. When I asked about my half-sisters and half-brother, who still lived near him in Kentucky, he gave me the minimum, things you would tell someone outside the family. "She's doing just fine." And, "He enjoys the new job, and we're happy for him." I, the absent daughter, didn't seem to warrant more than this. I know now that he cared about me, was undoubtedly desperate to get past his own grief, and simply didn't know how to have a conversation with me. But at the time, I fought stinging disappointment and couldn't resist the compulsion to yawn, my body's message that I was retreating. I longed desperately for a nap. I wanted to go home.

After lunch he pushed back from the table. "Let's just sit and visit a bit," he said. "I'm pleased to be here." But we ended up caught within long, awkward silences, each of us glancing around the room, too uncomfortable with the intimacy of a direct gaze.

It was time for me to get home, and this spurred me to ask Cyrus something I had wanted to know for a long time. I was afraid of the answer but pressed ahead anyway. I knew I might not have another chance.

"Why did you let Tom Briccetti adopt us?"

His head jerked around, and he faced me directly. I'd gone too far. This was not the way we were with each other, this direct, risking something so hurtful. "Was that just the way it was done then?" I knew that in 1961 mothers were usually awarded custody and fathers settled for summer visits. But even those visits had eventually ended for us, and I wanted to know why.

He pressed his palms into his eyes and rubbed, uncovered them and looked at me directly. "I didn't want to interfere with your relationship with your new father," he said. He had not met Tom Briccetti by then, so he couldn't have known whether it was a good thing to encourage a relationship with him. "I approved your adoption because I thought a full-time mom and dad would be better, and I knew they were fine folks, and both musicians."

I pondered his answer. He hadn't wanted to interfere. This fit with his personal style of deferring to others, not stirring things up. He'd needed to waive his rights, abdicate his role, in order for Dad to adopt us. Maybe he'd given up visitation because he'd been convinced it would be best for us children. There was no joint custody option then. Somebody had to lose. For all those years, though, because of the blurriness of my childhood lens, I'd assumed he was simply happier with his new family.

"Why did you leave us?" I asked, staring at my lap. I couldn't bear to see his face, see the pain I was causing.

"I did not leave you!" He was suddenly animated, and I sensed other diners staring at us. "I loved you three." His voice broke, and this was something new; I'd never heard him, or didn't remember ever hearing him, choking on tears. "I don't know why she left. Your leaving, your mom taking you and Mike from Burlsville, has given me unrest for thirty-five years." His last words were whispered.

Sweat surfaced on my brow, my nape. Under the table, I rubbed the skin on my palms until they stung, then stared at the pattern of creases I'd been born with, the heart line on each of my hands forking off into two branches like divining rods.

It couldn't be true, that my mother had been the one to break up our family instead of him. For an instant, I wanted to protest, defend her. But then my gut churned and I knew. I'd had it wrong all that time. I'd made a monumental mistake. Because I didn't remember leaving Burlsville as a four-year-old, I'd fashioned an explanation, and this mistaken account had colored my entire life, had made me a girl who had been left.

The Story of My Life had been based on a myth. The Abandonment Myth. But realizing this did not erase the loss. One loss simply had been substituted for another. Grief—for what had been and what had *not* been—began its ascent from the cellar where I'd locked it up, surged like current past my heart, burned my throat, and threatened to escape in tears. But I would not cry in front of him. I could not let myself be so exposed. I still needed to force feelings back inside, hoping they'd just disappear back into the dark.

I glanced up and found him staring out the window, his silhouette backlit by the bright day outside. For a while, we were silent.

"I'm sorry," I said to Cyrus, apologizing for getting it wrong. I was apologizing, too, for secretly blaming him for the breakup of our family. "I didn't know. I always thought you had left us."

He shook his head but did not speak. It was all we could manage that day.

Outside the restaurant, he pecked my cheek again. When he leaned in to hug me—a fleeting shoulder press with lots of back thumping—I patted his corrugated spine. "I love you," he said.

I knew I should tell him I loved him, but I couldn't form the words. It wasn't the truth, and I couldn't make it up. I couldn't, not even for his sake, pretend. Instead of the heat of tears and the spiky ball of pain in my throat—what I'd often felt upon long separations from my mother—after lunch I felt only numb as Cyrus and I repeated the stiff, pat-on-the-back embrace before I climbed into my car. I drove away, back toward my life, not knowing when or if I'd see him again, and as unpredictably as a burst of lightning, an aching pain in my chest set off an electric tingle down my limbs, lodging in my palms and Achilles tendons—the places that registered my deepest emotional pain. My eyes stung as if I'd wept. I craved sleep. Merging onto the freeway, I was heavy and drowsy, deeply weary. I was a four-year-old saying good-bye to my daddy. I was seventeen, knowing my stepfather was packing a U-Haul and driving it away. I was thirty-nine and I didn't know who my father was.

TWENTY

Filling in the Blanks

"Mommy, how do you get babies?" Benjamin asked one morning. He pushed his dump truck through paths he'd made in the sandbox while I hung laundry on a line. It was one of those rare sweltering spring days in Berkeley when the fog stayed away all day, when we turned on fans and groaned about the heat. Pam had built the sandbox for the boys, nestling it against the back of our house underneath a lemon tree that reached the second story and a plum tree that raccoons feasted from at night.

The appearance of Ben's baby brother two years earlier had prompted this question for the first time. That day, and again over the years when he asked, he and I squeezed into the armchair, often with a kids' book about reproduction, and I told him about a man's sperm and a woman's egg making a baby, adding a little more to the story each time he seemed ready for it. I was proud that my sons could identify their penis and scrotum along with their elbow, neck, and shin. I wanted them to feel free to talk about all their body parts, and not repeat my childhood experience, when those labels were off-limits, even shameful, when we whispered "down there" and "privates."

Bath time was often a prime time for this subject. One night, Ben let go of his floating toys and slipped his hands under the bubbles.

"What's this called?" he'd asked, lifting his scrotum above the water.

"That's your scrotum," I said.

"What's inside my scrotum?" He stretched the walnut-wrinkled skin smooth.

"Your testicles."

"Scrotum-testicles-scrotum-testicles," he chanted. Then he looked up and smiled. "I *like* my scrotum."

Another time, he asked, "Did we pop out of your stomach?"

"Nope, you came out of my vagina."

"Where's your penis?" he asked one day.

"Women have a vulva," I said.

Yes, the boys learned accurate labels. After a play date, Ben told us he had ridden in the seat that faces backward in his friend's car: their Vulva.

Because they had no father, I suspected certain words in my children's vocabulary appeared later than in their peers'. When Ben was two and a half, I took him to a birthday party where he met his friend Kai's father for the first time, and where Kai's father pushed Ben on the swing for a while. "Mama," he said to Pam when we got home. "Kai came to the party with his man."

Sometime later, we rented the video *Born Free,* the story of orphaned lion cubs in Africa. Ben was confused about the disappearance of the cubs' parents and asked, "Did the lion cubs' Mommy and Mama get killed?"

Now, at four, while playing with his truck in the shaded sandbox, he was asking for the baby-making story again, and when I finished telling him about the man's sperm and the woman's egg, he said, "Then how did you get me and Daniel?"

I dropped the damp toddler undershirt I was holding into the basket at my feet and turned so I could face him. I hadn't expected this question so soon, but I was proud to hear the ease with which he approached the topic, and I tried to come up with something that would satisfy him.

"You know how you put your money into your piggy bank and take it out when you need it?"

He parked his truck in a corner of the sandbox and looked at me. "Yeah," he said.

"The sperm bank is a place where a man put his sperm. We took some out when we needed it."

"Did you put it in your own vagina?"

Again, I had to take a moment to figure out how to answer. "Mama put it in my vagina."

He backed up the truck and loaded it with sand. His face was hidden under his straight blond hair, but I knew just how it looked, the lines of concentration between his eyebrows, lower lip thrust out. He was quiet. It seemed we were finished, and I looked back at the clothes on the line, lit with morning sun. When would we have the conversation about *how* Pam put the sperm in me, or the one about the donor, the one when Ben finally asked, *Who was* his *man*?

I regularly sent photos of the boys to Kentucky, wanting to keep Ben and Daniel in the Manfred family's consciousness. I knew Cyrus and Ursula displayed the photos on their fridge and on top of the piano. Recently, I'd sent new ones, and when my half-brother Cody dropped by our father's house one day, he studied the portraits of his California nephews. Over the months, Cyrus had told me people often commented on how much the brothers looked like each other. Everyone knew that the boys shared the same sperm donor, that they were full brothers. "Wow!" Cody said to our father when he saw the new photos of the alabaster-skinned boys with their matching Dutch-boy haircuts. "There sure was no mix-up in that lab!"

When they began to ask, we would tell Benjamin and Daniel about the donor's hair and eye color, his fondness for macaroni and cheese, his brother—their biological uncle—who works as a police officer. Although Ben, if he was interested, could ask the sperm bank for the donor's identity when Ben was eighteen and Daniel sixteen, I wanted both boys to reach legal age before we found the donor, to avoid any potential for a bizarre custody battle. And I wanted them to be mature enough to handle meeting the man we all thought about. I was already trying to convince myself that I'd be ready for that day when it came.

One afternoon while the boys napped, I came across a copy of Daniel's birth certificate in a pile of papers on my desk. Because state policy had changed after Ben's birth, Daniel's document from the State of California contained something Ben's had not. Back in 1993, the word "Withheld" on Ben's birth certificate had pronounced our family's illegitimacy. But on Daniel's birth certificate, the word "father" had been blocked out with six capital Xs from a typewriter, and the word "parent" was typed next to it. In the box underneath, Pam's name had been added. It was a start, and we had applied to the state for an amended birth certificate for Ben as well. We wanted both boys to have two birth certificates: one with both of their mothers acknowledged, and one with their father's name withheld because we didn't know when they would need one or the other. College applications. Marriage licenses. Or, God forbid, the Armed Services, where having two mothers might cause trouble for them.

This was 1997 and the season that Ellen Degeneres nearly ruined her career by coming out on national television. The religious right, as well as most of the general public, had been stirred up. The battle had begun, but our little family simply observed it from the sidelines. Neither Pam nor I was what I called an in-your-face lesbian, women who kissed in public, rode motorcycles topless in the Gay Pride Parade, marched stridently for the cause. I thought of those women as brave warriors and at the same time believed they were going about it in the wrong way. Too much force repelled people. Too much difference freaked them out. Our contribution would be more subtle. Every person who got to know us would see we weren't to be feared. We would infiltrate with stealth, change minds one at a time.

I took Daniel's birth certificate to the safe deposit box at our bank downtown and, inside the tiny cubicle in the basement vault, pulled other documents from the long tin box. Finding my own birth certificate, I traced my fingers over the raised seal of Indiana on the watercolor rainbow background. Like my children, I had two birth certificates: an original and a revised.

The second one, issued after my stepfather adopted me, I have come to view as a document of lies. My middle name, Anne, is missing its "e," and the space for my father's name states "Thomas Briccetti." There is no mention of Cyrus Manfred, my biological father. It is as if he never existed.

In my thirties, I had written to the State of Indiana for a copy of my original birth certificate and was denied. It was a closed document, the clerk's letter informed me, not releasable without a judge's orders. I phoned my mother and whined. "It's mine," I'd said. "They have no right to keep it from me." But she had saved one in her own safe deposit box, and within a week I held my original birth certificate. Katherine Anne Manfred.

An original birth certificate for Cyrus must exist somewhere, too, I thought as I placed my own back in the safe deposit box. More than likely his was locked in a microfiche file at the Health Department in Jefferson, Missouri. Despite Cyrus's continued reticence, even after his adoptive mother died a few months short of her 103rd birthday, I had briefly continued searching for his birth mother. But after no new leads, I had stuffed my notes, correspondence, and crossed-off to-do lists into the manila envelope marked MAVIS FOSTER and placed it back on the shelf in my closet with the family tree I'd begun in junior high school.

My family tree now included my two sons, but it remained half bare, as if a strange blight had attacked only one side, my father's side, denuding it. It would be several more years before I realized that my sons' genetic family tree looked exactly the same.

Folding Daniel's birth certificate so it would fit in our safe deposit box, the familiar urge to find Cyrus's birth parents pressed at me. Cyrus might have half-brothers and -sisters, a slew of kin somewhere. And, naturally, I wanted to be the one to bring us all together. In addition to the thrill of accomplishment, I wanted the attention the reunion would bring me. "She's the one," my new relatives would say at our reunion party, putting their arms around me, "the one we can thank for this." Then I'd gaze out at the hundreds of people I'd brought together, reliving what I saw as my amazing feat of perseverance and determination.

There was another reason I was compelled to make a last attempt to find my grandmother. It had to do with my children and what I believed was their birthright. On a family trip once, a flight attendant had leaned over while I buckled Benjamin into his airplane seat. "If we need them," she had said, "put on your own oxygen mask before assisting your son." I nodded, dismissing her. I already knew that a mother can't do her children any good if she's unconscious; she needs to take care of herself before she can take care of them. Likewise, if I didn't know my own roots, didn't know those from whom I'd come, I couldn't pass that knowledge to my children.

So it was more than eagerness to fill the empty branches of our family tree that compelled me, more than the desire to be reconnected with the missing members of our family, and more than a need to be acknowledged and not forgotten. Like the many cultures that practice ancestor worship—the Zulus, for instance, believe their lives are simply a conduit between their ancestors and their children—as an adolescent I had yearned for a connection to my roots so I might feel some groundedness, or steadiness, to balance the ruptures in my family. I wanted to search for the spirits of my ancestors and add their names to my charts so that I would feel embedded in my family's history, so that I might understand where I belonged. And *to whom* I belonged.

After having children of my own, though, I liked to think that it would be my gift to them if I found the rest of my missing family, if I was able to pass on the knowledge of the people whose woven ribbons of DNA we shared. Maybe one day I would even help my sons search for the people on the other side—their biological father's side. I had become that Zulu conduit after all. And particularly because of how I had made my children, I believed forging these connections was something I owed them.

TWENTY-ONE

Another Link on the Chain

In the fall of 1997, with the boys in daycare and preschool and my work schedule still part-time, I convinced myself I would make one last attempt to find my grandmother. She would be eighty-three years old, and I needed to hurry up and find her or I'd be sipping iced tea in front of her headstone instead of next to her on a porch swing. For the last time, I pulled out my creased manila envelope marked MAVIS FOSTER, its corners scratchy with molting Scotch tape, its edges disintegrating into a soft dust.

First, I shot off letters to the Fosters in the area surrounding the town of Fairdealing, Missouri. But, too impatient to wait for return letters in the mail now that I'd decided I had to find her *right now*, one afternoon I started telephoning.

"My name is Kathy Briccetti, and I'm researching my family tree," I said to the first Foster when she answered her phone. "I'm looking for a Mavis Foster; do you know her?"

"No, dear, I'm sure sorry." The woman's voice held only a hint of a Southern accent. "I don't know any Mavis Foster."

I called five numbers, amazed there were that many families sharing Mavis's surname around the tiny southern Missouri town.

But no one admitted knowing Mavis, and I began to suspect them of lying, hiding some big secret from me, the outsider.

"Is this crazy, what I'm doing?" I asked Pam that night. "Should I just let it go? I was perfectly happy before I knew about Mavis, and I have enough family." As I spoke, though, I knew this was a lie.

Usually Pam listened without comment. She often acted as a sounding board, listening until I figured out what I wanted to do. But that time she had an opinion.

"I've never really understood why you need to search for her. Why don't you let it go?"

She had finally shared an opinion, something I'd been asking for all along, but it was not the one I wanted. "You're right," I said, my voice hot with irritation. "You don't get it. You'd like it if things stayed the same; I bet you'd never do something as risky as this." I wanted to cry but fostered my anger instead. "You really *don't* get it." And with all the dramatic flair I could muster, I sighed loudly and left the room.

For my fortieth birthday, Mom and Mike presented me with Internet access so I could study adoption websites, search online White Pages for all the names in my Mavis envelope, and e-mail genealogists working on the surname Foster. The Internet was young in 1997, and there were not the hundreds of genealogy sites that there are now, so I mailed more letters to vital records offices, state archives, historical societies, and even to the Methodist church in Fairdealing, requesting marriage, baptism, and death certificates. Mike helped me search the Social Security Death Index online, but we found no Mavis Foster from Missouri. When nothing else panned out, I began to poke around the Internet for names of private investigators.

Before contacting one, though, I wrote a letter to the editor of the *Prospect News*, the newspaper that had carried Mavis's mother's obituary almost eighty years earlier, pleading for clues from readers.

I received no responses. Frustrated, I dug out the Adoptees Liberty Movement Association newsletter that the social worker handling Daniel's adoption had given me when I'd told her about searching for Mavis. I flipped it open to the list of adoption search meetings and put the next one on my calendar.

On a Sunday afternoon in October, I found the Korean church in the Oakland hills where the ALMA group met every other month. Clutching my raggedy manila envelope, I took a seat on a folding chair in the basement meeting hall. Floor-to-ceiling accordion partitions divided the space into smaller rooms, which I imagined were used for childcare during church services, evening AA meetings, and weekend rummage sales. Sunlight baked the rosebushes on the other side of the sliding glass doors, and yellow ginkgo trees flickered in the scorching breeze, but the basement space was pleasantly cool.

"Welcome to the East Bay ALMA chapter." From behind a lectern, the speaker scanned the audience, about twenty of us, and nodded once when her eyes met mine, acknowledging me, the newcomer. A thick braid, earthy brown, hung to her waist, and laugh lines around her eyes and mouth placed her around fifty, about ten years older than I.

"For our visitors," she said, "the Adoptees' Liberty Movement Association is a national organization formed to help adoptees and birth parents reunite. I'm Elizabeth McGuire, the chair of our branch. I'm an adoptee *and* a birth mother." She sounded proud of this dual heritage, the multigenerational repetition of adoption in her family.

"I found my thirty-year-old daughter, and we reunited two years ago. We write letters and call once in a while." Elizabeth smiled broadly. "I also found my birth mother." Her smile faded, and the lines between her eyebrows deepened. "But she doesn't want to pursue a relationship."

I read the pain on Elizabeth's face. This could be my story, too. My grandmother could shun me. And Cyrus, already reluctant about my searching, might become angry with me, want nothing more to do with me if I insisted on continuing. I knew I was stirring up too much, risking too much.

"I'm searching for my birth father now," Elizabeth said.

I wanted to know what her adoptive parents thought of her searches, whether they'd been supportive or had been hurt by them, but I didn't dare spoil the mood by asking a question. Elizabeth held the gaze of a woman in the audience wearing a nametag identifying her as an ALMA search assistant. Elizabeth looked as if she needed to draw strength from a compatriot before continuing.

"I was born on November 29, 1948, in Tulsa, Oklahoma."

The year and city, she explained, were key facts. Adoptees always included these bits of information when they placed newspaper classified ads, wrote to agencies, or sent cards to a potential birth mother. If a birth mother read the classifieds or received a card with an unknown name and return address, only she would know what that date meant, only she could decipher the coded message. It was a way of maintaining privacy and, if necessary, protecting secrets kept from husbands and children who might still not know about the adoption. I was an eager student, bobbing my head at each of her points.

Elizabeth invited us to introduce ourselves. We ranged in age from a high school girl accompanied by her adoptive mother to a man around Cyrus's age, late sixties, I guessed. Three people in the audience were searching for relinquished children, the rest for birth parents. No one else was looking for a grandparent.

When it was my turn, I rose from the chair. Looking over the group of strangers, I had a momentary lapse of courage. What was I doing here? I felt like a fraud, that I had no right to this sacrosanct knowledge. This was the adoptees' temple; they were the rightful recipients of this service, not me, the daughter of an adoptee, a step removed.

Years later, I would learn that when people join new groups, a common impulse is to look around, study the group, and determine how we are different from the others. I was also falling into my old habit of setting up myself as an outsider before I'd had a chance to join the group. Eventually, I would read that grandchildren sometimes do search for their parents' birth parents, and this would make me feel less alone and less strange for having such a strong drive to search for people a generation removed. But I didn't know any of this then, and I felt an urge to leave the ALMA meeting, forget about the search. Instead, though, I imitated the introduction script. "My name is Kathy Briccetti, and I'm searching for my father's birth mother. My father was born in 1930, in St. Louis, Missouri."

The others smiled and nodded, as if I belonged there as much as anyone else did. I sat down, relieved. After the last introduction, Elizabeth addressed us again. "We'll do our workshops in a minute. At that time, we'll pair you up with one of our search assistants—members who have found birth relatives and have undergone training in search techniques."

That was what I'd come for. Clues and secret tricks to help me find Mavis Foster. *Let's do that now*, I wanted to shout. *Don't make me wait.*

"But first," she said, "this month we have a reunion story."

A woman about my age approached the lectern, and Elizabeth enveloped her in a long embrace. Pulling back, she pinned a button the size of a teacup saucer to the woman's silky blouse, the heavy disc straining at the fabric like it might rend a hole in it. From my seat twenty feet away, I read the message: "I FOUND."

Something inside my chest took flight. I couldn't wait to leave, find Mavis, and come back again so Elizabeth could hug me and pin that clownish button on me.

The younger woman stood in front of the lectern clutching a five-by-seven framed photograph as if it were a life preserver. "My name is Claire," she said, flicking her wispy blonde bangs off her face. "I was adopted in 1959 in San Francisco. I found my birth mother last week." Her voice cracked, and she laughed again as she brushed away tears with the back of her hand. I fought the urge to weep with her.

"It was simple, really," she said, clearing her throat and straightening. "At the library I looked in phone books of cities all over California on the chance that she stayed around here and didn't change her name. I found her in Modesto, an hour's drive from my house."

"She kept her maiden name after she got married, hoping I would find her someday. She had other kids, but she always wanted to see me again." Claire was remarkably composed as she told this part of the story, but the switch that had dammed my tears had been opened to trickle setting. I pulled a tissue out of my pocket and dabbed at my eyes, feeling foolish. No one else was blubbering.

Claire had attended only one ALMA meeting. Afterward, it had taken her a week to locate her birth mother, reunite with her, and meet her half-siblings. I wanted to follow her, use her timeline.

"Oh," Claire said, almost as an afterthought, "I found my birth father, too. Sort of." All of us were rapt, and only the crisp leaves blowing past the open door broke the silence.

"He lived one town over from my birth mother. He was married, and they'd had an affair, but a week before I found my birth mother, he died." Someone gasped, and the audience emitted a collective sigh. "A heart attack."

Maybe I didn't want her story after all.

"So the day after I met my birth mom, I went to my birth father's funeral. I came in late and stood in the back of the church watching. I left before it was over. I didn't want to have to explain who I was."

I took some of Claire's sorrow and put it in the place I store mine. I imagine it as a tiny cabinet in my heart that is marked "Sadness," and within that cabinet is another, even smaller, compartment where I tuck "Regret." My habit of pushing away feelings was a part of the Midwestern cultural heritage when I was growing up. Now, friends from the Midwest who have also migrated west commiserate with me about our upbringings, how different the emotional cultures are among regions in the United States. How we feel more tightly wrapped up than the natives, gradually unwinding our psyches, learning how to untie swathed feelings the longer we live here. How different the West Coast—with its bare-your-soul, peace-and-love vibe—feels from any place else, and how this is no doubt part of the reason many of us were drawn here.

Claire flipped open a newspaper clipping that had been wedged into the back of the picture frame. "At least I have this," she said. She waved his obituary from the local paper in front of the group before folding it up again and putting it in her pocket. "I'll pass this around," she said and handed the photo to the seventeen-year-old girl searching for her birth parents. Then she returned to her seat as Elizabeth began introducing the research assistants.

When the photo reached me, I held it a long time, staring at the images of Claire, her birth mother, two half-brothers and a half-sister—strangers squeezed together on a couch in front of a framed painting of a bucolic scene, their arms wrapped around each other, captured forever mid-laugh. I find it suspicious that people are always laughing, or smiling hugely, in photos marking large events that must cause not only joy but ambivalence. I wondered how the people in Claire's photo were really feeling. Was it truly happiness, or was there also some uncertainty, fear even?

When it was my turn to meet with an ALMA search assistant, the woman first suggested I replace my worn manila envelope with a three-ring binder containing dividers and tabs. This would allow me to organize my papers into three sections: correspondence with individuals and agencies; a log of what I'd completed; and a list of what I needed to do next. She offered to hook me up with an ALMA member in Missouri who could search local records if I needed it, and, finally, she gave me something more valuable than everything else: the clue that would prove to be the most important one of my search.

"Look at the 1920 census," she said. "Because it's so difficult to find women, particularly if they've changed their name, if you can find your grandmother's *brothers* on the census, they might lead you to her."

* * *

Back in the Oakland hills a few days after the ALMA meeting, I drove into the parking lot of the Mormon Temple, a giant Disneyland-like structure visible from many spots in the Bay Area. I had visited the Family History Center fifteen years earlier, when I was researching my mother's family tree. Two closely shorn young men in ties and overcoats had met me then in the parking lot on a drizzly winter evening and, holding an umbrella over my head, led me to one of the genealogy centers for which the Mormons are renowned.

I walked unaccompanied this time across the parking lot in the brittle fall heat, remembering the orientation video from my first visit and praying I wouldn't have to sit through it again. I'd felt defensive watching the sections on the Mormon faith, as if I had to protect myself from being indoctrinated. I admired the Mormons' genealogy resources but hadn't heard yet that the church's goal was to create a worldwide database of genealogy records so that they might posthumously convert Mankind. Now I simply feared the ten-minute film would eat up my valuable search time. I had only three hours before I had to pick up the boys from daycare and preschool.

Inside the building, a notice read "No short skirts or halter tops." I glanced down at my culottes reaching mid-thigh and grabbed the fabric at my hips, pulling the waistband down low across my hips. *Please don't make me leave and come back another day.* I tucked my fanny pack in a locker, bringing the only objects allowed in the center: a pencil and a small notebook. I looked straight ahead and slipped inside.

In the Family History Center, I suspected that I shouldn't announce my search for a woman who had relinquished her baby for adoption, and sure enough, I soon overheard someone say, "We don't allow searches for people who are alive." As much as I loathed breaking rules, I couldn't stop. The rule was wrong. The information was my right. I had to have it.

The library resonated with hushed conversations, the cranking of microfiche machines, and the whirring buzz of film spooling through sandwiched glass plates. A volunteer in a belted, knee-length dress led me to an empty reader in the darkened alcove. It looked as if there would be no movie, thank God. What would this grandmother think if she knew I was looking for *my* grandmother, hoping to find her alive? Maybe she would secretly approve. Or maybe she'd kick me out, first posting my photograph on the bulletin board's Do Not Admit section. If she knew that my partner was a woman, that we'd conceived our children with frozen sperm and were raising them without a man, would she still welcome me to the Church of Jesus Christ of Latter-day Saints?

The woman's conservative dress contrasted with the ostentatious façade of the cathedral three hundred yards away, and I didn't understand this contradiction. Where did humility fit within one of the world's wealthiest religious organizations? Maybe I needed this bitterness to justify my breaking their rules since I needed the Mormons, needed their resources. "Thank you so much," I said, a little too cloyingly, after the volunteer loaded my first microfiche reel. My smile was so large my cheeks ached. After she left, I settled into my study carrel and, focusing on the 1920 census cards embalmed in celluloid, kept my eyes on the machine and pretended my search reached back in time, toward my dead ancestors, instead of the whole truth: that I was looking for names of living relatives so that I could meet them.

Hunched over, staring at the huge screen of spooling names, handwritten in a variety of historically loopy scrawls, I struggled to focus. After two hours scanning the cards in constant motion, my eyes stung and my head lurched with nausea. I had trained myself to pay attention only when the name Foster appeared on a page, but I didn't know how many more reels I could get through feeling this queasy.

M. F. Foster, Ripley County, I murmured to myself over and over like a mantra. Fosters were mixed up with Flynns, Fausts, and Franks, so I stopped scrolling every few minutes whenever a

Foster appeared on my screen. But none of the first names matched those on Mavis's birth certificate. Earlier, I had e-mailed a private investigator, and he was ready to start working if I couldn't find a lead of my own that day.

But finally, toward the end of the last microfiche roll, I saw it. FOSTER: Head of household: Mitchell F. I skimmed the names of his children: Oscar, 13; Esther, 10; Lois, 7; Mavis, 5; and Harlon B., 3.

"Yes!" I whispered, glancing at my neighbor, eager to show off my success. He looked up from his machine and returned my smile before turning back to his scrolling.

I had done it. Found Mavis's father, my great-grandfather. I'd hit the jackpot on this oversized slot machine that spit out information instead of quarters. This time the cherries had lined up for me. I grabbed my pencil and copied the Fosters' names from the 1920 census microfiche card into my small spiral notebook.

Mavis's mother's name did not appear with her husband's and children's, and I remembered that she had died two years before this card was filled out, during the flu epidemic of 1918, leaving her husband a widower and her five children motherless. Her obituary had mentioned one boy seriously ill with influenza. Had he died, too?

When I settled down enough to study my notes, I realized that sure enough, the 1920 census had unearthed the names of Mavis's brothers: Oscar and Harlon. The ALMA search assistant had said it might not be difficult to track these men down. Phone books at the library. The Internet. I could find them.

TWENTY-TWO

Connection

At home, the Internet White Pages produced hundreds of Oscar Fosters, too many to call or write. But when I searched for Harlon Foster, I found only six, and toward the bottom, one listing caught my attention: Harlon B. and Claretta Foster. This Harlon Foster had the same middle initial as Mavis's brother in the 1920 census and lived in Paragould, Arkansas. I pulled out the atlas and found Arkansas right below Missouri, Paragould maybe fifty miles across the border, probably a couple hours' drive from Fairdealing.

I should call, I thought, eager for quick results. But I knew a phone conversation might move too fast, and I could blurt out something and scare them off. A phone call without warning might pull the family tighter, buttressed against outside intrusion, and I'd never learn the truth. A letter would allow me to slow down and hint at what I wanted, proceed prudently.

Yes, Mavis is my sister, I imagined Harlon writing back. *Now, how do you reckon we're related?* He had been only fourteen when Mavis had had her illegitimate baby. Had he even known about her pregnancy? Maybe he'd been sworn to secrecy.

I'm your sister's granddaughter. Is she still alive?

I wrote to the six Harlon Fosters on the list. Then I wrote to Cyrus.

First, I enticed him with the names of Mavis's siblings from the census. Then I asked him what I really wanted to know: *Are you ready to contact the adoption agency now?* I was getting close on my own, and one more clue—something he could get from the agency—might lead us directly to her. I expected to wait for his return letter, but he called me a couple of days later.

"About your last letter," Cyrus said, "I'll ask for the non-identifying information if you want me to, but I just don't want connection with Mavis or my siblings, if I have any."

"Oh," I said, not understanding why he was still wavering when I was so close.

"It would probably do in Mavis, if she's alive," he said. "And it's just too emotional for me."

So that was it. He wasn't only afraid of hurting his adoptive mother's feelings by contacting his birth mother, and, like me, he didn't want to disrupt Mavis's life, but the real reason he was afraid was because of what it might do to him. He must have feared a repeated rejection, a blow strong enough to do *him* in. I could finally understand his reticence, but I wished he'd been able to tell me this earlier, instead of ten years after I'd begun searching—searching at times against his will, searching full of ambivalence and negotiating guilt and exhilaration. He and I were so different. While my approach was impetuous, his was more measured, guarded. Of course, I realize now he had more to protect than I did.

"She must be very healthy," he said, "because you and I, Mike, Sarah, Cody, and Melissa are darned healthy!"

"We sure are," I said, covering my disappointment with a cheery voice. "Yes, please do ask for the information. Then, after you get it, I guess we can decide what to do next." My voice cracked, betraying me. I hung up and let the tears come.

"I'd feel terrible if I opened up old wounds for Cyrus, or for Mavis," I said to Pam later that afternoon. We stood in the kitchen, watching through the window as the boys played together in the sandbox. "It seems like I'm the only one who wants to know what happened to her. Mike's interested, and he's found websites for me, but nobody really cares about searching for her."

Pam began cracking eggs for a quiche. "Cyrus might want to know but not want to know. You know?"

"Yeah," I said, picking up the three-ring binder from the counter and taking it to the desk. "I think." Underneath his fear, Cyrus was probably also curious. Maybe he really did want to know more about his birth mother, and I could act as intermediary, a protective filter. I didn't have to tell him what I found if it was too terrible. Mostly, though, my drive was selfish. I'd already spent a long time searching for Mavis, and now I was so close. I had to keep going.

A couple of weeks later, since my letters to the Harlon Fosters across the country hadn't produced any responses, I picked up the list and sat next to the phone. After Pam and the kids left for work and school, I dialed the first number, my heart thrumming so loudly inside my head I was afraid I wouldn't be able to hear the person on the other end. I didn't call the Paragould number first because I needed to practice my speech and gauge the reactions I received.

Harlon Foster from Carmel, California, sounded disappointed that he was not the right one, not irritated that I had bothered him. "Good luck," he said. "I hope you find your Harlon Foster."

His friendliness, the way he chatted with me as if we were indeed related, surprised me. And his intrigued—not shocked or horrified—manner relaxed me so that by the time I dialed the next number, my heartbeat had hushed.

After four more calls, I was ready to try the number in Paragould, Arkansas. It was this last number, the listing of Harlon B. and Claretta Foster, which held the most promise. I dialed, and the phone on the other end rang and rang, no answering machine picking up. I assumed they were an older couple, in their eighties, probably shunning a modern answering contraption, out for the day at a bridge club, golf game, or Moose Lodge luncheon. In case

I misdialed, I tried again, calmed by the hum of the ring every three seconds.

I hung up and settled in front of my computer to write a report for work, but I had difficulty concentrating. Every hour I pushed my chair back, grabbed the phone, and pressed redial. Each time, by the fifth ring the rhythmic drone had hypnotized me. I fantasized about Harlon leading me to my grandmother and talking to her on the phone. I wondered what her voice would sound like, what we'd say to each other. When and where we would meet. Each time, after ten rings, I hung up.

Where *was* this Harlon B. Foster who might be my great-uncle? In my typical style, now that I was ready, I wanted to talk to him immediately. I dialed his number again.

"Hello?" A woman's voice. My heart dove into my gut.

"Hi. My name is Kathy Briccetti and I live in California—"

"I got your letter. I didn't answer it yet," she said, her Southern accent raspy; I guessed she was a smoker. "My husband died a couple of months ago, and I've been up at my daughter's." She spoke rapidly, immediately taking over the conversation, behaving as if we'd been talking on the phone every day for years and were simply picking up where we'd left off the day before. "She just brought me home."

"I'm sorry about your husband," I said, praying she would not ask me about mine. "Are you Claretta?"

"Yes."

"Are you Harlon's wife?"

"Yes."

I couldn't wait any longer. "Does he have a sister named Mavis?"

"Yes, he did. But he died on the twenty-first of August; he had cancer. He was eighty years old, almost eighty-one."

I tried to listen, but my mind raced. I'd found my Grandmother Mavis's brother, but he was dead. Where was Mavis?

Claretta stopped talking for a second. In the background, another woman's voice had interrupted her.

"My daughter wants to know how you're related to us."

"Well," I said, taking a deep breath, "Are you ready for this?" I didn't want her to hang up from the shock of hearing that Mavis had been an unwed mother.

"Yes, I am." Her voice was firm and sure.

"Did you know that when Harlon's sister Mavis was sixteen she had a baby?" I sucked in my breath.

"Oh, yeah. We knew about that."

My breath escaped silently. "I'm that baby's daughter."

"Well, I'll be. I figured you'd be related through Mavis, seeing as you're out in California and all." She took off again, telling me about her two daughters, one a school teacher, the other an electrical engineer, and I scribbled notes on my legal tablet. Her comment about California didn't register; I didn't understand it, so I ignored it.

As soon as I could interrupt, I asked, "Where is Mavis now?" I wanted her to tell me that my grandmother lived an hour from me, that she would undoubtedly love to hear from me, that Claretta herself would call her right now and make the introduction.

"She died out there in California, about 1964 or so. Someone from the Red Cross called us. The boys, Harlon and Oscar, paid to have her sent back to Fairdealing on the train, and they buried her with their father."

My body turned heavy, as if gravity exerted a greater pull at that moment. I dropped my chin to my chest and closed my eyes, shutting out the sunny, optimistic sky outside the window. I would never meet her. I would not sit on her porch and chat over an iced tea; we would not catch up on each other's lives, discover the similarities in our personalities, exclaim about the physical features we shared. I thought I had prepared for this potential outcome, but my eyes stung and my throat began forming its ball of pain. I had wanted to be friends with her, like I had been with my Grandma Rose. I had so wanted to know her, my other biological grandmother.

The reality became clearer. Mavis had died decades before I'd started looking for her, but I'd missed her brother by just two months. If only I had worked faster, he could have been my link to his sister.

"How did she die?" I asked.

"I'm not sure, but I think it was a brain tumor or something."

I didn't know if I'd share this with Cyrus. He had reassured himself many times by saying, "She must be healthy; look how healthy we all are," but he was wrong. She had died a long time ago, and she had been young. I grasped another pattern. Inherited susceptibility to cancers, passed from mother to son to daughter. But Cyrus was healthy, no cancer there. Would it skip a generation, come after me?

"Harlon was a good man," Claretta said, picking up again. "He flew a single-engine F-40 in the war. He volunteered to go. He wasn't drafted. He went to Borneo, in combat, and came home in 1946."

Her voice softened and she choked up. Someone took the phone from her.

"This is Rhonda. How're you doing, Kathy?" The woman spoke with an easy Southern drawl, reminding me of my Kentucky relatives. "I'm a middle school teacher; I live in Memphis," Rhonda said. "My father was diagnosed with liver cancer earlier in the year, and my mom's been staying with me since he died."

"Yeah, I'm really sorry about your dad."

Claretta said something in the background, and then Rhonda spoke again. "My father jogged with the Olympic torch last summer when it passed through Memphis. It was the first year that average citizens could carry it. We have it on video. He hated that video because you could see his bowlegs. Do any of y'all have bowlegs?"

My laugh was more of a snort. "No, I don't think so." I loved her sense of ease, her humor, this immediate intimacy between us. She had simply accepted my word and begun filling me in on her family. Again I was surprised at a stranger's openness, her taking me at my word. There was none of the guardedness I'd expected. I was learning that not all families needed to keep secrets, put up walls. The passage of so much time, too, had undoubtedly softened the edges of hardened family secrets, if there had been any. And it was a different era, one in which people could be more open about premarital sex, unwed mothers, adoption. But still I dreaded telling these new family members about my situation.

"So, you and my father are first cousins," I said. "That makes us first cousins once removed."

"I guess that'd be right," she said.

"How did Mavis die; do you know? Your mom wasn't sure."

Rhonda lowered her voice, as if the phone might be tapped. "I believe that she died under suspicious circumstances. We heard she had been living alone in a hotel and she was hit over the head and died from that."

Murdered? I immediately pictured the Tenderloin District of San Francisco, its poverty, prostitutes, adult bookstores. I didn't like the image, couldn't put my grandmother in that scene, couldn't understand what she would have been doing there. I'd been hoping for more pride-in-my-ancestors moments, vignettes I could toss into conversations with friends. I wanted more Civil War heroes, abolitionists, securely middle-class professionals, not a down-and-out grandmother living alone in a hotel room in a run-down part of town. What could possibly have brought her to such a place?

In the background, I heard Claretta say something to Rhonda. "My mom wants me to tell you that one of Mavis's sisters is still alive. Her name's Esther, my aunt, and she lives in Houston. She's about, oh, eighty-seven or so, and she's in good health and still sharp as a tack, just bad knees, I believe. She has a son named Gary, my first cousin, who's in his fifties. He's a computer person. He's written a book. He'd be your Dad's first cousin, too, I guess. Hey, here's Mom again; she wants to say good-bye. Nice talking to you, Kathy. Make sure Mom has your address, and I'll write you a letter."

I scribbled notes as fast as I could. I couldn't wait to call Cyrus. I wanted more. How had Mavis really died? Had she had other children? Did anyone know about Cyrus's birth father? Before we hung up, I asked Claretta if she had a photo of Mavis.

"I doubt I do, but I'll look through my closet for one."

"Thank you. I'm so glad I finally reached you."

"Me, too, dear." She sighed. "But I wish you could have met Harlon. You would have loved him, and he would have been so tickled to meet you all."

I telephoned Cyrus. "I found her brother, Mavis's brother!" I said, almost shouting. Cyrus listened silently as I read to him from my notes. For as long as I could, I avoided the topic of Mavis's death. I'd had a little time to get used to the idea, but he would be hearing it for the first time. I wanted to let him down easy, and my steamroller style often rolled over my best intentions, so I fought the urge to blurt it out. I wondered if he would be relieved, or disappointed. Or both.

I finished reading my notes. It was time to let him know. "I'm afraid Mavis has already died," I said. "It was back in 1964, way before I started looking for her."

He was still quiet.

"Claretta said she may have had a brain tumor, and Rhonda said something about her being hit over the head with something." I hadn't wanted to tell him that part, but I couldn't stop myself; I felt compelled to tell him everything I knew. Then I slowed, backpedaling a bit. "Neither Claretta nor Rhonda were sure how Mavis really died," I said. "I wouldn't be surprised if both of their explanations were wrong."

I was ready for him to offer an opinion, share my curiosity, and join me in my fear for our health.

"I might have a half-sibling or two out there somewhere," he said. His voice was calm, almost hypnotic, and it was my turn to be quiet. I remembered climbing down from the Greyhound bus when it pulled into the tiny depot in Burlsville more than twenty years before, when I reunited with him and met my half-siblings. It looked as if it might be his turn to meet siblings, maybe even his own father.

"I'll type up everything and e-mail it to Ursula," I said. He didn't use e-mail much, preferring to stick with his frequent letters and to let Ursula manage the computer.

"That sounds fine. Thank you." His voice remained impassive, giving me no clue as to his feelings. I'd heard him turning pages on his own pad as he made notes, but that was all. No deep intakes of breath, no comments.

We hung up and I took a deep breath. I opened my Mavis binder, found my communication log, and with a black marker made a final entry. "FOUND: October 20, 1997." I shut the binder gently, leaned back in my chair, and, alone in the house, let out an audible sigh.

Over the years, Pam and I had covered the wall next to the desk with framed family photos spanning four generations, from my Grandma Rose to our young sons. After closing my binder, I stared at a photo of my mother and me taken at my doctoral graduation a couple of years earlier. She was the one I most strongly resembled. I had inherited her height, large bones, long feet, and loud, piercing laugh. Grandma Rose was short, and the only physical trait we shared was the bruise-colored skin under our eyes. Three generations of women—my grandmother, my mother, and myself—looked like we never got enough sleep. I wanted to add a photograph of Mavis to my family photo gallery on the wall next to my computer. More than ever, I wanted to see if I looked like her.

I also got a kick out of comparing my children's features with my own. Others often recognized more similarities than I could spot, but when Daniel was eighteen months old, I found a black-and-white photo of myself at that age and stuck it on the refrigerator.

The resemblance was uncanny. The angle of my jaw and slight under-bite matched his perfectly at that age.

When people say my sons look like me, I take pleasure in it, and at the same time worry about how it makes Pam feel. But if this lack of connection bothers her, she doesn't let on. Only once did someone mistake her for a biological mother. One afternoon when Ben was about three and she was pushing him in the stroller, a stranger passing her on the sidewalk cooed at Ben and then looked up at Pam. "He has your smile," he said. When Pam told me about this later that day, she looked amused, as if pleased for having fooled someone. I loved the stranger's innocent affirmation of our family.

When we brought Daniel home from the hospital, Pam and I had found that his fourth toes curled in considerably more than the others. The pediatrician assured us they'd soon straighten, and we ignored it until a year later when my mother came for dinner, plopped into a chair in the living room, and kicked off her sandals.

Glancing at the soles of her familiar feet, I saw something I'd never noticed before. "Oh, my God!" I yelled.

She planted both feet on the floor, ready to spring. "What's the matter?" She looked stricken, and I laughed so loudly Pam and the boys ran into the room.

"Look at Mom's fourth toe," I said. "It's just like Daniel's, curled in just like his." We all pulled off our shoes and compared toes. But there were no more matches. Only this little boy and his grandmother shared the genetic configuration that had formed their extraordinary fourth toes. I longed to see what other genetic similarities were swimming around among my missing kin and me. I wanted to resemble Mavis in some unusual way.

I have a small, faint café au lait birthmark on the top of my left foot, shaped like a scalene triangle with ragged lines, as if made with an Etch A Sketch. As a child, I believed this mark was a scar from the time I placed my bare foot into my grandfather's smoldering leaf pile next to the curb, thinking it was cooled ashes. My child's mind had no difficulty rationalizing a scar on the top of my foot with a burn on its sole. The adult me has long since abandoned this explanation but still occasionally wonders if this mark is purely random or whether it might link me to my missing grandmother.

The day I spoke with Claretta for the first time, Pam arrived home just before we needed to pick up the boys. Before she could toss her backpack onto the couch, I rushed to her. "I found her!" I shouted. She looked at me blankly.

"Found who?"

"Who have I been trying to find for ten years? Mavis!"

She stared, dumbstruck. "Get out of here; you did not."

"I did!"

She smiled, put her arms around me, and pulled me close. "Oh," she said. "I always knew you would."

"No you didn't." I laughed and then punched her on the arm.

TWENTY-THREE

Conduit

"Why, honey, I was just shocked and happy to hear about you all from my niece Rhonda." My Great-Aunt Esther's soprano voice warbled over the long-distance wires like a scratchy LP recording. I sat in the breakfast nook looking out the window at the creeping trumpet vine clinging to the garage near its roofline.

"I must be psychic," she said. "I was just thinking about that baby and wondering whatever happened to him. You know, I saw a television program last week about people who'd lost each other, and they were reuniting right there on the program. It got me thinking about that baby again. Honey, it's just a miracle, I can't believe this is happening."

She didn't have a Texas accent or an Arkansas drawl like Rhonda and Claretta. Her speech was flexible like Cyrus's and mine, as if it could go in either direction, north or south. "I have prayed and wondered about that baby," she said. "Honey, how did you find me? I mean, how did you find Rhonda?"

I told her and then promised to send a photo of Cyrus and his children. I would make a copy of the one taken ten years before, the last time all five of us kids—me, Mike, Sarah, Cody, and Melissa—had gotten together, when we posed with our father on the porch of the Kentucky house, the women seated on the swing, the men standing behind us. It was at that December reunion for Sarah's wedding when I had first asked Cyrus about his birth parents and he had shown me his adoption record. My search had taken a decade.

I asked Esther questions and filled more pages on my pad with stories about her family—my family—that I couldn't wait to share with Cyrus.

"Do you think we'll get to meet someday?" My Great-Aunt Esther sounded like a giddy young girl. "Honey, I'm talking your head off. This call is costing you a fortune!"

I laughed. "It doesn't matter. But before I forget, do you have a photo of Mavis? I'd love to see what she looked like."

"Honey, I'm sorry, I don't think so. We had a house fire in the seventies, and all those things burned up. And we didn't take too many photographs back then."

I placed my feelings in the little drawer in my heart labeled "Disappointment" and closed it.

"Kathy, I still feel like this is a dream. I truly do. Getting this happy news just after my sad news—losing my brother. You know, of all my brothers and sisters, I'm the only one left now."

Esther paused and I guessed that, like me, she was holding back tears. "God does miracles," she said, her voice trilling with joy. "Good-bye, sugar."

"I talked with your Aunt Esther," I said when Cyrus answered the phone. "She's funny and totally with it. She kept calling me 'honey.' I loved it. She lives in a retirement community outside Houston, a few minutes from her only child, Gary. He's about sixty years old and has four children and nine grandchildren, all living in the area. He'd be your first cousin, I think."

"That's just fine," Cyrus said. "It's good to know this."

I stood and peeked out the window at the boys pouring water

from the hose into the sandbox. Pam was pulling weeds next to them. It was another hot October day, and we had all the windows and doors open to catch any breezes.

"Mavis's family moved from Fairdealing to Kennett, Missouri, in 1924, when Mavis was ten," I said. "And that's where she later met your birth father. Esther thinks he lived out in the country, in a town called Senath." I turned the page upside down to read a note that snaked along the edge of the paper.

"I'm writing this down," he said, his tone undecipherable.

"When Mavis got pregnant with you, Esther was about twenty and had already moved to Poplar Bluff to work in a department store. Since Esther was gone, she didn't know much about the pregnancy and never saw you. But their sister Lois, the one in between Esther and Mavis, knew all about it. Esther kept telling me, 'If Lois was still alive, she could tell you much more about Mavis and that baby than I can.'"

"Anyway, I should start at the beginning." I arranged my notes, scattered across four pages. The squeals of the boys outside told me the water play was getting rambunctious. I heard the hose faucet squeak as Pam shut the water supply off.

"After Mavis's mother died, your grandfather, Mitchell Foster, married a woman the children called 'Auntie Nellie.' Esther thinks it was this stepmother who didn't let Mavis come home with her baby."

It was bizarre referring to Cyrus as "her baby," but it would have felt equally odd to say "Mavis came home with *you*." I was trying to protect his feelings by creating this bit of distance.

"Mitchell Foster owned the general store in Fairdealing. It had 'a little bit of everything in it,' Esther said. When Mavis's mother was pregnant with Mavis in 1914, the store burned down in the middle of the night. They rebuilt it, but it's no longer there. I guess it's been torn down. When I told her I'd like to see Fairdealing someday, she said, 'Don't blink or you'll miss it.' She's a hoot; I think you'll enjoy talking to her. Am I going too fast?"

"No, no, it's fine. I'm making notes as you speak." He was beginning to sound more animated.

"Mavis's mother died on her father's birthday in 1918, and the oldest son died within the same week, both of the flu epidemic." I skipped over the fact that she'd been four years old when her mother died, the same age Cyrus and I had been when we each lost ties with a parent. I didn't think he'd be as impressed by the cross-generational pattern as I'd been. *Quite a coincidence*, I could imagine him saying in an even tone, so I kept it to myself. "Do you want to hear more, or am I overwhelming you?"

"No, keep going. Unless you're tired of talking."

"No, I'm wired. I'm so excited I can't stand it." I laughed, too loudly, excited about what I'd been able to give him. "And get this! Mavis moved from Missouri to San Francisco and worked on ships during the war. I think she came out here at around the same age I did. About forty years before me, though." This coincidence I loved; I'd followed my grandmother from the Midwest to the West Coast, back when I didn't know she had even existed. It was another repetition in our family, reminding me of identical twins raised apart who end up working for the same company in different cities, driving the same model car, giving their children the same names. Genetics or chance, it didn't matter; these flukes excited me. While it wasn't crooked fourth toes we shared, our similar journeys away from home to the same spot linked me to my grandmother.

"She didn't have any more children." I paused to let him realize, as I had earlier, that this meant there would be no half-brothers or -sisters. I hadn't yet considered the other side, his biological father's.

"That's all I wrote down. If I remember anything else, I'll add it to my e-mail. By the way, Esther would love to hear from you."

"Yes, indeed," he said. "Thank you for calling with the news. I'll call her in a bit." Cyrus cleared his throat. "Thank you for getting this information; it's very interesting."

His muted tone countered my spilling-over exhilaration. I couldn't understand why he wasn't thrilled over my news. Maybe it was too much to take in.

The next week a letter arrived from Cyrus. *So many thanks*, he wrote. *Tears came to my eyes as I wrote Aunt Esther—It's the first time ever I've communicated with a blood relative besides you five kids. We must visit Esther! My Uncle Harlon and I would have hit it off so darn well—Sorry, in a way, that I lingered—but I think you understand.*

I rolled my eyes and moaned, but had to admit that, despite the frustration over his years of reluctance, I did understand.

A few days later, Melissa, the only child who still lived at home with Cyrus and Ursula, wrote me a note. *Dad is pretty excited about all this,* she wrote on stationery bordered by cavorting puppies. *What you've found about Mavis is so interesting.* From Cyrus's letter, I'd guessed at his wistful feelings—his disappointment at not having acted sooner—as well as his contentment at being accepted by his biological family. His excitement was news, though, and Melissa's words gave me what I needed: a proud-of-myself-big-sister-excellent-daughter feeling.

Soon after, I received an envelope from Cyrus containing a document I thought I'd never see. He had finally requested the non-identifying information about his birth parents from the adoption agency, and in a reversal of roles, he was sending me new information about Mavis.

I scanned the copy of the letter the social worker had typed after she'd scoured Cyrus's adoption file for information she could legally release. *Her father was the town's Justice of the Peace and had been very upset about the pregnancy,* she wrote. *He offered little support of your birth mother.* The social worker had omitted all the names from her predecessor's notes to make it "non-identifying." Cyrus's parents' names had been replaced by <birth mother> and <birth father>.

I showed the letter to Pam. "Isn't this ridiculous?" I said. "Who is she protecting now, after all this time? We already know Mavis's name, and I bet we have more information about the family than she has in her ratty file."

Pam laughed, even though I wasn't trying to be funny. "What else does it say?"

I kept reading. *Your birth father was twenty years old and the son of a part-time preacher and full-time farmer. He lived with his mother and father and two brothers and sisters on the farm.* I mentally filed this information for later, in case I decided to go back and look for Cyrus's birth father's family in the 1920 census.

It seems that your mother parented you at the maternity home from the date of your birth until November 1930, when she returned home. Her father would not allow her to enter his home with a baby, so she took you to the home of your birth father. You remained there for seven months, until June 17, 1931, when you were placed at the Children's Home Society of Missouri for the purpose of adoption. It seems that your birth father's mother was in poor health and the family simply did not have sufficient income to provide for a baby. You joined your adoptive family the next day.

I stopped. Mavis had mothered her baby for five months. Then she took Cyrus, or Jimmie Earl, to his birth father's family where he lived until they returned him to the adoption agency. He had been handed over to his new family on his first birthday. The image haunted me—a baby wrenched from his mother at five months, then relinquished again seven months later, this time from his father's family. He'd been a year old, not a few days old when he joined his adoptive family. He may have been calling people by name and responding to his own name, Jimmie Earl. Then one day someone whisked him away and handed him to two strangers who began calling him Cyrus.

I know what each of my sons had been like at a year—so deeply attached to their mothers—there was no question they would have been devastated had they been permanently separated from one or both of us, even if they remembered nothing later. How had his relinquishment affected Cyrus? Was it a scar on his soul?

I unfolded the other enclosure, a letter from the young Mavis, transcribed by the social worker to conceal Mavis's handwriting. It was dated July 26, 1932. Mavis had written it at eighteen, a year after she had last seen her son.

I tell you, she wrote to Miss Schroeder, the social worker who I guessed had befriended her during her confinement. *That was the hardest day of my life having to give him up. If I hadn't been such a fool to sign papers. His birth father arranged it. I certainly hope he feels all right over it. I don't know why I did it. The birth father and my Dad, everyone around me were telling me to hurry up and get it over with. I was crying so, I didn't hardly know what I was doing.*

My throat ached when I read the next line. *I'll remember until the very day I die about them forcing me to give my baby up.*

Even now, when every so often I flip to this letter in the binder where I keep it behind a plastic sleeve, I get choked up. And I feel this way every time I read a story about a woman who was forced to give away her baby. It was so wrong, the injustice, the inhumanity.

I find it telling that I react more deeply to this event so far in the past and relatively more removed from me than I do for comparable losses in my own life. I'm not choked up when I think about losing my first father. I empathize more with birth mothers and infant adoptees I don't even know than I do with four-year-old me. I jammed those feelings into the cabinet in my heart marked "Too Painful to Deal With," so I could forget them. But maybe it is precisely *because* I lost my father that I become weepy over these stories, my feelings of loss displaced onto another. Forgetting is a potent salve, and bathing wounds with its healing properties eases the pain, although it won't prevent scarring.

"I wonder what it was like for Cyrus to read this letter," Pam said when I paused. "He might have been relieved to learn that she didn't want to give him up."

Like me, I thought, he had not been abandoned after all.

"Wait, there's a little bit more," I said and read the end of Mavis's letter.

I guess he is adopted out by this time. If I could only get him back, I'll work at anything. Could I possibly get any kind of work there in the hospital or home I never will forget there. It seems like home to me. I regret very much leaving there. I'm going to get the address where he is and try to get a job up there and go see him at least.

I put the copy of her letter into a plastic sleeve in my binder, next to the three adoption records—my father's, mine, and my sons'—and then wrote a quick note to Cyrus thanking him for sending it. I didn't ask him how it had felt to read his mother's letter, and he did not volunteer it.

A couple of weeks later, in early November, Cyrus called. "I'm thinking about going to Houston in a couple of weeks to meet my Aunt Esther. Would you like to go?"

He had been so hesitant during the search that I'd always assumed I would meet the new relatives first. I would pave the way again, and then when he knew it was safe, he would go. He had written to Aunt Esther instead of calling because he'd needed time.

"I'd love to go," I said. I wanted to meet my grandmother's sister to get a peek at what my grandmother was like, to see what we might have in common, and guess whether we might have been soul mates. "But I need to find a long weekend from work, and with such short notice, I don't know if I can afford the ticket."

Cyrus bought a midweek airplane ticket with a senior discount. "It's the only time I can go," he said when he called again. "You could meet me there." But I couldn't get away at that time, and my disappointment at being left out quickly turned to anger. I pounded out a letter to him on the computer, ranting about the unfairness, and then ripped it up. That night, the boys in their beds listening to nursery rhyme songs on cassette tapes, Pam listened as I fumed.

"How can he visit her first, without me, when it was me who did all the work to find her? He didn't even want to search, then he didn't want contact, and now he's going off and leaving me behind."

"Because it's his aunt, do you think he should go first?" Pam asked. I knew she was treading carefully, assuaging my sadness.

"I know, it's his aunt, and only my great-aunt, and he's the adoptee, not me," I said. "I guess it's right that he go first to meet Esther, but I wanted to meet her, too."

Pam wrapped an arm around my shoulder. "Maybe he needed to go alone and just couldn't say so. You can go, too. Spring break, maybe."

"But it still hurts," I said. "It feels like he's dumping me."

"I don't think so, love," she said, pulling me close.

Although I couldn't admit it yet, I knew she was right.

A few weeks later, I pulled an envelope from Cyrus out of the mailbox and opened it while sitting on the front steps. The sun had warmed the December air, and I wanted to feel it on my face while I read his note. Even before I could unfold the letter, I felt a photograph inside, one taken during his trip to Houston, I guessed. I prepared myself for a photo of him and Aunt Esther with their arms around each other, and a space where I should have been standing.

But two photographs spilled into my hand, and when I looked at the first I knew I'd been wrong. Without checking for a note on the back, I knew I was looking at my grandmother. "Oh my God," I said aloud on the steps. "There she is." In a black-and-white snapshot with beveled edges, she perches on a craggy hillside boulder wearing a short-sleeved, tapered cotton dress, nylons, and open-toed black shoes. Her dress is too light for the cool breezes of the northern coast, and she looks out of place in the rugged terrain. Maybe she'd only recently arrived in California and hadn't known what to expect.

On the back of the photo she had written a message in pencil. *This was taken up on the side of a mountain. Beautiful spot.* Her handwriting reminded me of my half-sister Sarah's perfect childhood penmanship. Although Mavis's note suggested confidence, her smile betrays reticence. In the way of photographs from that era, she appears older than someone in her mid-forties. It could have been her hair, pulled into a loose bun, or the fullness of her features—a trait I did not share with her—that gave her this look. Posing for the camera, she appears happy, even smug, and this seemed at odds with what I knew about her. Forty years had passed since she'd lost her mother, thirty since she'd said good-bye to her son, and

I wanted to know what those years had done to her. Had she, like birth mothers whose stories I'd read, suffered from a hidden lack of joy and optimism that shaped the rest of her life? She would only live a few more years, and for the first time I considered the possibility that she had killed herself.

During my search, I had expected to find a white-haired grandmother in her eighties. Instead, this dark-haired woman is frozen in time, forever in middle age. There would be no photos of her with gray hair, no photos of her past forty-nine.

In the second photo, a younger Mavis, with chin-length black hair, wears a car coat and stands in front of a handsome uniformed man. He leans against a 1940s three-wheeled motorcycle parked next to the curb. Given the architecture of the building behind them and the slant of the sidewalk, I guessed it was taken in San Francisco. Hooked over Mavis's shoulder, the man's arm crosses her chest like a Girl Scout's sash, his hand casually cupping one breast. They are both laughing at the camera. She looks both like a wild and loose woman and a scared little girl.

With her dark hair and round face, I saw nothing tying her to me. I had wanted some spark of recognition, something that made me feel a connection to this woman, but there was nothing. She was just an anonymous woman in an old photograph.

When Pam and the boys got home, I showed Pam the photos. "What do you think?" I asked. "Do I look like her?" Maybe she would spot something I'd missed, something I couldn't recognize.

Pam studied the photos, and then me. She wrinkled her nose. "Not at all," she said. "Were you hoping to?"

"Yeah, I guess I was," I said. "But she died at forty-nine, remember. Maybe I don't want to be too much like her."

This was becoming the pattern. Excitement. Disappointment. Encouragement. Discouragement. I had wanted to meet her, but that would not happen now. I didn't know if I'd ever learn the truth about why she died at age forty-nine. Brain tumor or murder? I'd wanted to see if we shared physical characteristics, but those had not been evident from the photographs Cyrus had sent. We were both certainly unconventional in our own ways, and we had shared similar life experiences. I suspected our personalities might have been similar. Although I wondered what had ultimately caused her to leave the Midwest for California as a young woman, it was easy to guess that she had been disconnected from her kin. I wanted to know more about that, too. That was something we shared across the years.

I loved learning every new fact about her life, but there was also something missing every time I reached another mile marker on the Mavis journey. Instead of crossing a threshold and feeling satisfaction at what I'd learned, I needed more. Although I longed for emotional connection through my search for lost people, I still could not connect with the emotions that were stirred up by it. The search had only left me more untethered.

PART III

TWENTY-FOUR

Substitution

"Mavis could wrap our father around her little finger," my Great-Aunt Esther said from her place on the couch. On the first morning of my visit to her Houston condominium, we were sifting through a box of old photographs she'd found during Cyrus's visit, the photos she'd thought had been lost to a house fire. Esther wore gold satin pajamas and matching house slippers, and her loosely permed white hair framed her face. Gold ball earrings dangled from wobbly earlobes, and her eyes peeked through the upper half of thick round glasses, which magnified the tops of her cheeks. While Cyrus had stayed with Esther's son Gary and his family, because I was a female relative, I was staying with Esther. The intimacy suggested by this, and her immediate acceptance of me as one of her own, reminded me of visiting my Grandma Rose after her hip surgery, of how we'd bridged the gap of years between us simply by spending time together, grandmother and granddaughter.

"Whatever Mavis wanted she got," Esther said. "In Kennett, she climbed out of her window and ran around with some girls who were up to no good. She wanted the excitement and the acceptance of her group, I guess."

"By then," she said, "I'd left for Poplar Bluff to work in a department store. So I only know what my sister Lois told me, and that wasn't much." She pushed her glasses farther up on her nose. "Around that time I wanted to ramble a little. There definitely was an independent streak in us children. Papa encouraged it. With no mother for those five or so years, we had to grow up fast."

Esther moved to her tiny modern kitchen and plucked a piece of toast from the toaster. I wondered what had changed between Mavis's wild years and the day she brought her baby home and could no longer wrap her father around her finger. Had it been the narrow limits of his religion, shame from judgments of neighbors, or his second wife's influence? I had often imagined the scene on their doorstep, her father with his arms crossed, mute, blocking her way.

Esther returned to the couch and flopped down heavily. "We didn't have the love we should have." Her tone had changed, and she sounded weary. "Aunt Nellie was a good lady, but she never talked much to us. Dad was never an affectionate man. I missed that—not having a mother. I loved Aunt Nellie, but how I would have loved to have had a mother. I needed a mother. We all did."

"I should have done more for my sister," she said, tears forming. "Mavis would call me from San Francisco and beg for money. Once I sent her five dollars, but another time I refused and didn't send her anything." She removed her glasses and rubbed her eyes. "I should have taken better care of her," she said. "She had a hard life."

"I'm sorry. Should we stop?" I asked. "Do you want me to put the boxes back on the shelf?"

"No, no, no. I'm fine, sugar. I just miss her so much. But half the time we didn't know where she was. Lois tried to help her keep the baby, but couldn't." Esther paused. "Our dad could have done something. But I believe he never recovered from my mother's and my brother's deaths. Our whole family was like a bunch of orphans." Here she paused, eyes downcast, deep in the memories of the past.

To give her time to recover, I picked up one of the photos from the box. Mavis and her husband Jack Shaver posed in front of a life ring on the top deck of a ship, and on the back Mavis had written: *Mavis & Jack aboard the Sea Serpent.*

"I recall," Esther said, "that Mavis married a Jack, Jack Helms, before she went to California. I met him a few times. A nice man, but I do believe he might have been a gambler and a drinker. They must have gotten a divorce, because I remember when she married the second Jack, she wrote me and sent those pictures."

I wondered whether her husbands' names might lead me to more information about Mavis, as her brothers' names had.

Later that morning, Esther's son, Gary, joined us for a walk around his mother's complex. "This is my niece Kathy from California," Esther told everyone we ran into. "Remember Cyrus, who visited a little bit ago? This is his girl. She's the one who found me." She beamed and patted the top of my hand like my Grandma Rose used to do. I felt like a young girl, comforted and proud.

Gary was a tall man, like Cyrus, his first cousin, and he had the same handsome, sharp features and short-cropped haircut of my brother Mike and my half-brother Cody. He wore a tracksuit and appeared fit from the "old-timers'" basketball team he played on. Unlike his mother's flatter Midwestern accent, Gary's had more of a Southern pull. "My mother raised me on her own," he said, the three of us walking slowly in the late winter Texas heat. "My father took off when I was six months old." He gave Esther's elbow a squeeze and she smiled at him.

What is it with men leaving in this family? I wanted to shout.

"He was a gambler and philanderer," Esther said, surprising me with her candor. "We were better off without him." She glanced at Gary, and as if she realized she'd said too much, she became quiet.

"What was Mavis like?" I asked Gary, moving to what might be a less heated subject. "Your mom's told me a lot about her, but what do you remember?"

"I loved my Aunt Mavis," Gary said, smiling. "She swept through town every once in a while, and each time she brought me something. She was kind to me, and now I think she treated me like the son she had lost."

I imagined that son she lost, my father Cyrus, and thought about his loss and about those of Gary and Mavis. From Mavis's perspective, her sister's son, a boy who had lost his father, might have substituted in a small way for the son she'd lost, who in turn lost his own birth parents and then his adoptive father. It all sounded so sad, all these generations of loss, but I found it heartening that both boys had been raised by single women and had turned out relatively unscathed. Thinking about my own boys, I was beginning to see that boys raised by women were not damaged, not traumatized, not much different than a boy raised by a woman and a man. And if there was any trauma, it would more likely be from father loss than from mother—even two-mother—presence.

That night in Houston, Gary, his second wife, and his young stepsons hosted a dinner party for me at their house so I could meet most of Esther's twenty-plus descendants, my new cousins. Gary was her only child, but he'd had four children, and most of them had had children. That night we all came together over drinks and deep-fried crawfish, a Southern dish I tried for the first time and found delicious.

I wanted them to like me, and I wanted to be accepted by them. But even though they did whatever they could to make me feel welcome, inviting me along on a birthday party for one of Esther's great-granddaughters at Chuck E. Cheese and including me on family walks in the park, for example, I was aware of my outsider status. The children called me "Miss Kathy," a term of respect I was not used to. While most of the women wore a good deal of makeup, perfume, and jewelry even on the weekend, I wore none. When I compared my casual T-shirts and jeans to their coordinated outfits, I felt like a frumpy cousin. Some of them teased me about living in "crunchy granola" California, but I didn't reciprocate by kidding them about their grand affection for plug-in air fresheners.

After I'd first sent Esther photos of the boys, she always asked about them when we spoke on the phone. I assumed Gary had explained my relationship with Pam, but during my visit I wasn't sure if she truly understood, or if it was easier for her to believe that we were just single women raising kids together. It's something we never spoke of, something I'll probably never know.

One granddaughter slipped up after her third glass of sangria and told a joke about a drug abuser and a homosexual, flushing when she realized what she'd said and automatically glancing my way. I stayed silent, a goofy smile frozen on my face, pretending it didn't faze me, but I felt deep shame, as if there were something horribly wrong with me, something so abominable that no one dared mention it in public. It wouldn't have occurred to me to rock the boat, so ingrained, so *inherited* was my cautious style when it came to this subject. Plus, this was conservative Houston the year that Matthew Shepard was murdered in Wyoming.

Earlier, though, Gary had asked me privately about Pam, and I was frank with him, even though my heart beat dangerously fast and my voice wobbled as I told him how Pam and I met and about our commitment ceremony. When I finished, he smiled at me. "You're lucky," he said. "It sounds like you found the right person on the first try." My relief in his acceptance made me tearful. Looking back, I realize I may have misjudged the others. They may have been just as able to accept this part of me if I'd given them the chance, if I'd just expected it.

Before I left for the airport to go home on Sunday, Gary took a photograph of Esther and me standing in her living room. It felt awkward, bending to the side to grasp the shoulder of this old lady I was only just getting to know. I was exhausted at the effort it had taken over the weekend, meeting people—my kin—telling my story and hearing theirs, sleeping two nights in a strange bed. But I was also invigorated. I'd gotten just what I'd wanted from this trip. While I was disappointed that I would never meet my grandmother, it felt as if I now knew her a little better. On the way to the airport, Gary told me more about her. "The lady I knew," he said, "was an effervescent person." I liked the word "effervescent." Friends have described my personality as bubbly. I've always been loud and outspoken, sometimes getting into trouble with my strong opinions offered too readily. I liked to believe that I was effervescent, too.

Gary also told me he sometimes felt like the son Mavis had lost, and on that trip to Texas, I, too, had felt as if I'd found a stand-in for someone. After several months of exchanging letters with Esther following my visit, I became close to my spunky, affectionate great-aunt, who without a second thought had welcomed Cyrus and me into her life. She began to replace her sister Mavis, first in my mind and then, gradually, in my heart. She began to feel less a great-aunt and more like a grandmother. And it was shortly after this that I came to realize something else. I was indeed a part of my Great-Aunt Esther's family. Like the dwarf Pluto spinning far off on the edge of the galaxy, I was distant, and not even a true planet, but I was still part of the whole.

TWENTY-FIVE

Searching for Ghosts

Even before the pilot announced our descent into St. Louis, my inner ears balked at the thicker, heavier air of the lower altitude. I furiously chewed a stick of cinnamon gum, and, when that didn't work, pinched my nostrils together and blew. The right eardrum squeaked, popped, and then released in an ecstatic hiss. But something deep inside the left ear began to throb. The descent was too fast. I forced a yawn, jiggled my jaw and chomped my gum, but my left ear would not loosen its grip, and the pain, like an ice pick puncture, turned my eyes watery.

I remembered a trip on another airplane when Benjamin was three, and we had begun our descent onto Maui when he began thrashing his head against the seatback. "Ear hurts!" he screamed over the throbbing engines. The mint I gave him to suck didn't help; he spit it onto the floor of the plane and batted at his ears, the pain laid bare on his face. As a baby and toddler, he was plagued with a series of ear infections, and finally the pediatrician explained why. "Narrow tubes," he said. "They don't clear efficiently. Probably hereditary."

As my plane landed in St. Louis on a cloudy day that July, I imagined my defiant eardrum rupturing, forcing a hospital detour from my true mission, my journey to a tiny town in southern Missouri, where I would search for the grave of Cyrus's birth mother, and where I would begin my search for his birth father. Before desperation turned to panic, I yawned once more and my left eardrum imploded, the agony instantly releasing into a deep ache and, finally, to a dull throb.

I massaged my left ear as we taxied up to the gate. Since the moment I'd first held my grandmother's birth certificate, I'd wanted to see Fairdealing, Missouri, her birthplace and the place where she was buried. I would also go to Kennett, the town in the Missouri boot heel where Mavis became pregnant at fifteen, where I would find Cyrus's birth father. I would do this, I was sure, even though all I had was a name that my eighty-nine-year-old Great-Aunt Esther had pulled from her memory.

This trip to Missouri at age forty was another quest of identity and reconciliation. I was still trying to make sense of all the ruptures in my family, how we had become so scattered, how we might reconnect again. As if studying a machine built by da Vinci, with all its wheels and cogs and interdependent parts flowing smoothly, I wanted to map out our parts, and in particular, see where I fit.

I'd left the boys, three and five, at home with Pam to make this five-day trip. I needed to do this alone, couldn't be bothered with parenting chores or negotiating the needs of others while I searched for what I needed. "You're so lucky," a friend, another mother, had said during a recent dinner. "Taking a vacation. Alone time!" I'd tried to explain that it wouldn't be a vacation but more like a business trip, which she did regularly for her job. Mine was a private mission, I knew, but it wasn't like I'd be lounging next to a swimming pool reading *People* magazine. True, I was able to leave mothering duties behind, but it was still a working trip. Something was driving me, impelling me so strongly that I needed to leave my preschoolers with their other mother and fly across the country searching for ghosts.

At first Pam had looked horrified. *You're leaving me alone with two preschoolers to do what? And for how long?* But when I offered to forget it altogether, she'd put her arms around me. "Go," she said.

I had pulled her close, full of guilty gratitude.

At the airport in St. Louis, I rented a car, found a light rock station, and slogged through construction traffic to my stepfather's sister's house on the near south side of the city. Joan Briccetti and her partner, Kathy, were putting me up for the night before my drive to southern Missouri. Ten years earlier, Kathy had found the address of the Children's Home Society, the adoption agency in St. Louis, so I could write that first letter, the one that had begun my search for Mavis.

The irony of beginning the Missouri trip to meet Cyrus's kin from the home of my stepfather's kin was not lost on me. I felt disloyal to Dad, like I did when I first hyphenated my name and wrote to him using new return address labels with my surname, Briccetti-Craig, on them. *You're rejecting my name*, he'd written in a letter. *And it feels like you're rejecting me*. I didn't understand. I hadn't gotten rid of his name, just added another one to it. Besides, if I married in the traditional manner, I might have hyphenated my name. Or I might have thrown his out altogether and taken my husband's. Now I believe that he felt me pulling away, and he was fighting it.

I was afraid my searching for blood kin would hurt him, too, so I didn't mention it during our infrequent conversations. In retrospect, though, I believe he might have surprised me. He might have understood my need to search for my blood relatives. Had I told him, he might have wished me luck, accompanied me to the family reunion. But, back then, I feared telling him. I imagined him saying that what I was doing was akin to killing him.

Joan gave me a tour of their turn-of-the-century three-story brick house, and in the dining room I spotted a collection of framed photographs arranged on a small side table. I picked up and studied a recent photo of Dad standing alone, bundled up in a familiar leather jacket and knitted scarf. I hadn't seen him for almost three years, and I expected to see him as he always looked: youthful and dashing. Instead this image startled me: he looked gaunt and old, like a man beginning to shrivel up. Only sixty when the picture was taken, his skin stretched tightly across his cheekbones, accentuating the deep hollows. Lines raked across his brow, and his hair, still long and fine, looked thinner and duller than I remembered.

My first thought was that he was dying and no one had told me. The idea of him ill, something destroying him from the inside, jolted me. I hadn't written him in months, and I had let another birthday pass without even e-mailing.

A few months before this trip to Missouri, Pam and I had attended a performance of the San Francisco Symphony, and beforehand Mom had asked me to give her regards to the harpist, a man who had played in the Indianapolis orchestra with her. At intermission I waved to him from the edge of the stage. He joined us, crouching to come level with our heads.

"I'm Kathy Briccetti," I said. "You might not remember me." I'd been a child when we lived in Indianapolis.

"Sure I do."

"You played with my mother in the orchestra in Indianapolis."

"Yes, and Tom Briccetti is your father."

"Stepfather," I said, my tone harsher than I'd intended. Why had I needed to make that distinction, after all those years of calling him Dad and explaining to others that he felt like my true father? But our relationship was changing, and our remoteness was changing me. I was building a higher wall between us. Even more likely, I was experimenting with giving up a father.

The morning after arriving in St. Louis, I popped my AAA maps into the glove box of the rental car, flipped on the air conditioning, and waved good-bye to Joan and Kathy. Patsy Cline's voice blared from the car's speakers, and I tapped the steering wheel, singing along with the cassette Joan had loaned me for the trip. "I'm always walking, after midnight, searching for you." I laughed at this, what seemed to be my theme song. How many more years would

I be searching for the living and the dead? I couldn't answer this question then because I didn't know yet what I was searching for, what I needed to find.

The sporty rental car smelled new. It had no child seats, no cracker crumbs scattered on the floor, no peanut butter smeared into the upholstery. And, best of all, I wasn't listening to *Sesame Street* characters singing in an endless loop about parts of the body. A Styrofoam cooler filled with water and fruit sat on the floor behind me, and within easy reach on the passenger seat, a giant bag of peanut M&Ms. Feeling light with freedom, I sailed south on I-55. The landscape became more lush the farther south I traveled, with fresh fields and leafy forests hugging the highway, and jungle-like kudzu vines threatening to creep across it. The hills at home in California this time of year were dry and bronzed like savannas. But in southern Missouri, the air was moist and the forested countryside a stunning, fertile green.

On the trip, I wanted two things: to stand at my grandmother's grave and see what would happen, and to find my grandfather, Cyrus's birth father, so he could tell me about my grandmother. My life felt full, so I wasn't seeking a replacement family, but I was still seeking something I lacked, something I felt I was *owed*: getting to know, or at least meeting, the people who shared my genes. I wanted their stories and wanted to tell them mine because this was all we had to share. I know now that many adoptees believe their history belongs to them, that they shouldn't be denied access to their beginnings. I have aligned myself with them. On the surface, we all want information. Below that we want repaired ties, genetic affiliation, a shared history. I especially wanted this connection to something larger.

That afternoon, I stopped at a Dairy Queen. When I climbed out of the air-conditioned car, a blast of dense, wet air and the scent of tar pavement melting in the sun threw me back to summers growing up in Indiana. I had grown accustomed to the ocean breezes of the Bay Area, but here the heat battered me with its ferocity.

Inside, while spooning up the frozen curlicue peak on my strawberry sundae, I watched two toddlers race down a slide into their parents' arms and flashed on my boys, now just past the ages that Mike and I had been when we'd moved to New Jersey with our mother. I missed my babies, and for a second I believed I was a horrible mother for leaving them for my latest whim, for abandoning them because I couldn't let this thing go. But sitting there at the Dairy Queen, I also knew they were going to be fine. They knew I always came home. And gradually I realized something else. The spell had been broken, the blueprint torn up, one part of our family's legacy ended. My children would not be the fourth generation to lose a parent before kindergarten.

TWENTY-SIX

Motherland

Farther into southern Missouri, confederate flag license plates began appearing on the fronts of pickup trucks and tractor-trailers, and the racks behind drivers' heads that at home held fishing poles and lacrosse sticks, here held shotguns. A few miles outside each town, I began anticipating the ubiquitous Harley-Davidson billboards, biker bars, pawnshops, and "one-stop" shops selling boats and guns.

Billboards with ten-foot photos of aborted fetuses occasionally flanked the highway, and approaching one small town, a mock cemetery appeared with thousands of tiny white crosses in rows and signs denouncing the "Murder of Babies." In case I didn't truly appreciate that I had arrived in the Bible Belt, there were bumper stickers that spelled it out: "Real men love Jesus" and "Liquor leaves you breathless, drugs leave you senseless, Jesus won't leave you regardless." I hoped I wouldn't get stopped by a highway patrolman and asked why my husband wasn't driving me. I felt as if I had a great deal to hide.

An hour after passing the limestone quarry outside Poplar Bluff, and turning on to a two-lane highway, I began looking for Fairdealing. I'd just crossed the Ripley County boundary, and remembered Esther's warning not to blink or I'd miss the town. The stretch of highway I'd just traveled on had cut through the Mark Twain National Forest. I knew from my AAA map that I was close to the Lake of the Ozarks, where my stepfather and his third wife, Jennie, had rented a vacation cabin in their motorcycling days and where I had visited Dad briefly one summer after their divorce.

Three houses appeared on the right side of the road, and then a small square building the size of a trailer materialized, an American flag drooping on a pole in front. A sign on the post office read Fairdealing, Missouri, 63939. I had arrived.

My first task was to locate the cemetery where my relatives were buried. In particular, I wanted to find Mavis's marker, study the birth and death dates—1914 and 1964—run my hands over the rough stone, make a pencil rubbing. Nineteen-sixty-four was the year I turned seven, the year of my last summer trip to my father's in Kentucky, and the year my half-sister was born. Also that year, Esther's son Gary and his first wife were living in Tampa, a few miles from us in St. Petersburg. Supposedly, we are all connected by, at the most, six degrees of separation; how many times in our lives do we pass kin without knowing it?

I didn't want to ask directions at the post office because I believed I could find the cemetery by intuition, by being open to a mystical force pulling me to my grandmother's final resting place. Usually a map-lover, I had no map of the tiny town, and for once that did not bother me. There were only two gravel roads, one on either side of the highway, to choose from. Surely I could find the cemetery. The road I picked meandered past several farms, and I drove a mile off the highway before admitting that I'd chosen the wrong road, hadn't been as tuned in to the mystical force as I thought I'd been. I headed back, cut across the highway, and tried the other road. Small manicured lawns embraced diminutive houses, separated from neighbors by fields of waist-high wild grasses. Two blocks from the highway, I spotted a church steeple and pulled the rental car into an empty parking lot. Instead of intuition, it seems I'd found the cemetery by process of elimination.

A one-room white clapboard building with a modern belfry above the front entrance, the church looked as if the congregation had rebuilt it sometime in the fifties. Once the Fosters' Methodist church, the building currently served as a Baptist Mission.

When I climbed out of the car, a stark sun baked into my skin, and I pushed against the heavy heat. A flowering vine woven into a short picket fence was in bloom, scenting the thick air with a cloying perfume. Taking my camera from my fanny pack, I photographed the front of the church and the sign behind it marking the entrance to the Fairdealing Cemetery. Behind the church, a shiny jungle surrounded the half acre of neatly tended plots. I wandered over uneven ground and perused cracked, lichen-covered gravestones, hunting at random for familiar surnames.

Across the freshly mown grass, a balding, slightly stooped man clambered down from a parked backhoe and began shoveling gravel onto a walkway between sections of the cemetery. Although he must have seen me arrive, he made no move to approach. I made my way over the bumpy ground toward him, stiff grass once again finding its way past the soles of my sandals, and I made a mental note: closed-toed shoes for cemetery traipsing. When I reached him, the man rested his shovel against the backhoe and pulled off dirt-caked gloves. His sleeveless undershirt was lined with sweat and his face glowed crimson from the heat. The depth of the lines in his face made him appear eighty, but he might have been younger, prematurely aged in the sun.

"Hello," I said, giving him a wave even though only four feet separated us. He stared, his face expressionless.

"I'm looking for the Fosters," I said, squinting from the glare. I glanced at the part of the cemetery I hadn't checked yet. "I haven't seen any of their markers."

"Sure. I'll take you." He behaved as if he saw this every day: a stranger climbing out of a rental car, taking photos, and asking for directions to plots in a cemetery that didn't hold more than a hundred gravestones. He wiped his forehead with a clean handkerchief and led me to the corner I hadn't reached.

"I'm looking for my grandmother's marker. She was a Foster, but her name was Mavis Shaver when she died."

He gestured to a spot behind me. "That'd be them right there. This here's called the Ward section, but the Fosters are mixed in there, too." His words slithered out in the drawl of the Deep South.

I spotted a granite double marker with the name Foster at the top. Two carved rectangle slabs sat underneath, one for Mavis's mother and one for her father. "Yes, this is it. Thank you," I said. "I'm here from California. This is my great-grandfather's grave." I suspected I sounded too eager, giddy almost. And I was conscious of my Northern accent, like I had been when I first visited the Kentucky family, how it announced that I was not from here.

"I'm Junior Clayton. Been caretaking here and over at the cemetery in Naylor for forty years now, I reckon."

Junior Clayton looked like he enjoyed the break from his labor and might like to chat awhile. I wanted to find my grandmother's marker, and I wanted to see it for the first time alone, so when he turned and headed back to his shovel across the cemetery, I was relieved.

I perused the collection of markers, concentrating on Mavis's parents' graves. On the other side of her mother's marker I found one for Nellie Pennington, Mavis's stepmother, the woman the children had called Aunt Nellie. And then I spotted it: a simple slab, lying flat, tamped into the bumpy ground. Black lichen highlighted the letters of the name etched into the marker. Mavis F. Shaver.

I'd found her, my long-missing grandmother. But she was just a collection of bones now, thirty-four years dead, a supine skeleton laid out somewhere under my feet. I'd imagined—hoped—that when I finally stood in this spot I would sense an instant metaphysical connection to the grandmother I had never known. I wanted to experience a jolt of recognition, a feeling that we *had* known each other somehow. Instead, I wiped sweat off my forehead with the back of my hand and stood there thinking about her skeleton. I wondered whether her coffin had disintegrated yet, whether her bones had settled gently or had fallen roughly when the bottom of the coffin finally gave way.

From the photos I'd carefully studied, I conjured up her thick, dark hair, her full, round face, and her ambivalent smile. I had an urge to sit on her grave and whisper a message to her. *I'm your granddaughter. I wish we could have known each other.* Instead, I said this in my head, hoping it would evoke greater emotion, wishing I would feel something—something deep and significant. I realize now I was after a Hallmark greeting card moment, a condolence card for myself. *Missing you, now that you're gone.* Instead, I felt only self-conscious as I checked for neighbors peeping out the windows of their double-wides at the stranger poking around the graveyard. I had wanted a movie-of-the-week story to tell the people back home, something poignant, something that would justify what felt like windmill chasing. But there was no burning in my throat, no throbbing of my Achilles tendon. Instead, it was more of a feeling like, *Well damn, I'd hoped for more, but this is kind of cool, seeing where this person is buried, where she came from. Now I can add this to my family history file. Maybe Ben and Daniel will like to hear about this someday.*

I peeked at Junior Clayton across the cemetery. His back to me, he was swinging a pick ax into a hill of dirt. He probably didn't give a rat's ass that I was taking photos of grave markers. He didn't care whether I was having a spiritual moment of revelation or not. When I look back on this scene, I understand I didn't have a momentous reaction that day because I had been trying too hard, forcing feelings that didn't exist. The graveyard experience had not been all I'd anticipated, and I was disappointed about that, but my expectations had been unrealistic. I'd wanted a metaphysical experience when I'd never had one before. I wanted to be hypnotized when I was utterly unhypnotizable.

I crouched next to my grandmother's marker. It did feel as if an invisible cord had connected her life to mine, but I was no longer sure it had guided me to a cemetery in southern Missouri. My personality—a particular mix of obsessiveness, impulsivity, and persistence—had brought me there. I sometimes still like to get lost mulling over our parallel lives, but at the same time I tell myself that I'm being too dreamy. They could be simply coincidental events in our lives, I know, but I enjoy imagining that it might be more, something outside our familiar domain, something in the realm of spirits, that connects my grandmother and me.

Fiddling with a sprig of grass next to the marker, I remembered a letter of Mavis's that my Great-Aunt Esther had given me. In 1953, Mavis had written to her stepmother from San Francisco. "Dear Aunt Nellie," it began. Using a pencil on a small tablet, she wrote that she had just come out of the hospital following surgery to remove her gallbladder and gallstones. Twice she thanked God for her recovery, and this suggests what gave her the strength to make it to forty-nine. But she also admitted weakness. "Aunt Nellie, I almost died," she wrote. "I didn't want to fight, but now I do. I thank God I'm alive, and I'm ashamed I ever felt any other way." Her words touched me. She didn't want to live then, ten years before she would die of mysterious circumstances. What had made her want to die? And what had made her change her mind? I had to know.

Crouching beside Mavis's grave, I recalled her vow to remember until the day she died how she'd been forced to give up her baby. Wondering if she did indeed think of him on the day she died made me mourn from time to time, but mourn for her, not for me. I did not miss her, and I felt nothing standing at her grave because I had never known her, had never had the chance to know her since our paths had never crossed and she died long before I even knew of her existence.

That day at the cemetery, I asked myself, how can you miss what you never had? But I didn't understand yet that I *had* missed something, something large enough to propel me on a ten-year search for her. But it was not Mavis Foster who I'd been searching for. I suspect now Mavis was a substitute and that I'd really been searching not for another grandmother, my fourth, but for fathers, fathers I *had* known. Fathers who I *did* miss.

I brushed the rough surface of the grave marker with my palm. A part of me believed she knew I'd come to meet her. "Good-bye," I whispered to the grandmother I never met. "I'm sorry I missed you."

On my way back to the car, I thought of the other grandmother I hadn't known, Hazel Manfred, whom I'd met only a few times and whose death and memorial I had not been privy to. The last time I had seen her, Cyrus had taken Michael and me to visit shortly after her one hundredth birthday. "You were beautiful babies, beautiful, beautiful babies," she said with her characteristic lisp. "I kept your pictures on my bureau." I hadn't known this, and learning it that day connected this woman, my adoptive grandmother, to me in a new and deeper way. She, too, had loved and lost us.

When it was time for us to leave Grandma Hazel's room, I couldn't form the word "good-bye" for the unexpected burning in my throat. It had shocked me then, this grief at our parting. Now I know I was grieving not only the likelihood I would never see her again, but also the relationship that could have been but never was.

TWENTY-SEVEN

Fatherland

That night, I brought a pizza and salad to my room in a motel a few miles down the road from Fairdealing. I had scattered my notes across one bed, and I sat on the other with the phone to my ear listening to Benjamin tell me about his day at preschool. Hearing his sweet chatter made me miss my boys, and again I questioned what I was doing so far from home, what the purpose of my mission was. When Ben finished talking, we exchanged noisy kisses and Pam took the phone.

"How're the boys doing? Running you into the ground?" I could hear Ben and Daniel screeching and shouting, playing their wild animal game. For a second, I was glad to be far away, glad for the quiet, the abdication of parental duty.

"They're fine, but I need to get them in bed. How's the trip going?" She sounded rushed, so I hurried.

"It's amazing. I saw Mavis's grave. I'll tell you more when I get home, but I met people I'm related to here. Get this, even the postmaster is a cousin."

Pam was quiet, and I couldn't tell if the boys had grabbed her attention or if she was just bored by all this.

"The retired couple who lives across from the cemetery, they're also related to me. They saw my letter to the editor, just never responded. They sent me to another couple down the road, other relatives, and they gave me an antique plate with the name of my great-grandfather's store on it. They've all been so nice. Treating me like family. But I guess we *are* family, right?" I laughed. "I'm glad I came, and it feels like I'm almost done with all of this." I paused. "But I am still curious about Cyrus's birth father."

"Great. Listen, I'd better go. They're chasing each other with 'magic wands,' sticks from outside. Sorry, I can't talk right now."

"Okay. Go. Talk to you tomorrow. Love you—"

But she'd already said good-bye, and I was left with the sound of air pulsing through wires.

My Great-Aunt Esther had given me the name of the man who could be my grandfather and, since I'd been robbed of the opportunity to meet Mavis, I wanted to find him. I wanted to know more about her, and I still held out hope that I could reunite Cyrus with someone from that side of his birth family.

"I'd love to know," I had said to Esther on my last evening at her condo in Texas, "if you knew Cyrus's birth father, or who he was."

"Oh, honey, I wish I did." She removed her eyeglasses and wiped the lenses on the hem of her silky pajama top. "When Lois and I lived in Hot Springs, she told me all about walking with Mavis and the baby over to his house. Lois wanted to know what happened to him, too. But I never even saw him."

"Do you know the father's name?" I'd asked.

"It was Jimmy Lynn or something like that. I believe they lived out in the country outside Kennett, in Senath, if I recall. But, sugar, you know I'm an old lady and I could be wrong. But I do remember hearing that name." She put her glasses back on. "Jimmy Lynn," she said. "Yes, I believe his name was Jimmy Lynn."

The name Mavis had given my father, before his adoptive parents changed it, was Jimmie Earl Foster. Jimmy Lynn sounded about right.

Esther also had told me their family had moved to Kennett from Fairdealing for her father's work and that in Kennett Mavis had climbed out her window to run wild with her friends, to meet up with Jimmy Lynn. "I do believe Mavis carried that baby in her arms all the way out to Senath, where the Lynns lived," Esther said. "Of course you could drive it now in a few minutes."

So, over country roads laid perpendicular like the lines on graph paper, I left the rolling hills of Fairdealing behind and followed the level route between hundred-acre farms in the southeastern tip of Missouri. In mid-afternoon, air conditioner blasting and radio blaring, I arrived in Kennett, a town of just over 10,000. I found a motel on the edge of town and, after a few laps in the pool, I sat cross-legged on the queen-sized bed in my room. I pulled the thin telephone book onto my lap, opened it to the listings of Lynns, and scanned the column until I reached James Allen Lynn. Could that be Jimmy Lynn, Cyrus's birth father? Or was it one of his sons? It looked as if I could simply dial James Lynn's number and reunite with this side of the family tomorrow.

I reached for the phone and pulled it onto the bed beside me. Again, as I had the year before when I dialed Harlon and Claretta's phone number, I had to concentrate on breathing slowly and steadying my voice. I spent an extra few minutes arranging my piles of papers. Then, because I knew in my eagerness I'd forget to say something important, my name for instance, I wrote out a simple script.

Calling Claretta and meeting Esther and her family had boosted my confidence and given me courage. I dialed James Lynn's number. After three rings, a woman answered, and I began reading from my notes.

"My name is Kathy, and I'm looking for a Jimmy Lynn—"

"My husband is deceased. I wish you people would—"

"I'm sorry, just give me minute, please." The dial tone buzzed in my ear. Although sorry for disturbing his widow, I was frustrated that she'd mistaken me for a telemarketer or a bill collector and hadn't given me a chance to explain. *Which* James Lynn, I wanted to know. I considered calling her back. If this dead James Lynn was my grandfather, then I might never know more about Mavis. If his widow refused to speak with me, this could be the end of my search.

I returned to the phone book. My second call was to Hazel Lynn, a woman who shared a first name with Cyrus's adoptive mother. Another coincidence and one I hoped would bring me luck.

"How exciting that we might be related," she said when I explained the reason for my call. Now widowed, Hazel had been the third wife of Jimmy Lynn's brother, Wilford; she was a sister-in-law of Jimmy's. I made notes to keep it straight. "Why don't you come over?" she said. "I have an album I can show you."

Following the AAA map to get across town, I couldn't believe she was inviting a stranger to the house where she lived alone. I was used to the city, locked doors, keeping strangers out. Of course I wanted her to let me come, I had so many questions, but I also wanted to call her next of kin and tell them to scold her.

"I made lemonade," Hazel said from the kitchen as I settled onto her plastic-covered couch. Despite her age—I placed her in her eighties, the same generation as my Great-Aunt Esther—she navigated her tiny house without difficulty, carrying two icy glasses from the kitchen on a tray.

"Jimmy Lynn died about seven years ago," Hazel said, setting the tray down. "Liver cancer," she said. "He was eighty or eighty-one."

The news brought a familiar feeling—disappointment over not meeting one more member of my missing family. But it also brought relief, since I wouldn't have to expose what might have been a secret, his getting a girl pregnant all those years ago. My disappointment also was tempered by the fact that I still wasn't sure he was the right man. I had no proof, only the word of my eighty-nine-year-old Great-Aunt Esther—who had heard it secondhand herself.

"Was he the James Allen Lynn I found in the phone book?" I asked, recalling my brief phone call to his widow.

"No, that was Jimmy Lynn's nephew, his brother Wilford's son.

My stepson. He died earlier this year. He was in his sixties. He had a heart attack."

I was thoroughly confused but jotted notes so I could decipher it all later alone in my motel room.

"Yeah, Jimmy Lynn, the one who might be your granddad, was a wild one; it wouldn't surprise me if he had a baby no one knew about." Her eyes crinkled, as if with delight at her brother-in-law's promiscuity.

Hazel pulled out her photo album and flipped through it, pointing out Jimmy Lynn and his brother Wilford. Her easy manner relaxed me immediately, and I showed her photos I'd brought of young and present-day Cyrus. Neither of us found any physical resemblance between the men, nothing we could point to and say, "Yes, look at that forehead, look at this smile." Despite that, Hazel was sure I had found the right man. "Honey, Jimmy Lynn fooled around on his wife the whole time they were married."

Before I left, Hazel suggested I call one of Jimmy Lynn's sons who owned a large soybean and watermelon farm just outside of town. He was two years younger than Cyrus, making him sixty-six. She suggested I call him when he returned from the farm around ten o'clock that night. "And tell him," she said with a grin, "that I need another watermelon."

Back at the motel that night, I called the number Hazel had given me. Don Lynn had a soft, gentle voice and sounded weary from his work.

"No, I haven't heard of any out-of-wedlock baby," he said. "But then, my father would not have mentioned it."

He listened as I outlined the relationships as I understood them.

"So your father, Cyrus, would be my half-brother," he said.

"Yes," I said, "and you'd be my half-uncle."

"So I would." He sounded reticent but also intrigued.

"Could I meet you and show you a picture of my father?" I spoke quickly, afraid he'd say no.

"Sure, come on out to the farm tomorrow. It's out in Senath, about ten miles outside of Kennett. You may have to ride around with me, but we can talk in the truck. I'll ask Betty—my wife—to bring some photos."

I checked my notes. Senath was the town to which Mavis and Lois had taken the baby, my father, to leave him with his birth father's family.

The next morning, on my way to the old cotton gin he used as a staging area for loading watermelons, I tried to imagine what Don Lynn would be like. I assumed he'd be wearing a wide-brimmed straw hat and driving a beat-up tractor, an old man with wizened features.

When I pulled the rental car next to the barn, I noticed a man with hair a blend of blond and gray wearing sunglasses and a long-sleeved button-down shirt, dampened from sweat, talking on a cell phone. The scene seemed incongruous, too California-like for a farm in southern Missouri. Clearly I didn't know the first thing about modern farming.

I stepped out of the car and he held up a finger. I backed up, trying to keep out of the way, and watched the action in the loading area. A woman, who must have been Don's wife, Betty, her head just clearing the steering wheel, maneuvered the pickup and its trailer full of watermelons next to an eighteen-wheeler waiting, empty. With her neatly pressed sleeveless blouse and her short bobbed hair, she looked unperturbed by the heat.

The faded ochre barn stood alone, surrounded by fields as far as I could see. Betty and I appeared to be the only women for miles. In the adjacent loading area, twenty shirtless men shouted to each other in Spanish as they tossed watermelons down a fire brigade line. In the fields across the highway, more men bent over sprawling plants. They were in constant motion, their rhythm broken only when they stopped to wipe sweat out of their eyes or take long pulls from tall water bottles. I put my hands in my pockets and backed up another step as a second eighteen-wheeler moved into place, its tires spitting up chunks of gravel from the road. In my leather sandals, khaki shorts, and navy T-shirt, I was overdressed. I was a city girl far from home.

Don worked on unhitching the trailer from the pickup, rich umber dirt clinging to its sides like splattered paint on a white canvas. The uncoupling completed, he strode over with an outstretched palm. We shook hands and he motioned for me to hop in the truck. Taking Betty's place in the driver's seat, he started across the watermelon fields, and as soon as the loading area disappeared behind us, I began talking.

"Thanks for letting me come out today. I hope I'm not getting in the way."

"No problem," he said, looking over and smiling. "I hope you don't mind riding around with me. This is our busy season. We work dawn to dark."

I studied his face as he wiped the sweat off his forehead with the back of his hand. The lines in his forehead reminded me of cornfield furrows. He was as fair-skinned as I was, and his face was flushed a strawberry red from the heat. Other than our hair color, I didn't recognize any physical traits that we shared.

"Like I said on the phone, I'm curious about who my father's birth father was. I guess it could have been your father, but I'm not even sure I have the right family." I brushed damp hair away from my temples.

We cruised the rows of watermelon plants, the dust from the field settling on my damp skin. Behind the wheel, Don silently surveyed each row, looking for what, I didn't know.

"Farming goes back three generations in my family," he said. "If it is the same family, your father was the lucky one. He got out of here. It's a hard life."

We drove in the fields for fifteen minutes, stopping once so I could get out and examine a soybean plant up close. On the way back, Don asked me the dreaded question. "Who's watching your children at home?"

Figuring I had nothing to lose, I told him the truth about Pam and the sperm bank. "I see," he said after a moment staring out the windshield. "Sounds like your kids are pretty lucky."

His graciousness surprised me, and I realized I had some rearranging of expectations to do.

At the barn, I tried to stay out of the way. I found a place next to a dozen waist-high cardboard crates brimming with heavy melons. Wanting to make myself useful, I joined Betty in slapping small oval stickers on watermelons before the men tossed them into the eighteen-wheelers. "This trip of yours sure is interesting," she said, not breaking her pace. "Don's cousin is doing some family tree research; I'll ask him if he's come across your grandmother's name."

When he returned, Don asked me to back up the pickup a few feet so he could reattach the trailer. Afraid I'd hit the gas too hard and bash the truck's bumper into the trailer's hitch, I balked. I didn't want to make a fool of myself or damage his truck. But when I understood that this might have been a small test of his to see what I was made of, I climbed in, put the truck in reverse, and eased it back so he could make the connection.

After a few minutes, Betty took a break to root around in their no longer new Lincoln Continental. She returned holding two framed photographs of Don's father, a short, stocky man with thinning black hair. From my fanny pack, I pulled snapshots of my tall, thick-haired father. Don joined us and we compared the men's noses, foreheads, and eyes. "I don't see much resemblance," Betty said.

I wanted to show Cyrus what Don Lynn, the son of Jimmy Lynn, looked like, and I also wanted to study Don's face later, to search for similarities I couldn't see in person, so I snapped a picture of Don and Betty. Smiling for the camera, the two of them posing in front of the watermelon crates, Don draped his arm around Betty's shoulder and, despite the heat, pulled her close.

Just before noon we shook hands again and then I headed for my car. "Thanks for talking with me," I said over my shoulder. "Maybe someday we'll get this figured out."

"I'll write to you," Betty said, "if any of the cousins can tell us anything." As I opened the door to the car, Don called for me to wait a minute. He pointed to the pile of melons and shouted over the eighteen-wheeler's idling engine to the nearest man. "Grandy!" The man stared back and didn't move. It took me a second to realize Don was trying to get me a large watermelon. *Grande*. With his southern Missouri accent, it came out like a person's name.

"Grandy!" Don said again, pointing to a pile of watermelons and opening his arms wide. The man nodded and leaped off the pile, immediately grabbing a watermelon and looking to Don for approval. Don took it from him and presented me the bulky gift.

Don and Betty, arms around each other's waists, waved good-bye as I pulled onto the highway, heading north toward St. Louis where I would share the watermelon with Joan and Kathy before heading home. I glanced in the rearview mirror and watched them turn back to their work. Then focusing on the road ahead, I let out a loud sigh. *Damn*, I whispered. *Will I ever know if I've found my kin?*

My mother met my plane in San Francisco. "Tell me all about the trip," she said, turning off the NPR station and easing her Honda Accord onto the freeway toward the Bay Bridge. "Did you find what you'd hoped to?"

Taking my time, I told her about Fairdealing and Kennett, the people I'd met, the cemetery, the sticky heat.

"It's an incredible story," she said, her enthusiasm about my search making me feel less strange for conducting it. "What will you do next?"

"I don't know. I could stop searching, I guess. It was great to find out about Mavis and to visit her grave; I could just settle for that."

My mother glanced at me and smiled as if she knew what I was going to say next.

"But," I said, "I really want to know about Cyrus's birth father.

Wouldn't it be cool to see his picture, too? See if any of us—Mike, me, the boys—look like him?"

"I guess so." She shook her head slightly. "You sure are determined."

I suspected it might have made her uncomfortable, my work to find relatives on her first husband's side. I knew she still struggled with guilt over her two divorces. "I feel horrible about doing that to you and Mike," she'd said when we finally talked about it, sitting in her garden several years earlier.

"You were miserable," I said. "I understand why you left your marriages. If you had stayed, things might have been worse for all of us."

I didn't tell her that if any damage had been done, it had not been caused by the divorces but by the loss of my father and the charade that followed: pretending that he no longer existed. When the visits with Cyrus ended, it was as if he had died. But there had been no memorial service, no grave to visit, no album of photos to linger over; he'd simply disappeared. Missing in Action. And no one talked about it.

If I were to blame someone, I could hold my mother culpable, although not for leaving my father—I understand why she did that now. Of their three-month courtship, she had said once, "He swept me off my feet." Later, she admitted that at twenty-five she was the last of her friends still single and had felt pressure to marry or risk becoming an old maid. When I asked her why they had divorced, she said only, "We just got married too quickly." She did not elaborate.

I might blame my mother for severing my ties with my father so completely, but I don't, because I know now she was a product of the times. It would not have occurred to her (or Cyrus for that matter) to challenge the status quo, and I have no doubt that at the time, she was doing what she thought was best for all of us.

When Pam and I had house-hunted with her in the Bay Area, I'd feared her new home would be too close, that the proximity would threaten my autonomy, that she would demand too much of my time, that we would not find mother-daughter equilibrium. But I was wrong. Four miles has been the perfect distance between us. And I can finally appreciate the significance of her move. Not only because now that I'm a mother I sometimes dread the future when my sons might be far away from me, but mostly because I understand that despite the distance over the years, both geographic and emotional, she has never, not for one moment, been an absent mother.

Mom took the University exit from the freeway, heading along the frontage road and then turning east, toward the hills and my house.

"I still don't know if Jimmy Lynn is Cyrus's birth father," I said, looking out the window at the familiar route up Cedar Street, passing the park where Ben's team practiced soccer. I ached to see my boys but would have to wait until they got home from school. "I guess I'll just wait for the Missouri folks to talk among themselves. Someone must know something about a baby who got adopted."

She glanced over at me. "I'm sure you'll hear something soon."

"I don't know," I said. "I really don't know."

When Pam and the boys got home, Ben demanded a whole-family-even-the-dog hug. It had been five days, the longest I'd been away from them. Inside our love huddle, I squeezed them and breathed in their scents, a jumble of baby shampoo and little boy sweat, before giving Pam a long embrace. "Thanks for letting me go," I said. "It was just what I needed to do."

I gave the kids stickers I'd brought back for them and then plopped down on the floor to give airplane rides—Mommy's reconnecting ritual. I didn't even need to click my ruby slippers; their shrieks and giggles brought me truly home.

Understandably, one might find it odd that I craved family ties—even ties to the dead—so much that I left my partner and children behind to seek them. But the dichotomy makes perfect sense to me. It's like the cartoon of a writer that I saw somewhere, its caption reading, "Someone who devotes himself to a lifetime of solitude for the sake of communication." My quirk was comparable: I left family to find family.

Two weeks later, I rode a BART train to San Francisco and walked two blocks to the Department of Health, an early 1900s office building six stories high on the corner of Grove and Polk. The sun's heat was thwarted by a conglomeration of clouds, and a coastal wind whipped between downtown structures. I zipped up my fleece jacket and pulled up its collar. In the Bay Area, we bragged about our natural air conditioning while the rest of the country suffered from the heat, but on some days, I wished it was just a little warmer, more summer-like.

I found the building easily and, once inside, headed toward Room 105, the Office of Vital Records and Statistics. After joining a short line under a sign marked "Death Certificates" I handed my request to a woman behind the counter. Barely glancing at me, she took my check, stamped the form, and pointed down the hall.

Five minutes later, I held my grandmother's death certificate. Mavis F. Shaver. February 6, 1964. Cause of death: fatty infiltration of the liver and coronary arteriosclerosis.

There was no mention of a homicide, and the form made no mention of a crushed skull or brain tumor. Something was wrong with her liver, and she had hardened arteries, but I still didn't understand what had killed her.

At home that afternoon, I e-mailed my Uncle Al Briccetti, my stepfather's brother, a physician. He knew about my search and had found it intriguing.

How does fatty infiltration of the liver cause death? I wrote.

That evening he answered. *Most likely the liver was damaged by alcohol.*

This surprised me. I hadn't known anyone who'd died from alcoholism, and it changed my image of my grandmother. She had worked on ships during the war, making her a Rosie the Riveter. I had imagined her as independent, strong, not an alcoholic hitting the ultimate bottom. Like her, millions of children lost parents during the flu epidemic, but not all of them went on to lead tragic lives—divorces, alcoholism, and early death. At first I was disappointed at what I saw as weakness in her character, but soon I began to forgive her. She had given up a child. She had divorced twice and was single again before she died. She might never have recovered from her grief. The combination of all her losses may have been too much to bear, making her turn to alcohol to numb the pain.

After hearing from my uncle, I e-mailed my Great-Aunt Esther's son, Gary, about Mavis's death certificate, and let him decide whether or not to share its contents with his mother. A few minutes later, his reply popped up in my mailbox.

The Foster family became dysfunctional after Papa Foster's wife died. Mother believes he never recovered after his wife and son died, and he almost lost two other children in the flu epidemic. After his wife was gone he began drinking from a flask he kept in his office. He didn't drink out in the open, and he didn't get out of control. My Aunt Lois married a guy who'd been married twice before. She met him in a bar. She died a full-blown alcoholic.

This news stunned me. Esther had told me that Lois died of cancer, but she hadn't mentioned the alcoholism. The two young sisters who walked Mavis's baby out to the house in the country both had become alcoholics. It was a sad legacy, and while I ascribe to the medical model that alcoholism is a disease, probably genetic, I still wonder how often grief activates it.

Gary also wrote about his last contact with his Aunt Mavis:

The last time I talked with her was via phone in San Francisco sometime in 1963, when I was getting out of the service. I don't know why I didn't stay over and visit her, but I was anxious to get home. I knew what I'd find and I didn't want to see it. Anyway, she was drunk when I called her, and that made my decision easier.

I couldn't imagine my grandmother as a Down and Out Drunk. I preferred thinking about her when she was sixteen, when she tried to bring her baby home from the Children's Home Society in St. Louis.

"You may not enter this house with that child," I imagine her father saying, standing on the top step of their porch with his arms crossed. "That bastard child," he might have whispered. Her mother and a brother had died in the influenza epidemic when Mavis was four, and now her stepmother, perhaps hidden in the shadow cast by the porch roof, did not intervene in this homecoming standoff.

I also imagine Mavis turning and heading back down the dirt driveway. I can see her sister Lois hopping off the porch to catch up with her. On that day in late fall of 1930, the two girls must have taken turns carrying the baby a dozen miles out in the country, past pungent dairy and cattle farms, alongside bare soybean and watermelon fields, to an even smaller town. It wasn't even a town, really, but a cluster of houses holding down an intersection of two unpaved roads, damp dirt tilled into naked rows creeping out behind the houses. The girls would have knocked on the door of the home of the baby's father, Mavis would have placed her baby in his grandmother's arms, and then I imagine she and her sister turned around and walked back home, both of them crying most of the way.

Seven months later, on a late spring day in 1931, just before her son turned a year, Mavis was summoned to this house to collect him. One of the other children was ill, and the family too poor to keep her baby any longer. In my imagination, they look like the Joads in *The Grapes of Wrath*: torn dresses, cardboard strung around holey soles, sunken eyes. Then, my Grandmother Mavis returned to St. Louis, and the day before my father's first birthday, handed him over to a social worker at the Children's Home Society.

The times—before and during the Depression—were harsh, and I understand why Cyrus's birth father's family couldn't keep him. But what must it have been like for Mavis when her father rejected her and forced her to give up her baby? How deep her pain must have been to make her run as far away as she could and eventually drink herself to death before age fifty. And what about Cyrus's birth father, I wondered. The missing man. What had it been like for him?

TWENTY-EIGHT

Carrying On

During my first pregnancy, I had fretted about what would happen if I had a boy. Who would show him how to pee standing up and how to shave? I worried that other families would shun us in the park because we were a two-mom family and that kids at school would say cruel things to him because he didn't have a father.

Peeing turned out to be the easy part. One day, as Benjamin sat on the toilet with his feet on the toddler step stool, I said, "You know, men usually stand up to pee and you will, too, someday." The next day, as I walked by the bathroom, I saw him standing with his legs pressed against the toilet bowl, leaning over it, his face straining with the effort of concentration. A couple of years later, Daniel simply copied his big brother, and thus the skill of peeing standing up was mastered in our house.

Other tasks—like explaining our family to the boys' friends as they got older—were more challenging. One day as I drove Ben and his friend Abe from kindergarten to their afternoon childcare, my thoughts were interrupted by Abe's voice from the back seat.

"Who is Benjamin's real mom?"

I hesitated. "Both of us are," I said, using a singsong voice to hide my unease. "He has two moms."

He pondered this for a few seconds. "No, I mean who gave birth with him?"

"Oh, I see what you're asking. I did. I gave birth to him."

"So how did he get his other mom?"

We pulled up to the after-school program. "His other mom and I made him and Daniel. Do you know how babies are made?" I unbuckled my seatbelt and opened my door.

He giggled. "No."

"Don't forget to take your lunch box with you," I said.

Benjamin joined in. "Is it like how kitties are made?"

"Yes, all mammals are made the same way."

"Is it like how monkeys are made?"

"Yes."

Abe's turn. "Snakes?"

"Turtles?" asked Ben.

"No, those are reptiles; they lay eggs outside their bodies."

Laughing, the two boys ran to the locked redwood gate and waited for me to catch up.

A week later, Ben and I walked onto the school playground just before the bell and met up with Abe and his father, Nick, who was dressed in a suit and carrying a worn daypack. Next to the play structure, Abe stopped.

"I know how you got Benjamin and Daniel!" he shouted. "You married a man and had them, and then you got a divorce, and that's how you and Pam got them." He was a precocious child, much more verbal than Ben. At that moment I wished he wasn't so damn smart.

I knelt next to him and Nick leaned over him, resting his arm on his son's shoulder. "They had a little help from a doctor," Nick started.

"Actually, a man gave us his sperm," I said, looking into Abe's face. "Like a present. And I put it inside of me and that's how we made Benjamin and Daniel."

I glanced over at Nick to make sure I hadn't gone too far. He was nodding.

"What do you think about that?" I asked Abe.

"That's *weird!*"

The word was a punch to my solar plexus. I glanced at Ben standing beside me. His head was tipped back in laughter, as if Abe had said a bathroom word. Did he really think Abe was funny or was he covering up embarrassment? Did this hurt him as much as it hurt me?

"No, it's *different,*" I said.

"Yeah, it's different, not weird," Nick said. "Benjamin and Daniel are beautiful boys." He sounded flustered.

Abe picked up his backpack and ran to his classroom line. I kissed Ben on the top of his head and watched him catch up with Abe. Nick gave me an apologetic look. "Oh well, at least it's a start."

"A good start," I said, and we parted ways at the schoolyard gate.

TWENTY-NINE

Letting Go

I'd been a Briccetti for more than three decades—most of my life—but now I considered changing my last name from Briccetti-Craig to simply Craig. I told myself I wanted a name that people could pronounce and that I didn't have to spell every time I ordered something over the phone, but I was really experimenting with possibilities. I wanted to shed my stepfather's name like a skin I'd outgrown. I didn't consider taking back the name Manfred—that name didn't feel like mine anymore. I wanted to claim my adult name, my own name, the name I shared with my children instead of a father.

I had called my stepfather "Dad" ever since he'd adopted me when I was nine, but in my twenties, I began to vacillate between calling him "Dad" and "Tom." In letters, I'd avoid the dilemma by simply leaving off the salutation entirely. By the fall of 1998, our communication consisted mainly of sporadic e-mail. In my most recent message I'd replaced, "Love, Kath" with simply "K."

Mirroring my conflict, he had begun using "Dad" and "Tom" interchangeably when signing his letters and e-mails, but until recently he had still tacked on affectionate tags like "Lots of love." But that winter when I sent him a copy of one of my first published essays, he'd replied with an unsolicited critique. It had made me furious, and in a change of character, I fought my diffident style and called him on it, asking him not to criticize my published work. The subject line of his next e-mail read "IRE," and for the next three months we battled point-by-point, shooting long e-mails back and forth like artillery fire, me finding courage to tell him how it felt to be teased, to have my feelings discounted, him defending himself and calling me oversensitive and paranoid, or wondering if I was fancying myself another Sylvia Plath or Doris Lessing already. I cried in frustration in front of the computer screen. We finally agreed to drop it and to stop communicating altogether. He closed his last note with *Give my best to Pam and the kids. Tom.* It was almost a relief, but anger vied with the frustration, leaving me simply sad. Pam soothed me, but it felt like my adoption papers had been crumpled up and tossed away.

I recounted those e-mail exchanges to my mother on the phone one evening. Her silence signaled her discomfort with the subject, and I didn't expect her to say much. I'd become used to her quiet during emotional times. Years earlier, I'd had to ask her not to talk me out of my feelings. After breaking up with a boyfriend, I had cried on the phone when I told her about it. "Oh, honey, don't cry. It'll all work out," she'd said.

"It doesn't help," I said, "when you tell me not to cry, to forget about it, to get on with things." My voice wobbled from nerves; I had not been this direct with her before. "It would help if you could just listen. Or say something like, 'I know it hurts.'"

Although she'd sounded wounded, she agreed, and the next time I poured something out, she didn't jump in to appease me. "Oh, I see," she'd said.

I understand how difficult it is to push against generations of precedent, one's family's molds. Mom's mother's family had settled on the plains of Alberta, Canada, suffered harsh conditions, had to be tough, had no time to "process their feelings," especially the more vulnerable ones. If you needed to boo-hoo about something, you went off on your own and took care of that in private. The only time I saw my mother cry was on the day President Kennedy was assassinated and she picked me up from first grade when the school closed early. The news commentary came over the car radio, but it was her sniffles I heard the loudest. My mother's family definitely believed in the "stiff upper lip" and in "getting back on the horse." And they were not physically demonstrative. My mother told me once that as a child she had been physically comforted by a neighbor who'd embraced her after a fall, and that she had experienced the feeling as novel.

On the phone, Mom listened. "I'm relieved to have it out in the open at least," I said. "I've asked myself if he were to die tomorrow, is there anything else I need to say?" Then I answered my own question. "No, I don't think there is."

What I didn't say was that losing him again that way brought back the pain of losing him before. It was as if I had no father at all; it was as if he *had* died.

That spring, Pam had to get to work early every morning, and I was driving Ben to kindergarten and Daniel to preschool, a forty-five-minute undertaking, before I headed to work myself. I couldn't remember whether it was my night to cook dinner, didn't know how we'd get Ben to his after-school program in the middle of the day, had no idea how I'd get all of my work done, prayed I could sleep just one night without waking up two or three times, brain racing, afraid I might be having a heart attack when pressure squeezed my sternum toward my spine. It felt like I was stuck in a small room with concrete walls steadily moving toward each other.

Just before making an appointment with a therapist, though, my panic settled. I had begun to coach myself, began to put things in perspective. On my walks in the hills, I thought like my mother would, reminding myself that I had a partner, two children, a dog. I was not an orphan and had never been. I'd had two fathers, sometimes present, sometimes MIA, and I'd had an ever-present mother. I finally slowed down and began to take stock of what was existant in my life instead of dwelling on what was missing.

* * *

One Saturday evening in early April, after returning home from Daniel's soccer game, I played back a phone message on our answering machine. It was Don Lynn, the watermelon farmer from "Missour-a" whose slow and easy speech flowed out of the speaker. "Uh, there are some people here who would really like to talk to you. Call us back as soon as you can."

I heard amusement in his voice. Riding in his truck across the fields the previous summer, Don had mentioned a nephew who dabbled in genealogy. Maybe he had discovered our link, figured out whether Jimmy Lynn was really Cyrus's birth father. Or maybe Don's sisters had visited him during the holidays and they'd started talking, and someone said they knew about that baby. Now that their parents were dead, maybe that person could finally leak the secret. Or someone had found something, like a document with rust-colored edges folded in half and stuck in the back of a worn book, or a letter in a strongbox in the back of the garage. *My darling Mavis,* it might have begun.

It was too late to return his call, so the next morning, praying he wasn't at church, I phoned Don Lynn.

"Hello there!" he said. "How's the weather out there in California?"

"Just fine." I looked out the window at cinder clouds. *Give me the damn news,* I wanted to shout.

"Well, now," he started, in no hurry and making me crazy with curiosity. "You're probably wondering why I'm calling you."

"Yes!"

"Well, then, I'll tell you," he said, his smile coming through in his tone. "The other evening Betty and I went out to supper with my cousin Dale and his wife Barbara. Betty and Barbara were sitting together at the end of the table talking, and right before dessert Betty said to Barbara, 'I have an interesting story to tell you.'"

"Yeah?" *What was the damn story?*

"So Betty tells her about your visit last summer and your story about how your grandmother carried her baby all the way out to

Jimmy Lynn's house and handed him over to them. And as Betty's talking, Barbara keeps nodding and smiling, bigger and bigger, and when Betty finishes the story, Barbara looks at her and says, 'That wasn't Jimmy's baby, that was Wilford's baby.'"

"Oh, my goodness." I said. I knew Wilford's name from my research the previous summer, but couldn't piece it all together. It had been months since I'd looked at the notes in my three-ring binder.

"Turns out, before he died, Wilford told his sons that he had another son but didn't know anything about him or where he was. When Dale asked for the woman's name his father told him he had forgotten. Of course, he just might not have wanted them to know. He may have been lying."

"Wow! Now how are you and Dale related?" I was lost in this tangle of relationships.

"Dale's my cousin, my first cousin. Wilford was my uncle, Dale's father. He died about fifteen years ago. Hazel Lynn was his third wife."

I scribbled on a scrap of paper next to the phone. Hazel Lynn had served me lemonade in her tiny house, had told me that Jimmy Lynn cheated on his wife. But if Don was right, it was Hazel's husband who had fathered the out-of-wedlock child during his first marriage. It was sweetly ironic.

"You know, after you visited and left that photo of Cyrus and you five kids? Later on Betty commented that Cyrus looked more like Wilford's side of the family than my side."

Last summer, when we had swapped photographs, we'd seen no physical resemblance between Cyrus and Jimmy Lynn. As an older man, Jimmy Lynn had black hair and a round body and looked nothing like Cyrus.

"Kathy, my cousin Dale just walked in. And it looks like he's going to rip this phone out of my hands if I don't hand it over. I'll talk to you later."

"Kathy, this is just too good to be true," Dale said by way of introduction. He had the same Southern drawl as Don, but his voice fell on a higher register. "It was the story of the woman carrying the baby to Senath that gave us the connection," Dale said. "Kathy, I believe we're kin."

I drew in a deep breath. His words made me smile. I *was* related to these good people on the other side of the country.

"I'm just so excited to hear about you all," he said. "I couldn't sleep last night after we figured all this out and then Don left you the message." *Me, too*, I wanted to say. "Before my father died, he owned a furniture store in Kennett, and one night when we were closing he told me that he had another son but didn't remember the girl's name and didn't know what became of the baby."

Didn't remember the girl's name, or didn't want to say? How could you forget the mother of your baby?

"I wish we could be sure," I said. I'd paid attention lately to reports of DNA testing on the news. One of the Lynns might still have an old hairbrush of Wilford's that we could send in for testing. But I didn't know how to bring it up with Dale.

"Those DNA tests would tell, right?" he said. "I'd take one. If it wasn't too expensive. Yeah, all of us brothers could get together and do it." His voice bobbed with eagerness, and I laughed. "I guess they would."

Near the end of our conversation, Dale asked, "So Kathy, y'all got any money?" For an instant I was confused. Then he chuckled on the other end of the line, and I understood.

"No, I'm afraid not. I was hoping *you* did. You're not related to Loretta Lynn by any chance?"

"I wish!" Our laughs overlapped across the wires.

"So if you're Cyrus's half-brother, then you're my uncle, right?" I asked.

"Yes, I believe so. Or, your half-uncle." He laughed again.

Don and his siblings would be Cyrus's half-cousins, and I'd heard mention of Dale's brothers, so that meant Cyrus had several half-brothers after all. *If* all this was true.

Dale handed the phone over to his wife, Barbara, the woman

who had put the pieces together when she heard Betty Lynn's story about my visit.

"I'm looking at the photo you sent Don, and your Dad's nose looks like Wilford's. He's in the shadow, though, so it's hard to see his face clearly. I'd like to see another photo of him. I'll send you pictures of Wilford and all the boys, so you can see what you think."

I hung up the phone and let out a whoop. I found Pam in the backyard. "I think I've found Cyrus's birth father's family. The Lynns. Or they found us—after I found them."

"What are you talking about? Who? I'm lost."

"I was, too, but now I understand it, I think. Jimmy Lynn wasn't Cyrus's birth father, his brother Wilford was. But Wilford was married, and his wife was pregnant, so to protect his brother, I think Jimmy Lynn said it was his baby. I think they may have lied to the adoption agency." I thought for a moment about the possibilities. "Or the adoption agency made changes to the records. Covered up for the birth family, I mean."

Pam shook her head. "That's rich. Is he still alive? Wilford? That's your grandfather, right?"

I nodded. "He died a while ago. But he's got a few sons, and that means Cyrus has brothers."

The disappointment at having missed meeting my Grandfather Wilford didn't sting as much as it had when I'd learned about my Grandmother Mavis's death. I felt a distancing, and I was becoming accustomed to the broken connections. This man was more a name on my family tree, an ancestor, than a grandfather to me. And the excitement of forming new connections, especially for my father, eased any residual regret.

I wanted to tell Cyrus right away, but he was traveling in Mexico with Cody and wouldn't be home for several days. I called Ursula at home in Kentucky and spewed out everything so she could pass the news to him the next time he called home. While I waited to hear from him, I wondered about Mavis's having named her baby Jimmie

Earl Foster. Foster had been her own last name, so I understood that. Now it seemed that she had named her baby Jimmie after the brother of the married man who had gotten her pregnant, to protect him. But where did Earl come from? I hadn't seen it in any of my genealogical notes. Had she made it up? I wanted to believe that sixteen-year-old Mavis was sending a message into the future. Scrambled, Earl could make the word "real." This is not his real name, not his real daddy; *don't be fooled,* she could have been saying in code to her son and to the rest of us, her future descendants. But I see now that I was still grasping at ways to connect her to me, and, apparently, I was getting a little carried away.

To celebrate this latest success, Pam and I took the boys to our favorite Mexican restaurant. At Juan's Place, Pam and I clinked margarita glasses and the boys added their root beer glasses to the toast. They didn't know what we were celebrating, just that they got to drink soda, eat as many chips as they wanted, and order flan for dessert.

"You did it, love," Pam said, taking a sip of her drink. "Good job."

I looked at my hands, fiddling with the paper napkin on my lap. "Thank you for taking care of things when I went searching; I know that wasn't easy." I looked up. I still didn't know what she made of my travels, whether she saw them as whims to be tolerated, or whether she had some sense of their meaning to me.

"I didn't really get it. I still don't, really, but I'm happy for you." She held my gaze. "And you're welcome."

In mid-April, Cyrus made another trip without me. When he invited me to join him, I declined. This time it seemed right that he go by himself. It was his turn to travel to Kennett, Missouri, to meet his three surviving half-brothers and their families. These were his only blood kin besides us five kids and the grandkids, and I understood his eagerness to meet them. And, for once, I was content to have simply brought them all together, to listen to their reunion stories. I would meet these relatives another time.

His half-brothers staged a family reunion in Kennett to welcome Cyrus into the family and gave him a tour of the town where he lived until he was taken back to St. Louis to be adopted. His cousin, Don Lynn the farmer, and Don's wife, Betty, stopped by, and the widow of Cyrus's oldest brother—the woman who had hung up on me when I called from the motel the summer before—came to meet him.

Hazel Lynn, Wilford's third wife, the woman who invited me over to look at photographs and served me lemonade, had died several months earlier. I speculated whether she'd known about her husband Wilford's baby born out of wedlock, but I would have bet he'd kept it a secret from her, too.

The patterns of secrets continued to frustrate me, and I briefly plotted to petition the Missouri court to open Cyrus's adoption records. One little peek could uncover the final missing piece. Perhaps in her letter, which the social worker had censored, Mavis had written the true birth father's name. But while this thought tickled at me, my satisfaction with all I had discovered overshadowed the desire to push on with the search. I was winding down.

One evening, near the end of his trip to Kennett, Cyrus telephoned. Laughter burst in the background; it sounded like a party in progress. I sat in the desk chair, swiveling it so I could stare out the window at the backyard.

"This is just fantastic," Cyrus said. "These guys are great. One of the young cousins saw me get out of the car from across the yard, and he thought I was Dale. It seems we have the same physique and even walk the same."

He handed the phone to Dale.

"Kathy, we don't need none of that DNA testing; Cyrus is one of us!"

Cyrus returned to the phone, as exuberant as I'd ever heard him. "Thank you for this," he said. "Thank you for finding my brothers."

I laughed. "You're welcome." I wanted to spin the chair,

pretending it was a carnival ride like my boys would. Instead, I sat quietly and let myself feel his gratitude fill a space in me. I'd been proving myself my whole life to everyone and especially to my fathers. Because of what had felt like their elusiveness, like a puppy from the pound I pined for them, chased them, struggled to please them.

A week later, I received a large envelope from Cyrus. In it were photos of him and his three half-brothers posing together in someone's kitchen, their arms draped across each other's shoulders. Antique dinner plates, like the one my relative in Fairdealing had given me, hung on the wall above the cabinets.

My Uncle Dale's most noticeable features were his Amish-like beard, owlish glasses, and his nose. Cyrus and his half-brother did indeed share this long family nose—the nose that Barbara said Wilford had, and the one I'd inherited from Cyrus. Finally I could see a resemblance, a physical connection to these relatives.

I studied the glossy black-and-white photo of Wilford, Cyrus's birth father, my grandfather, taken in 1955, when he was fifty. A hulking man, he lounges in an armless floral-print chair, one leg crossed over the other and arms folded tightly across his chest—a self-assured, almost cocky pose. He would go on to live until almost eighty, married three times, widowed twice. He had lived thirty years longer than Mavis, and this knowledge lit a flicker of anger in me. She had suffered and died alone, far from her family, while he appeared to have enjoyed a long life surrounded by four sons and several wives. Did he grieve, too, in ways I could never know, for the son he never knew, that piece missing from his life? Or had he pushed away those feelings, lived as if it had never happened?

We think he looks like Cody, Ursula had written on a Post-it stuck on the back of the photograph. This time when I studied my grandfather's face, the resemblance was obvious. Indeed, his eyes and thin-lipped smile had been passed down to my half-brother.

Inside Cyrus's envelope, I also found a copy of the *Daily Dunklin*

Democrat, the Kennett, Missouri, newspaper. When I glanced at the front page, I understood why he had sent it. In a photo taken at the Lion's Club pancake breakfast, his fork poised over a plate of pancakes, Cyrus sat next to his new brothers.

Thank you for everything you did, all your hard work, he had written on a piece of stationery with a sketch of a cello on it.

Sitting alone in the breakfast nook with the pages on my lap, I nodded. "You're welcome," I whispered.

THIRTY

An Ordinary Life

I held up a T-shirt imprinted with a photo of my two blond children on the front, and the sales clerk glanced back and forth between me and four-year-old Daniel, who was doing chin-ups to peer over the counter. She smiled and raised her eyebrows at him.

"He looks just like you," she said, meeting my eyes. "Is your husband tall, too?"

I glanced down at Daniel while running through possible answers in my head. I still changed the subject when strangers asked about my husband. Often I nodded or said "umm-hmm" and prayed that we'd move on to something else. But at the shop on University Avenue, for the first time in front of a group of strangers, I did something different.

"I don't have a husband," I said softly, turning my gaze to my checkbook. "My partner is a woman, and we used the sperm bank to get pregnant." I said this in a clarion voice in front of Daniel and the other customers, and the clerk didn't slam shut the cash register drawer and refuse to serve me. No one even looked my way. Emboldened, I tore out my check and handed it to her. Daniel rested his chin on the counter and looked up at the clerk.

"We know the donor is a little taller than me and has brown

hair," I said, even though she hadn't asked about his hair color. With what I hoped was an air of nonchalance, I spoke as if I had this conversation every other day, but blood banged against my eardrums, and my neck and face turned warm. It was the first time I had come out like this, in front of a half-dozen strangers. I waited for a sharp intake of air from someone in the store, or an awkward silence. But before I could continue, the woman beside me, rummaging through a bin of shirts, looked my way.

"I have a friend in the same situation, but she's having a hard time deciding whether or not to use the sperm bank." I couldn't place this woman's accent. I guessed Russian and pegged her as a grad student at Cal.

I nodded. "Yeah," I said. "It's a hard choice, whether to use the sperm bank or ask a friend for a really big favor."

She nodded.

The sales clerk, an Asian American woman who looked about my age, jumped in to the conversation. "I have friends who used the sperm bank and they have a beautiful boy. I think he has some Asian in him."

A man in his twenties with a beard and a long braid down his back approached the counter and nodded. "Cool."

Never before had I spoken so freely about this with strangers. Pam, the boys, and I belonged to a social group of one hundred gay families who got together at the children's museum, zoo, and holiday parties, and at these gatherings we shared stories about ovulation predictor kits, co-parenting, and domestic versus foreign adoption. We occasionally signed petitions and drafted letters to the editor about gay marriage. But most often we just sat back, watching our kids swing, slide, and run across the grass at the park, while we parents talked about toilet training, ear infections, and starting kindergarten.

My family and friends knew the details of my donor inseminations and pregnancies and had accepted my partnership with a woman. But out in public, in the grocery store and the library, I'd been too afraid to speak freely. I didn't know who would cluck their tongues and mutter something like, "Goes against nature," and who would smile and say, "What beautiful children they are!"

But with the clerk and customers in the store, it was as if we were discussing whether the rain would keep up for the rest of the day or quit soon. It was a perfectly acceptable exchange, sharing stories—a little unusual or special, but perfectly acceptable.

I felt a loosening of tension around my rib cage I hadn't realized had been there. To have my life accepted as just another ordinary life, to have it viewed as common and regular, was a singular moment. I couldn't wait to tell Pam. She, too, had not yet spoken with strangers about our family. When Ben was a toddler, a woman passing on the sidewalk told Pam he looked just like her. Recently, more than once strangers had assumed she was the boys' grandmother. Pam usually just nodded. But now that the kids were getting older, we needed to be more direct, more honest. I wanted to tell her how well this had gone so she could try it, too.

Except for the time I told my story to the woman at Totland Park, I'd been silent about my family in public since Ben was born almost seven years before. But something in me changed that day at the T-shirt shop. I had risked the truth and survived. The next time someone asked about my husband, I would try the same response again. "Nope, I don't have a husband," I'd start, looking them directly in the eye.

As I took Daniel's hand and we walked to the door, I glanced back at the clerk and the customer, their heads bowed together like confidants picking through the sale bin.

"See you later," I said with a little wave.

"Bye," the clerk said. "Hope that rain stays away for the rest of the day."

THIRTY-ONE

Markers

"There's something I need to tell you." My mother's strained voice over the phone line frightened me. She'd just had a routine biopsy, and I braced myself for bad news.

"What is it?"

"Tom died." She paused. "Uncle Al asked me to call you and Mike."

"What?" I swiveled in my chair and faced the window. I'd heard her but needed a few seconds to comprehend.

"How?" I imagined him racing his motorcycle through the mountains of northern Italy.

"Al thinks he had a heart attack at home and died in the ambulance on the way to the hospital in Perugia. Supposedly he clutched at his chest and said, 'It hurts.'"

I had never heard my father say that anything—the time a stray cat bit his wrist to the bone or the divorce from my mother—had hurt him.

My chest began to ache. "When?" I asked.

"Today." She paused to let me absorb this, and in my typical fashion, I took refuge in my head. I needed to get it all straight before I could feel it.

He was only sixty-three. It was his Type-A personality that had killed him. And the smoking. He hadn't gotten cancer like I'd feared he would. Remarkably, he'd agreed to a set of lung X-rays a couple of years before, and had promised his brother, the physician, to give up smoking if they were damaged. The X-rays showed completely healthy tissue, surprising even his doctor. How he loved to tell that story, laughing at his luck, laughing in death's face.

It was near the end of May, a few days before Memorial Day, and in a complete change of character, he'd been anxious already about the following year, 2000, concerned that computers wouldn't be able to handle the switch to the millennium, that with a series of crashes, the world's infrastructure would collapse. I wonder now if he'd had a sense of foreboding about his own body's gradual shutting down, the blockage in his heart growing; maybe he'd felt death approaching. But I didn't really believe this. My father lived as if he were invincible, tempting the fates continuously. I'm sure he thought he could beat anything.

He'd had a minor stroke five years earlier, and this should have served as a warning, but as far as I knew, he hadn't made any changes—didn't stop smoking, didn't start exercising, pushed himself hard still. The image of him hunching over a musical score on his desk, dropping his baton and clutching his chest, vulnerable, mortal, is what first prodded at my shell of denial.

"He never responded to my Easter greeting," I said to Mom, my voice wobbling. "That's what I regret, that we'll never finish the discussion, or argument, we started." I paused. "But I'm glad I told him what I needed to say in those e-mails; if I'd waited, it would have been too late." My mother listened as I morphed the negative to positive, and when I was finished she sighed, her own feelings undoubtedly as complicated as mine. "I'll be here," she said, "if you want to talk more later."

That evening, I plodded through the dinner routine, supervising hand washing, setting out the broccoli and macaroni and cheese Pam had made. The boys' chatter at the table distracted me from brooding, and Pam shot sympathetic looks from across the table. I choked up only a few times when memories of my father—scenes I hadn't recalled in years—resurfaced. Like when we moved from Florida to Indiana and detoured to Six Flags Over Georgia for the day, the four of us racing back into the line for the log flume over and over. And my eleventh birthday when he came wobbling down the driveway on the banana seat of my new purple Stingray bicycle, peddling with legs splayed like a giant spider. How he taught me to love orange juice mixed with grape juice and to twist the stem off a pear and eat it from the top down. How instead of calling the cops on our teenage neighbor's rock band practicing with the windows open on summer nights, he hauled an unused air conditioner out of our attic and installed it in their garage for them. How at our picnic table one evening he'd slapped our ancient aunt on the back, dislodging the hunk of steak from her windpipe, giving her a few more years.

And I remembered something I hadn't thought of in years: his voice coming through the speaker in my sixth grade classroom when he produced the citywide Music Memory program in Indianapolis, teaching elementary children to recognize pieces of classical music. I'd been both proud to be his daughter and at the same time embarrassed at the attention the program brought me. I remembered with pure enchantment, though, my mother performing the violin concerto he had written for her in Florida. She had looked like a princess that night in her ice blue satin gown, but the image I hold onto even more doggedly happened a minute after the music stopped, before their bows, when my father set his baton on the podium, grasped her hand, and brought it to his lips. It was a moment stopped in time for me, witnessing, along with hundreds in the audience, that instant of exquisite tenderness between my parents.

When I learned to drive, he taught me that accelerating on turns produced more traction, and although I've never confirmed this with a race car driver, I think of it often as I speed up slightly when taking some of the turns on Bay Area freeways. He also taught me what I'd first assumed was an old wives' tale: to get rid of a wart, lick it every morning before getting out of bed. I'd had a small wart on my inner forearm as a child, something I'd been ashamed of, and I'd tried shaving it off with a razor, a painful and bloody mess, but I usually just hid the imperfection under long-sleeved shirts. When I finally took his advice, within a month the wart was gone.

I remembered leaning next to him on our couch on Sunday mornings in Florida when he read Bible stories to Mike and me for a few months, his brief attempt at nonsectarian religious homeschooling. He had not attended mass for most of his adult life, having abandoned his Catholic practice before we'd met him. However, he was a man full of contradictions. On Good Friday one year, he insisted on complete silence in our house at the noon hour, observing the time of Christ's crucifixion. I still don't know why he chose that day and that particular year, when I was nine or ten, to lapse into such an obscure Catholic ritual. He never did it again. And the only time I saw him in a church was at his mother's memorial service, when he stood in front of the altar and addressed the crowd, his voice trembling. It wasn't the stories on the couch I loved so much as the time spent with him then, listening to his expressive voice, watching his eyes follow the words on the page and then look over at me, his broad, full-of-love smile, his complete acceptance of me at those moments. I had been mad at him for so long, I'd forgotten.

That afternoon, shortly after learning of his death, I phoned my friend Nancy, who'd been in that sixth-grade classroom with me, and years later had taken me for the pregnancy test. "Tom's gone to a better place," she said. "And he's probably trying to run it," she added, making both of us laugh.

After dinner, I spoke with Mike on the phone for nearly two hours. We had grown apart over the years, but on the evening of our father's death, we plunged into memories of growing up with him, examined our relationships with this difficult man, shared our feelings of loss.

"Remember the notes we hid around the house," I asked, "telling him not to smoke—'cancer sticks,' I think we called them?"

"You did that, not me," he said. "It sure pissed him off to find those notes—in the piano, in his sock drawer." Mike still sounded angry at our father. When my brother was a rebellious teenager, he had lived with Dad briefly after the divorce but eventually returned to Mom. Dad had failed each of us in different ways. On the day of his death, we were both calling him Tom.

After our conversation, I finished loading the dishwasher, snapped the door shut, and stood alone in the middle of the kitchen, staring at nothing. In the next moment it felt as if someone had lowered a weighted coat over my shoulders. With no warning, my body was too heavy to move. A deep sadness shifted in my center, something old mixed with something new. Tingling pain built in my chest, whirling into my fingers and shooting to my Achilles tendons. When I finally began to sob, Pam found me and held me in a long embrace. The boys silently joined us, wrapped their arms around my waist, and pressed their heads into my sides. I kissed the soft hair on the tops of their heads.

I had asked Dad once how to say "I love you" in Italian. *Ti voglio bene.* I practiced it over and over, and even used it when we spoke on the phone, since those words, coded as they were, slid out easier.

Besides the sweaty-palmed middle-school boys who took ballroom dance lessons with me in Indianapolis, he's the only man I danced the waltz with. I had always thought he would live well into his eighties, a Picasso-like figure hunched over his desk composing music. *You have to come back; we have to finish our conversation.* He was playing a trick, teasing me as he had so many times. It was another of his dramatic acts to get attention, I wanted to believe. He'd call me in a while. "Just kidding," he'd say, laughing, *thhh-thhh.* "Gotcha!"

I hadn't seen him in four years. Our argument wasn't finished yet, and my missing him was still wrapped up in my anger. He would not see my children grow up. He and I would never reconcile. So much for telling myself that our falling out hadn't made any difference, that I could do without him just fine. His death knocked me down.

But I recognized another feeling, too. Relief. My surviving him would be what finally made me an adult. I was no longer his little girl. No longer subject to his judgments, his one-upping. And I would never again hear him say, "Kithi, *ti voglio bene.*" I was torn apart.

Eventually I moved to my desk and, alone again, stared out the window at the trumpet vine steeped in the sunset's subtle blush. The light was perfect at that moment, extracting the leaves' range of colors—the older leaves a deep moss green, the newer ones shiny emerald. It was too much, the clarity of the moment. I had a sudden urge to lie down on my bed, pull the comforter over me, and will the numbness back.

That night as I lay in bed, I conjured up an image of the morgue in Perugia, a modern facility inside an ancient brick building. In my mind, his corpse lay on a metal gurney in a refrigerated mausoleum. He was not lying flat on his back but curled on his side as if returning to the womb. Small and powerless and stiff. It took this image, and that of his last moments, writhing and helpless, to begin to convince myself that my indomitable father was gone.

In August, three months after his death, about a hundred relatives and friends from across the United States, as well as from Germany and Italy, converged for a memorial in New York. Mike, Mom, and I had flown together from California. Although she had been divorced from my stepfather for twenty-five years, Mom wanted to join us. "I'd like to be there," she said, "for you and Mike." That morning in White Plains, she and I had taken a walk around the hotel grounds, and I finally let myself cry in front of her. "Go ahead," she'd said, putting an arm around me and remaining stoic. "It's good to get it out."

Unlike the hills of California, which were turning golden near the end of the summer, New York's landscape was glistening in greenness. The muggy air and lush lawns reminded me of living in the Midwest, where summer meant rain not drought, verdant vistas not desiccated hills. As we entered the building that housed Pius X Hall, a small auditorium at Manhattanville College in Purchase, the absurdity of gathering to remember my father in a hall named for a pope was not lost on me.

Inside the auditorium, my Uncle Al's second wife, Mary, introduced Mom to a circle of relatives: "This is Tom's former wife." Knowing of his three marriages and scores of girlfriends, the group remained silent, not sure how to respond. "Our favorite ex-wife," Mary added, and the group relaxed into laughter.

Reintroduced to the Briccetti cousins I had met years before, now grown with children of their own, I felt a twinge of regret that we had lost touch so many years ago. Meeting their kids made me miss mine; Pam and the boys had stayed home. We couldn't afford to bring the whole family and, truthfully, I didn't want them there. For that weekend I wanted to not be a mother, or even a partner, but only a daughter again.

In the hallway before the memorial service, someone showed me photographs of my father, the last ones taken of him, at a restaurant with a group of friends in Perugia. His last girlfriend looked at least my age, late forties even. In a wacky little twist, she looked like my mother, her dark wavy hair, her head tossed back in uncensored laughter, my father with his arm squeezing her shoulder. His face, though, is gaunt, lined, and ashen, as if his heart wasn't supplying enough blood to his skin. The photos reminded me how far apart we'd grown, how little I knew him anymore.

Shortly after his death, I had found his website again, something I hadn't done since just after he'd published it, and then I'd given it only a cursory look. The second time, waiting for it to load, I expected to see nothing but text, his CV, and his conducting schedule, so when his photo materialized, covering the screen, I recoiled. He was dead, but he was right there, staring at me like a ghost.

Before the memorial service, I met again the symphony board president at whose house Dad and I had had dinner when I'd gotten off the train on my way to California in 1978. After two decades, I was curious to hear her memories of that night, what the twenty-year-old me had been like during that visit. I thought she'd talk about what a polite and charming young woman I'd been, an eager-to-please girl with good manners who knew how to smile through dull evenings filled with symphony orchestra business. An interesting girl who was headed west to start her fascinating life. Instead, what she said surprised me. "You were so sad that night. I remember you sitting in the corner of my couch crying."

I didn't believe her. It was so far from my image of myself, so far from what I know to be true about how I behave in public, that I was absolutely sure the woman was mistaken. She was now in her seventies; she must have had me mixed up with another young woman who had visited her house around that time twenty years earlier.

But now that I try to recall that evening, what was going on during that trip—my leaving home for California, meeting Dad's latest girlfriend, trying to get to know and connect with him again—it's possible that the symphony board president was right. I would not have been bawling on her couch, that's just too out of character, but perhaps I did sit there quietly sniffling, suffering young adult angst. "Your father sat right next to you on the couch and put his arm around you," she said as we stood together outside the auditorium. Her smile told me that she admired him for this loving, fatherly gesture, and it annoyed me that, even after death, he was viewed in such mythical proportions. She was just another woman who had fallen under his spell. And I was still so hard on him.

Stephanie, the former girlfriend whom I'd met in Italy, attended the memorial with her husband, a man close to her age. As part of the memorial service, she would be playing a clarinet piece my father had composed for her. When I'd heard this, the haunting jealousy resurfaced; she had shared with him so much more than I had in recent years. She had been closer to him, had reaped his love while I'd fought with him. It was an absurd, one-sided rivalry.

Before we entered the auditorium, Stephanie told me that she'd found her birth mother in France when she was living with my father, and that he had gone with her to meet her for the first time. "He was great to me," she said. "I couldn't have done that without his help." *Lucky you,* I wanted to say. But I couldn't hate Stephanie any longer; she was one of the few who had contacted me after my father's death. She'd telephoned me from Europe the day after he had died, and we'd talked for nearly an hour, remembering how difficult he could be, how aggravating, and how much fun. And now, all these years later, I understand that my father might have helped me search for my biological grandmother if I had let him.

Many of my friends hadn't known what to say after he died and instead remained silent. One had asked, "Now, which father was he?" as if his death didn't warrant grief since he had been only my stepfather, one of two fathers. *You have another one left,* she seemed to say, when what I wanted was for someone to say, *I'm sorry your Daddy died.* I wanted someone to appreciate my loss, but I imagine now that they simply didn't know what his death meant to me. And, of course, I wasn't entirely sure myself.

A large floor fan hummed in a corner of the auditorium, and people fanned the clammy air with programs. As Mom, Mike, and I settled onto wooden seats with their desktop armrests folded away, a college student snaked wires from a microphone to a recording unit next to the stage. Someone else arranged music stands near a grand piano. The memorial, a concert of alternating speakers—family and friends—and performances of my father's music, would be recorded and copied onto cassette tapes for those of us who wanted them.

He would have loved this, his pieces being performed in tribute to him, all of us speaking about him, and it occurred to me he must have planned it, spelled it out in his will. But then I remembered that I had seen that document, and while he'd given precise directions about his cremation and the interment of his ashes—down to the "white, covered, ceramic urn," the artist he'd commissioned to paint it, and the precise metric measurements of the ceramic wall tile to be affixed near his ashes, which would be sealed in a wall of his own house's catacombs—he hadn't given any orders about his memorial service. It had been organized by his brother and sister, who had known best what he would have liked.

I saved my copy of his will so I could always remember the way he managed details until the end and even beyond. *The wall tile,* he wrote about his crypt, *shall be made by Maria Antonetta Tattichi, and should portray the north elevation of my house as seen from the bottom of Via del Paradiso, a bit of the house, a bit of Piazzale degli Apostoli, the sky, and underneath should be my name, dates, and the words: 'Amava la vita e la musica'.*

He loved life and music. Although he often tempted death, he did love life, and rode it with the power of a king. Music was the only true constant in his life and, I suspected, the only true love. No matter where he was, or with whom, the man was his music. The rest of us simply fell in line behind her.

When my uncle had traveled to Italy the month before, he'd asked me if there was anything of my father's I wanted him to send me. I'd already received the G. H. Rothe print of a ballerina, which Dad had left me, but there was one more thing I wanted.

"I'd like one of his batons," I said to my uncle. "There should be several on his desk." I remembered the orange juice can covered with macaroni and glitter that I'd made for him, in which he'd kept his collection of batons, pencils, and even a cigar or two. I remembered the feel of the cork-covered handle and the slick wood of the baton, which as a child in his studio I had waved, pretending to conduct an orchestra. When I received one in the mail, I lifted a wood-handled baton I'd never seen before and ran the length of it beneath my nose, inhaling. I'd hoped to be able to smell him, remnants of the cigarettes and cologne that made up his scent, but it was gone. Nor could I feel anything of him when I held up the baton. *He* was gone.

During the service, my Aunt Joan spoke of growing up as Tom's younger sister. She told of the time he convinced her to stand on a ledge at the Empire State Building while he held her legs so she could peer down the side of the building. "He was phenomenal. He was hard to handle. It all came with the package." She paused, grief silencing her.

A former student spoke of my father, his conducting mentor. "A couple of months ago, I sent Tom a CD of our opening concert—the Beethoven Ninth," he said. "A few weeks later he sent me an e-mail, which I was a little nervous to open, knowing how critical and brutally honest he could be. But he raved about the performance and the quality of the orchestra and said, 'Whatever they're paying you there, it's not enough!' Of all the reviews and feedback I've received about this project, none meant more to me than Tom's praise."

I could hardly hear the end of the story because I was still stuck on the words about my father's criticism and brutal honesty. Relief made me want to laugh; it hadn't been only me he had criticized, nor only me who knew how painful his words could be. I relished this confirmation. But along with relief came envy; I wished he could have recognized an accomplishment of mine the way he'd done with his student.

Other friends and family members climbed the stage to share stories. Some had known him as a young man and some only more recently. Many of us could claim him only for a period of his life, and together our stories made up the puzzle that was my father.

I was surprised to learn that one of his works had been nominated for a Pulitzer Prize, that as a young man he'd won a fellowship to Yaddo, and that he'd had pieces commissioned by the National Endowment for the Arts. His failure to mention these honors when he was alive, if it was due to modesty, seems out of character for him.

I would have expected him to drop those tidbits into conversations with the dinner guests we entertained. It is this dichotomy that made him who he was, his possession of humility and arrogance, the conjoined-twin features that I could finally start to reconcile.

When my uncle introduced me, I climbed the steps, afraid of tripping over the wires from the recording equipment. I loved the image, though, of us non-performers appearing on a stage like those on which he spent so much of his life. But far from wanting to laugh, as I stood behind the podium and unfolded my brief note, I hoped I could get through it without breaking down.

"For years we called him Ditti." Laughter rippled through the crowd, encouraging me. "But before that, back when I was six or seven, and he started hanging around our house in Florida, he was The Man with the Beard. When he adopted us, Mike and I started calling him 'Dad' and then, for a while, 'Ditti.' A few years ago, I called him on the phone from Rome on my way to Perugia. I wanted to impress him with my Italian, so at the end of our conversation I said, 'Ciao, PA-pa.' I knew he was smiling when he said, 'That's pope. I'm your pa-PA.'"

The audience laughed. I was glad I'd kept it short, and I was relieved to have it over.

I never renounced my last name—Briccetti—as I'd once believed I would. True, I'm Cyrus Manfred's firstborn child, but my father is Tom Briccetti. Despite his leaving, our estrangement, and his death, he will always be my father. Our name is just too much a part of my life, my identity, for me to divorce myself from it. But he'll never know about my difficulty almost letting go of it, my tendency to use it more often than the recent hyphenated tag-on. He'll never know how I have held on to this connection to him.

A year after his death, I had a dream about him. In it, he and Mom and I are listening to Mike play the piano in the living room of our house in Indianapolis. Sitting next to me on the loveseat,

Dad pets my head, smoothing my hair like I do with my children now. Then he leans over and kisses my cheek. It is so real; I'm with him again, living this tender moment. But then he disappears, and I'm alone in an archives library where I have found a photo of the four of us standing side by side, posing. I run my finger over the image of me, towheaded, missing my top teeth, wearing a pink cotton sundress, holding his hand. In the photo, though, I'm younger than I was when I'd first met him. This doesn't seem odd until, finally, I begin to stir out of the depths of dream and understand the temporal mistake. As I awaken, it becomes clear, and I realize that in my dream I'd merged Dad with Cyrus, folded two fathers into one. *Clever girl.*

THIRTY-TWO

Surrender

On Christmas morning, 2000, as my two shrieking boys were turning their stockings upside down, the phone rang. I assumed it must be the wrong number. Our relatives called later, when they knew we'd be finished opening presents. Pam brought the phone to my spot on the couch.

I didn't recognize the male voice, he was singing something I couldn't decipher, but his accent made me think of the relatives in Missouri. I could barely remember all their names, much less identify one of them from a voice over the phone.

"Who's this?" I said in my office receptionist voice. I didn't want to offend him in case he was indeed related or had a prize to give me.

He sang a bit more, and then laughed. "This is your Uncle Dale, Kathy. I'm just tryin' to sing you this song I made up."

I couldn't hear him over the shouts of the boys so I retreated into the kitchen, the door swinging behind me. We wished each other Merry Christmas, and then Dale turned serious.

"I just wanted to thank you again, Kathy, for finding us and getting us together with Cyrus." He told me he'd visited Cyrus in Kentucky the previous summer. "I'm just so happy to have met my long-lost brother."

Dale passed the phone to his wife, Barbara. "Kathy, we are so grateful to you. I have to tell you something. Dale used to walk around the house saying things like, 'I wonder where my brother is. I wonder if he lives around here, if I've seen him and not even known it. I'll probably die without meeting him.' Kathy, the brothers are just thrilled to have been brought together."

I allowed myself to smile as I stood alone in the kitchen, festive noises from the living room drifting in. This was why I'd searched, to forge connections, both in person and by proxy. Originally I'd thought I'd feel more complete by connecting myself to the people in my past, but this, too, joining others together, gave me a sense of completion.

"We saw the photos of your boys Cyrus showed us last summer; they are just beautiful, they truly are. Now you all will have to come and see us. And bring those boys so they can run wild."

Dale returned to the phone. "Be sure to wish Pam a Merry Christmas for us."

"I sure will," I said, hanging up the phone.

My search was over. Speaking with and meeting those new relatives on both sides satisfied my urge for knowledge and connection. I'd been on a dual quest: to find strangers and to have them accept me. The Lynns, and all the others before them, had more than satisfied that need.

I never returned to an ALMA meeting for the badge-pinning ceremony. And I never hung a photograph of my Grandmother Mavis on our wall. I don't look like her, I have come to realize; I look like my parents and my children.

I could have continued with more detective work. I could have tried to track down people who knew Mavis Foster in San Francisco, could have sequestered myself in the library's historical collection searching for stories about shipbuilders, and could have visited the Rosie the Riveter monument a few miles from my house. But instead I would place the folders, binders, scribbled notes, e-mails, and letters on the shelf. I'd send holiday cards to my new family, even though they were still strangers. I'd call Aunt Esther on her last few birthdays, and that would be enough.

My two fathers didn't cross paths until almost thirty years after my adoption. In 1990, when I was living with Pam in California, Dad guest conducted the Lexington Symphony in Kentucky, and Cyrus drove the short distance to meet him for the first time. During a break between rehearsals, Cyrus made his way backstage to Tom's dressing room. When Cyrus told me this story a couple of months later, I could clearly see the two men, such opposites in physique and personality, shaking hands. I could see Tom grasping Cyrus's hand with both of his, like he did when shaking the hand of a soloist after a concert, the maestro congratulating the musician while the audience applauded and shouted its bravos.

"He's a decent man," Cyrus said to me, "and a fine conductor. I was tickled to meet him, and I believe he enjoyed meeting me."

How I would have loved to witness that moment, those two men clasping hands, greeting each other for the first time. It reminds me of what Cyrus lost, what he surrendered. I used to see his giving us up as a passive act, and in some ways it was; it's possible that he gave us up because he'd been given up, and powerlessness was part of his personality. But relinquishing us was also a selfless act. He thought he was doing the right thing for his children.

Cyrus told me their meeting had been brief. As he was preparing to leave, Cyrus turned to Tom, and the two men looked directly at each other.

"Thank you, sir," Cyrus said, "for raising the children."

"Thank you," my father said, "for letting me."

THIRTY-THREE

Home

Both my sons still called me Mommy. I'd thought by ten and eight they would have switched to calling both of us Mom, but it had become the way they distinguished us. To their friends, though, they had begun calling us by our first names. "I'll ask Pam," they'd say when invited for a play date, or "Kathy said I have to do my homework first." Occasionally they'd say, "I have to ask my moms." I loved that; it sounded so natural, so ordinary. I did still want to be called Mommy, the intimacy of the label bonding me to my sons, and I hoped they would not be teased at school for it, and that it would not end abruptly because they'd been shamed.

Being the mother of sons also means being called "Dude," "Homey Dawg," and "Home Sista.'" It means having to grab Ben in football tackles to get something resembling a hug. My tall boy has a stocky build, and until I found the Lynn family, I'd always assumed that the sperm donor had been responsible for that, but now when I look at a photo of Cyrus's birth father, Wilford, I can see the resemblance between him and his great-grandson. In that photo, of Wilford lounging on a chair with one leg crossed over the other, his knees are the size of saucers, his body a linebacker's. It appears that my boy may have inherited his size from both sides of his family tree.

Being the mother of sons also means having to translate grunts into English, and not getting too riled up over burps, farts, and scatological language. It means being teased mercilessly and taking it. Recently when I asked Ben, "How did you get so cute?" he fired back with perfect preteen attitude: "It must have been the sperm donor."

My sons rarely fear getting hurt; when they wrestled on the living room rug and on the neighbor's grassy yard, they grimaced with what looked like agony but was actually what I came to realize as simply a release of tension, a kind of primal ecstasy, totally foreign to me. I grimaced, too, as I watched them, imagining an emergency room visit. But they almost always emerged intact, scuffed and grass-stained with sweaty, red faces and blissful smiles.

They have had their feminist moments as well, moments that particularly pleased us, like the day Daniel ran into the house with a fat bristly caterpillar climbing up his forearm.

"Wow!" I said. "Where'd you find him, love?"

"Mommy," he said, as he guided the iridescent green and black creature from one hand to the other. "This caterpillar could be a girl, so you can't call it a him."

"Oh," I said, raising my hands in surrender. "My bad."

In an after-school woodworking class that year, Daniel built a bird feeder and a snowboard, and Pam helped him paint them at home. Ben took apart old stereo receivers with his Uncle Mike, from whom he learned words like "integrated circuits" and "capacitor." When I picked up Ben at the end of day camp, he was driving the electric go-cart he and his group had built and tinkered with during the week. His hands were greasy, and a smudge remained where he had swiped at an itch under his nose. "Mommy, guess what!" he shouted as he putted past me in the parking lot. "Our car caught on fire today!" He was ecstatic. "The first time in the history of the camp!"

If my children had a father, I might not be as quick to notice, and to point out, that they are turning into boys with gender-typical interests. I might not feel the need to reassure myself, and others, about how "normal" they are. I might not seem more inclined than most to prove that we're raising healthy young men and, more importantly, that we haven't damaged them.

"Mommy, some people don't know what the sperm bank is." Daniel, eight, frequently blurted non sequiturs from his seat in the back of the van when it was just the two of us. At the time, the boys rarely talked about our family being different, and for years they hadn't asked about the sperm donor. But it was the short car trips across town, like that day's drive up the hill to summer sports camp, that provided a safe venue for Daniel.

"Yeah, like who?" I asked, trying to find him in the rearview mirror. I couldn't see his face; it was hidden behind the headrest of the middle seat. "Who doesn't know about the sperm bank?"

"My new friend at camp. Ryan."

"Were you talking about the sperm bank with Ryan at camp?"

"No."

"Then how did it come up?"

"I told Ryan I have two moms, and he asked how you made a baby."

I was proud of my youngest, the tag-along in our family, who, since he was an infant, had watched and listened. Even though he'd been privy to many of the conversations we'd had with his big brother, and of course we'd talked directly with him, too, I didn't know how much he understood about how we had made him. But in the car that day, he sounded mature, sure of himself, and far from traumatized.

I remembered an earlier conversation at the dinner table a year before, when Daniel did not have such a good handle on the gay thing.

"Have you seen the movie *Gay People Say No*?" Daniel asked that night. At seven, he often told us long, detailed stories that made no sense because he left out key words and ideas.

"What?" I asked, spearing a green bean with my fork.

He repeated it, and Ben snickered with the pleasure that comes with the anticipation of pulling something over on one's parents. Something was up.

Then I got it. I set my fork down. I remembered similar tricks on the playground when I was in elementary school, but we said "retarded" and "queer" to insult each other. Our sons were bringing home the new version, "You're so gay." Every time I heard it at the school where I worked, it stung a little.

"No, Daniel, I haven't seen that movie."

He laughed in triumph. "That means you're gay!"

Quickly, I held my palm up toward Ben.

I smiled and shook my head at my younger son.

"Honey, what does gay mean?" I asked.

"It means you're retarded," he said.

I wasn't sure he was clear what retarded meant, we'd have to tackle that next, but I wanted to see this through.

"And these are bad things?"

"Yeah."

"Daniel, gay doesn't mean you're retarded. You know that. What does it mean?"

He smiled. Something clicked, and he realized his mistake. "It means you love a woman."

Clearly he didn't have it all down yet, and the three of us gawked at him with raised eyebrows. "What about me and Mama?"

"Yeah," Ben said. "*They're* gay." He sounded smug.

"Oh, yeah," Daniel said.

I knew he was embarrassed to be caught not realizing something so obvious.

But on the way to camp that day, I was proud of him when he told me about Ryan's question.

"Some people don't even know what gay means," he said, and I slowed the van. We were getting close, and I wanted to be able to finish the conversation, hear what else he had to say.

"Most adults know what gay means," I said. "But, you're right, not all kids do."

"Josh thinks if you touch someone's butt you're gay."

"No, if you touch someone's butt you can get in trouble because you're not supposed to touch people's private parts. But it doesn't mean you're gay."

"He doesn't know that gay just means a man loves a man or a woman loves a woman," Daniel said.

"Some people don't understand; that's all it is." I glanced into the mirror again but still couldn't see his face. "They don't know that being gay is not bad. Probably because they don't know any gay people." I paused. "Some churches tell people it's wrong to be gay. And, this is really sad, some parents teach their kids that gay people are sick."

"That's stupid."

"You might have to tell the kids what gay means, so they'll know."

"Yeah," he whispered.

"Did Ryan know what the sperm bank was?"

"No, he's a bum."

"Bum" was the new word for someone who didn't know something.

I pulled up to the drop-off spot. "A bum, huh?"

"Maybe," Daniel said, leaning over for a kiss before he climbed out of the van. "Maybe he knew, and he just forgot."

One evening later that summer, Daniel squeezed between Pam and me on the couch. She and I had been talking about her father, who had been ill. Daniel interrupted. "Who's *your* father again?" he asked me. I reminded him that Grandpa Tom, my stepfather, had raised me and that Grandpa Cyrus, my biological father, lived in Kentucky with Grandma Ursula.

"I want to meet my biological father someday."

Pam and I stared at him. "Okay," I said, hiding my surprise at his straightforwardness. "You might be able to. We can get his name and address from the sperm bank when you're eighteen."

"Cool." Daniel sounded matter-of-fact; it seemed this topic was not as loaded for him as it was for me. He could not yet understand the ramifications that preoccupied me. How would the donor—my sons' father—compare to their fantasies about him? Would they be glad we found him or wish we'd never looked?

"Why do you want to meet him, Daniel?" Pam asked.

"I just want to see what he looks like." He twirled a clump of his hair around a finger.

"Me too," I said.

"I do too," Pam said.

Daniel looked at each of us in turn. "You do?"

I knew his curiosity stemmed from a different source than ours, but I had to step away and look back on this conversation before I could remember that it was more than just simple curiosity for him. This was his father he was talking about. The other half of him. I knew about that absence, and I knew about that longing to know.

But how can you miss something you never lost? In comparing my experiences with that of my sons, I see similarities but significant differences, too. What we have in common is that as children we are powerless and blameless. Adults make the decisions, and these decisions are shaped by cultural expectations of the time. There is a long history of children remaining with their mothers instead of their fathers when parents divorced. Although joint custody is much more common now, the mother-child bias remains deep in our cultural psyche.

My children were never relinquished for adoption, never formed and broke a bond with a parent, so I tell myself they will be saved the lifelong pain of abandonment that many adoptees and orphaned children suffer. I might be fooling myself when I say that my children cannot grieve something they never lost, that it could be a different kind of pain they feel, but I still see the difference between having a father and losing him and never having him to begin with. My children might grieve an *idea* but not a person. Like children whose fathers die before they are born, my sons were denied having a father in their lives, but they have not lost someone. And here is where I must take responsibility. I decided to make them in the way that I did, and I decided to raise them without a man, without the man whose genes they share. My hope is that we two mothers can give them what they need and can help them if they feel that something missing must be filled.

"Maybe he's rich," Daniel said that night on the couch, squeezed between Pam and me, "and he has a mansion, and he'll give me a motorbike and a bunch of money."

As a mother, I could have believed that his response signaled deep unhappiness with us, that we were not giving him enough of what he needed, that he was lacking some deep connection, but as a psychologist, I knew his response was typical for his age. Kids, even those living with both of their birth parents, often make up adoption fantasies, and many dream of being rich. When disenchanted with their parents, they daydream about who their *real* parents might be. There must be an explanation, they think, for these horrible people doing them wrong. Babies Switched at Birth. A Secret Adoption.

Those times that Daniel stormed up the stairs after being sent to his room for misbehaving and he shouted, "You're *terrible* parents; you need to read more parenting books!" I wondered if he then did what I used to do. I wondered if he flopped on his bed and conjured up scenarios of meeting his true parents, the ones who would give him whatever he wanted, deny him nothing. As a child, I played with the idea of finding my *real* father, the wealthy king of some obscure island, who would grant me all of my wishes. Maybe my boys longed to find *their* father, a basketball pro or computer genius, so they could live with him—a *cool* guy—because their mothers were *so mean.*

"Or he could be poor," I said on the couch. "Maybe he's hoping you're rich, and you can buy him a car."

"Yeah." Pam joined in. "Maybe he's a bum."

The three of us laughed, and Daniel headed outside. "Naw," he said, looking over his shoulder before he disappeared out the door. "Your mother's a bum."

I often imagine the four of us meeting the sperm donor. I want to see in his face the suggestion of my children's origins: Ben's arched eyebrows, Daniel's impish smile. And more than superficial qualities, I want to recognize idiosyncrasies of personality that he's passed on to the boys: Ben's demand for the predictable, the tug of Daniel's deep emotions.

I wonder what the donor would think of our little family. Donating sperm in the San Francisco Bay Area in the early 1990s, he must have guessed that some of his offspring would likely be raised by lesbians. If we ever meet him, I would want him to like us, and, as ridiculous as it sounds, I would want his approval. I could imagine showing off the kids to him. Look, I'd say. See what a good job I did? I'd want him to smile and nod. *Thank you for raising the children.*

THIRTY-FOUR

Blood Strangers

In the summer of 2005, I took Daniel to Kentucky to visit our family there. Cyrus met our plane at the Lexington airport, and once we were buckled into his Corolla, the three of us set off on the drive to the house in Burlsville. I'd forgotten the beauty of the Kentucky landscape: the lambent green horse farms and creosote-soaked fences meandering for miles—containing, dividing, and protecting. Triptychs of ebony barns, blood red roofs, and white farmhouses punctuated the landscape on both sides of the highway.

"It's all the limestone under the grass that makes it so green and good for the horses," Cyrus said, as if he'd read my mind. The interstate cut through limestone hills, dynamite bore marks still visible: rows of vertical lines, straight as fence posts, sketched into the blasted rock. We crossed the Kentucky River on a massive concrete bridge towering two hundred feet over the water. We passed the park where thirty years earlier I had played in the sand with my new siblings.

Ten-year-old Daniel called Cyrus "Grandpa," but I was still unsure how to address my biological father. A few years earlier, he had signed a letter, "Love, Dad," and I had bristled. It's too late, I thought. You can't have that name back now. You're not my Dad anymore. I wrote back to him, *Dear Cyrus*. Eventually, he signed his letters "Dad/Cyrus," which seemed to match our uncertainty. He'd been "Cyrus" to me longer than he'd been "Dad," and I would have felt unfaithful to my stepfather, even after his death, if I'd called Cyrus "Dad."

Please call me Dad, he wrote in a letter more recently, *unless you use Dad with Tom, therefore Dad-Cyrus is fine 'cause I certainly understand. Tom has been your dad for a long time—so whatever—I love you and Mike even if you call me Ralph, Phil, Bob, or Joe.* This had made me smile.

I studied his profile as he ferried us back to his home, hands whispering above the steering wheel, head quivering with tremors of age. I was still self-conscious around him. I knew we'd never form a true father-daughter bond; instead I'd have to accept our unusual relationship. I was trying to convince myself not to worry about what to call it but to simply enjoy our time together.

Sarah and Melissa and Cody and all their children joined us for a barbeque on our second day. Mike had flown from California, too, and for the first time in thirty years, all five of Cyrus's children were reunited.

"Quick, get a camera," someone said before dinner. "Who knows when we'll all be together again." We took many photos during our visit; my favorite is the one in which the five of us posed with our father. This time we settled the men into the couch while we women stood behind them. I keep the three photos of the six of us in a single frame on our wall of family photos next to the computer. Like pilings supporting a bridge, they mark the span I have known this family. In the first photo, when we six formed a tottering human pyramid, I am seventeen; in the next, after Sarah's wedding, I am twenty-nine; and in the one we took during that last visit, forty-seven. For thirty years I have been getting to know this family. And, as we posed that evening before dinner, I felt the familiar tug of regret that we didn't live closer to each other, that we didn't know each other better, that we'd lost all that time.

One afternoon during our visit, I sat alone on the porch swing, gently rocking with a bare foot on the smooth cement floor. It was the same kind of swing I used to ride sideways like a bronco during my summer visits when I was a child. Now, because I had no memories before age four or five, I had begun to ask Cyrus questions in letters, feeling bolder from the distance writing allows. My earliest memories begin after our separation: learning to tie my shoes on the steps of the apartment in Fanwood, New Jersey; the mail carrier delivering the snow cone maker I won in a coloring contest; and Cyrus's crazy old duck, Honk. But even these memories were devoid of images of him. It's as if losing him had made his face blur, like a coin sinking into a muddy river bottom, just out of reach.

Ursula joined me on the porch, placing two glasses of lemonade on the black wrought-iron table. She looked the same as she did when I stepped off the Greyhound bus on that scorching afternoon in 1974, except that her kinky charcoal hair had turned a smoky gray, and the skin around her eyes and jaw had loosened.

I took a glass of lemonade and rested it on the arm of the swing. "Ursula, what has my searching for Mavis been like for Cyrus?" It was easier to ask her than to ask him directly. Cyrus often put her on the phone when he and I hit a lull or we couldn't think of anything more to say; this usually happened after only a couple of minutes. Ursula and I could chat for much longer.

"You know, Kathy, Cyrus has just lost, lost, lost in his life," Ursula said. "The people he's loved. First his birth mother and that family, then his adoptive father, then your mom and you two kids."

I thought about how baby Cyrus, or Jimmie Earl, had spent his first five months with his birth mother, then the next seven with a large extended family, including his two half-brothers, one a toddler, the other an infant. How he was taken from them to become the only child of an only child, his only family his new mother, grandparents, and a father who left when Cyrus was four years old.

"Do you think that's why he didn't want to search for his birth mother?" I asked Ursula.

"Could be," she said. "Maybe he couldn't face another rejection." She took a sip of her lemonade. "Also, Grandma Manfred was terribly possessive of him, her only child. When he was growing up, she was a stage mother," she said. "Taking him to recitals and concerts but very jealous of other people taking Cyrus's attention. She wanted him to herself. She didn't even go to his wedding to your mom because she was too upset about losing him."

I knew that Grandma Manfred had changed her son's name from Jimmie Earl to Cyrus, her maiden name. This seemed like an attempt to label him as her own, something she felt she needed to do since she hadn't given birth to him but was adopting him. It was her way of branding the year-old child as her own.

"When she was about seventy," Ursula said, "she told Cyrus her doctor said she was going to die any time because of a weak heart and that she wanted to move to Burlsville to be near him."

I remembered visiting my Grandmother Manfred in the senior center, next door to Cyrus and Ursula's house. She couldn't have gotten much closer unless she had commandeered a bedroom in their home. "We learned later that the doctor had said no such thing, that she had lied just to come here, had even faked angina attacks to get Cyrus's attention." Ursula and I laughed out loud, knowing that her mother-in-law had gone on to live thirty more years, past one hundred, receiving frequent visits from her son.

"She made him feel guilty," Ursula said, "saying over and over things like, 'I gave you so much.'"

No wonder Cyrus had been beholden to her, paralyzed, really, by her power over him, and it explained why he couldn't betray her by searching for his birth mother.

"It's possible," Ursula said, "that her husband left her and Cyrus because she was so overbearing. She had to have things her own way, and he may not even have approved of adopting a baby."

Daniel came racing out the front door, letting it slam behind him.

He climbed up in the porch swing with me and started rocking it.

"I see," I said to Ursula. And, finally, I did.

Cyrus joined Ursula and me, settling on the swing. Daniel climbed down and ran into the yard after the neighbor's cat. Cyrus and I tried to coordinate our long legs, pushing in unison, but we were out of sync. Instead we jostled it sideways in a jerky dance.

"Whatever happened to your adoptive father, William Manfred?" I asked, thinking of the grandfather I never met, who left his family when Cyrus was four.

"I saw him once in St. Louis when I was about sixteen and he came to one of my recitals. He wrote me beaucoup letters over the years. He was drafted into the Army in World War II, but because of his age he didn't get sent overseas."

"When did he die?"

"The last we knew of him, he lived in Rogue, Missouri, selling cars. He died in 1950 or '51 of cancer, I think. I was at Oklahoma University, and I was about twenty years old, so he would have been around fifty-three or so."

"Did you go to the funeral?"

"I thought about taking my '38 Ford down there, but Mom talked me out of it. I wouldn't have known anyone anyway."

I felt a flicker of anger toward his mother for dissuading him from saying good-bye to the father he had known only briefly.

For a long time I'd wanted to ask him something, and I understood I needed to do it then. "Why didn't you want to search for your birth mother?" I lowered my gaze, afraid I'd gone too far.

"Because I had three fine parents," he said with a trace of defensiveness in his voice. "My mother Hazel and her parents raised me and they did a fine job."

Ursula jumped in. "What y'all don't understand," her voice held a trace of vexation, "is that they don't need any more family." It seemed she was speaking for all adoptees. "Their adoptive parents are their real parents. There isn't any more room for these new people."

"I *do* understand that," I said. Angry hurt heated my temples. "Everyone has their own perspective, I guess, and the birth mother—some birth mothers, at least—want to know why their child doesn't want contact with them."

"Oh, sure," she said. Her voice softened. Possibly she could see in the set of my mouth how her words had stung. "You're right. Everyone's different."

I did not tell her that if I had felt there was no room in my life for more people, I wouldn't have ridden the bus to visit Cyrus when I was sixteen, and I wouldn't have searched for the Fosters and Lynns. Cyrus would have lived his life without knowing why he'd been adopted, who his people were. I couldn't imagine such restraint.

That night, when Daniel and Mike were jumping on the trampoline in the backyard, I settled on the couch and looked around the living room. The artwork on the walls had changed, and the furry bear on wheels had been banished to the basement to save its patchy, over-loved hide.

Cyrus joined me, pulling a photo album off the shelf. He sat next to me on the couch and slowly opened the book across our laps. At seventy-five, his hair—silvery now—had continued to recede on both sides, leaving a combed-back peak down the middle. His head trembled, but his grasp on the photo album was steady.

The album, its edges frayed and its pages slipping free from the binding, held baby pictures of Michael and me. Documenting the junctures of our lives, the album was skimpier than those containing photos of his youngest three children, the children he had raised. I turned the pages. In one photograph of me at about eighteen months, I'm smiling at the camera, standing inside his upright cello case, its lid swung open like a door, about to step out of my makeshift playhouse. But I didn't recognize the little girl with the blonde bangs cut too short over her forehead; she was someone I didn't know. I had never seen this photo, had not grown up with it, could not claim it. It captured a child before her life took a different direction.

In another photo, I'm sitting on my father's lap while he plays the cello, and this one stirs something in me. The image, little girl and her daddy smiling at each other, is so tender it evoked an aftertaste of loss.

Then, as if that wasn't enough to meddle with my carefully warehoused wistfulness, Cyrus turned to a creased photo of a sleeping baby, tummy down, swaddled except for head and one clenched fist. In the photo, he sleeps beside me on the couch, his hair black and full, face unlined, splayed fingers shielding my supple scapula, embracing his firstborn one-handed. His thumb and my wrist are the same circumference. I was his first baby, and I finally understood, looking at the photo, that this man was never going to abandon me. I knew he had loved me and that our leaving must have almost destroyed him. I forced the tears back, and my throat, weary of damming sorrow, turned raw.

"Could I borrow these to copy?" I finally managed.

"Sure," he said, springing up. "I'll put them in an envelope for you."

Looking at Cyrus's photos of me as a young child had disturbed the place where I had neatly tucked memories away, protected myself with a cushion of forgetting. They made it real that I had had a father and lost him for a time. I wanted to leave Cyrus's living room then, go out the front door and walk in the night air, forgetting it all. At the same time, I wanted to stay on the couch remembering it all.

During our visit, Daniel stayed up late each night with his Uncle Mike and Grandpa Cyrus. I had thought that he would feel shy meeting all the new relatives—grandfather and grandmother, aunts, uncle, and cousins, but he met them all with such effortlessness. Before I'd unpacked, he had warmed up to his grandparents and they to him. Ursula made him pancakes every morning no matter what time he woke up, and cooked his favorite foods every evening. A legendary California Cousin, Daniel wooed his five Kentucky cousins, all younger than he except for one quiet teenager. Daniel bounced on the trampoline and then rocked on the porch swing with them, his arm laid protectively across the chest of Melissa's four-year-old son.

I did not feel this ease. I had told myself for so long that I didn't know these people, they were strangers, and I still reminded myself of this instead of just getting to know them. It was an outdated protective device I couldn't shut off. I needed to remind myself to breathe, to unclench my jaw.

I was a child again in my father's house; I was forty-seven, but my emotions were tangled between the past and the present. I was envious that Daniel was such a hit when I felt uptight, nervous, old. When my father embraced me, my toes curled inside their shoes. My son drew a bow across his grandfather's cello, at perfect ease with his family, while I stood back, snapped another photo.

On the last day of our visit, my half-brother, Cody, invited us to go canoeing on a tributary of the Kentucky River. I declined, preferring to read on the front porch. Plus, I thought, it might be fun for Daniel to spend a morning with his two uncles.

I had hiked with Cody the previous day, and when we paused on a boulder to take in the view of a picture-postcard valley, he'd asked me what it was like for my boys not having a father. Cody, a handsome thirty-seven-year-old father of two children with two different women, neither of whom he had married, had a strong Kentucky accent. But he was no Southern country bumpkin; he had been raised by liberal parents, was well-read, and his political views sounded more like a San Franciscan's than a rural Kentuckian's. On our hike we lamented the state of the country under Bush Jr., the absurdity of the gay marriage debate, and the shame of the Iraq war.

Cody had not been around much when his son, the shy teenager, was young, and he regretted it. "Kathy," he said in his appealing drawl, "I was just so young. Now I know better. I know he needs his Dad."

"My boys don't seem to miss having a father," I said, feeling only a touch of defensiveness. "They've told us that their friends think they're lucky to have two moms, that dads are meaner than moms." My tone felt too strident, so I tried to soften it. "I know it might change when they get older," I said, "when they're teenagers and want to know where they came from."

Cody and I climbed down off the boulder and resumed our walk. I didn't tell him about Daniel's fascination with the two generations of *Star Wars* trilogies. For months Daniel had been repeating one of Darth Vader's lines at arbitrary moments, apropos of nothing. "LUKE," he would mimic in James Earl Jones's deep, rasping voice, drawing out each word. "I AM YOUR FATHER." I had kept to myself my fears that Daniel's obsession with this particular line might have indicated a kind of deep, father-loss grief. It's only a movie, I convinced myself, a movie millions of boys love. And my boy just happens to be fixated on the revelatory moment in a blockbuster movie, when the orphaned boy/hero discovers the identity of his father, a good man who had turned to the dark side and left his son behind. I didn't mention this to Cody. But, in truth, it did worry me, and it reminded me to prepare a little more for the possibility that Daniel would someday want to unmask his own father, would want to find the donor so that he might see his face.

While it seemed that Cody believed me, he seemed eager, almost desperate, to take Daniel out for some guy time. I imagined him thinking *We'll make a man out of him.* Although I didn't share his desperation, I agreed to the plan for Mike, Cody, and Daniel to go canoeing.

"Do you have sunscreen?" I shouted from my spot on the porch as Cody started the engine. "He doesn't have a hat."

"Naw," Cody said, shaking his head. "We'll be in the shade most of the time."

Yeah, right, I thought.

A few hours later, they returned, spent and smiling. "How was it, love?" I asked Daniel, pulling him into a hug that he shrugged off.

"Great," he said. "I got to drive!" His face was dirty, sunburned, radiant.

"What?" I said, my voice a squeak. I shot a glance at Cody, who was retreating to his truck, grinning sheepishly.

"Yeah, Uncle Cody scooted over, and I got to drive. All by myself!"

Daniel had driven a truck out in the country. He had held a snake that Cody had plucked from the dirt road. And he had paddled a canoe in the middle of a river in the sun between his two uncles.

Back at the Lexington airport before our flight home, Cyrus unloaded our suitcases from the trunk and placed them at the curb. I busied myself with making sure that Daniel hadn't left his backpack in the car, that I had the boarding passes in hand. "Say good-bye to Grandpa," I said. "And say thank you for everything."

Daniel hugged Cyrus around his waist, and Cyrus bent down to squeeze him around his shoulders. "Good-bye, fine grandson," he said. "We enjoyed your stay. Come back soon."

Cyrus straightened again and found my gaze. I embraced him, feeling the brush of his jaw as he kissed my cheek.

"Bye-bye, honey," he said. "We all love you all very much."

I hugged him quickly. "Love you all, too. Thanks for everything," I said. "I'll bring Ben next time. So you can get to know him, too." It was easier to place the children between us; they were the buffer so I didn't have to be alone with my father. And alone with my confused feelings.

"That would be so fine," he said.

I handed Daniel his backpack, grabbed the handle of my suitcase, and began rolling it behind me as we walked toward the airport door. When I stopped and looked back at Cyrus, he was standing next to his car watching us. He and I waved at the same time. Then I lowered my gaze and turned away. I reached over and draped my arm across Daniel's shoulder as we made our way into the airport and headed home.

THIRTY-FIVE

A Happy Childhood

"Mommy, wait," Daniel called as we climbed the hill to our house after school one afternoon that fall. As usual, he lagged a few paces behind. "I want to show you something." When I turned around he leaned over slightly, placed his thumb under one nostril to close it off while he blew air out the other. A tiny glob of mucus spiraled from his nose to the ground.

"What are you doing?" I shouted. "That's gross, Daniel!"

"Uncle Cody taught me," he said, beaming.

"Don't do that here, on the sidewalk," I said, praying none of the neighbors had witnessed this, my parenting lapse. "Honey, use a tissue."

It was apparent that Cody had given Daniel one more gift from that uncle-bonding and boy-toughening trip in the truck and canoe in Kentucky. It seemed he had taught my son how to blow his nose like a rancher. Although embarrassed by witnessing this rural skill put into practice in the city, I had to admit that, in part, I was pleased. It was definitely not something I would have taught him.

In December, Pam, the boys, and I walked up Solano Avenue one evening to eat dinner at our new favorite Mexican restaurant, Cactus. We were all accustomed to Bay Area panhandlers and their mantra, "Spare any change tonight?" and we passed several on the sidewalk on our way to the restaurant. But that night we were presented with a twist. In front of the bookstore, a man sat under the awning on an overturned milk crate. Onto a large piece of cardboard he had taped a sprig of mistletoe tied at the top with a red bow. In his hands he held another linty green sprig.

"Mistletoe?" he called when he caught my eye. The four of us continued toward the restaurant, all of us staring ahead. "Take some home to your husband?"

"No husband in this family," I called back to him, amused at my impulsive response. Usually I simply shook my head or said "no thanks." I laughed, though, and the kids picked up on it and joined me. Pam smiled. But the man was quick, sharp. Berkeleyized.

"Lover?" he called to our backs. "Partner? Really good friend?"

He laughed as we pulled open the restaurant door and left him to his wares, a far cry from a different man who years ago had shouted "Fuckin' lezzies!" to Pam and me when we passed him on the sidewalk one night.

Using a senior discount airfare, Cyrus visited us the following February, during the week of the 2006 Winter Olympics, and stayed with Mike at his house. We made plans to see him on Sunday, when Mike would drop him off at our place. That day, Ben's soccer game was cancelled, and the rain slapped at the picture window. When Cyrus arrived, we drove up the hill to the children's museum, an activity in which, because of the weather, nearly every family in Berkeley with children under thirteen would be taking part. I drove deliberately, like when I first strapped my babies into car seats, aware of the fragile, precious cargo I was carrying. With Cyrus riding next to me, I came to a complete stop at stop signs and climbed the hill to the museum slowly. I was aware of the wet road, the guardrails, and where the rails were absent. I imagined the plunge we'd take if we slid off the road. I knew that I was driving for my father. That I wanted to show him I was a good driver, a good mother, a good girl.

His recent decline in hearing made it even more difficult to chat with him, and I remained quieter than normal. Earlier, I'd often filled the spaces with nervous chatter, but I didn't need to do that now, there was no point. Besides, I realized, I was becoming comfortable with the silence.

On the way to the museum, I glanced at his profile and for the first time realized that his lips were thinner than I had remembered, thinner than my mother's. They looked just like mine.

On the slippery steps down to the museum, we walked side by side, Cyrus grasping the railing, me staying close in case he needed a hand. When he slipped, I reached out instinctively, but he caught himself. The rest of the way I lightly grasped his elbow, like I'd done with my grandmother years ago. Inside the museum, he occasionally grazed my shoulder with his fingertips to make a point, reminding me of a hesitant suitor, someone who longs to be closer, longs to show his love, but is afraid of being rebuffed.

During this visit, I did not feel the need to impress him—except, it appeared, with my driving expertise. I remembered driving home after seeing him at Mike's, after our lunch at the Chinese restaurant years ago, and how my body had stung with grief. But this time, as I drove Cyrus back to Mike's after dinner at our house, I felt as if I were ferrying an old friend.

I was eager to drop him off, though, shrug off the weight of obligation. We had little to talk about, my father and I, and I didn't understand Mike's e-mails to friends that week, all proclaiming that his father Cyrus was in town and suggesting get-togethers with neighbors and friends. Mike had been twenty-one months old when we left Cyrus, and Cyrus had told me recently that little Michael didn't seem to remember him when we visited the first time after the move. Thinking of this now makes me pause. I'm sentimental,

I guess, picturing my chubby baby brother climbing into the car to drive away from our Daddy and then forgetting him.

My brother was a man who had finally found his father, who wanted to know him before he died, wanted to make up for lost time. And now that our stepfather was dead, perhaps it was his last attempt at having a father. I, on the other hand, the Reunion Queen who had for years kept the paths between our homes cleared, had become content with our distance, with our relationship the way it was. I accepted that the time we had lost would never be found. I was content with having a father who felt more like a friend.

I believed this until, at my doorway, I said good-bye to Cyrus. We embraced; he released his grasp before I did and, when he felt me lingering, pulled me close again. But that was not what tugged at my emotion. It was not what softened my resolve that I was okay without him. What began to poke holes in my shell happened after he said good-bye and lowered his glance.

"Oh goodness," he said, looking up and grinning, his face bright, his voice not sure. "Bye-bye, honey." It was the way he said the word "honey" that pulled me back into regret. His voice was so full of love, his eyes, too, that I could not mistake it. He sounded like the man I must have known all those years ago, the one who said good-bye as if I were heading to the park. As if he wanted to say, "Bye-bye, little girl. I'll see you later. I love you. I always will."

Driving in Berkeley recently, I spotted a bumper sticker with an aphorism that sang out to me: It's Never Too Late to Have a Happy Childhood. I loved it. We make our own realities. We can alter our histories, or at least how we interpret them. We don't have to wallow in self-pity over the past. It's the old glass-half-full philosophy my mother raised me to practice.

Ever since I thought my parents and brother had laughed at my lack of musical talent after I chanted that cheer in our Indianapolis kitchen, I hadn't sung in front of anyone. This ended when my children were born. It was only then, in a rocking chair that squeaked out the beats with each push backward, in a room lit only by a soft night-light, and with my arms wrapped around a baby in fuzzy pajamas, that I tested my voice. I invented melodies and words as I rocked *(You are my sweet, sweet love...)* and sang songs I remembered from summer camp *(Kumbayah, my Lord, kumbayah...)*. When I couldn't remember all the words, I hummed to fill in the blanks. Ben clapped his hands and smiled. Daniel nestled his head into my neck and fell asleep. No one laughed.

One day, I couldn't get a melody out of my head; it repeated in an endless loop. It was a classical piece I'd heard in a movie, maybe in a scene with soldiers on horseback riding in full armor. The music haunted me, and I wanted to buy the CD, but first I needed to identify it, so I called my mother and described it to her.

"The chorus really belts it out," I said. "The bass drum booms in a few places, and the music is so moving it gives me goose bumps."

"I'm sorry," she said, regret ringing in her voice. "I don't know what that could be."

I remembered my family sitting around the dinner table humming parts of orchestra music to each other. "I played the section that goes dee da-da-da dum," my brother would say, humming a few bars, and my parents would immediately recognize the pieces. I always sat in awe of their secret language.

On the phone with my mother, I said, "If you promise not to laugh, I'll try to hum a little of it for you. I'll probably botch it, but here goes." After a couple of false starts, my voice began to sound like the notes playing in my head. But I wondered what it sounded like to my mother on the other end of the line. I hummed it once more and waited.

"Oh yeah, that's Carl Orff. *Carmina Burana.* You carried that tune nicely."

It was what I needed. In my living room, I began to sing with my sons ("Yellow Submarine," "Down by the Station"), and I didn't stop even when my brother visited. I twirled my boys around as we drowned each other out, our voices sometimes rough and ragged, other times soft and dulcet. I got pajamas on a four-year-old by making up a song ("Jump, Jump, Jump into the Jammies"), and while we waited in traffic my children and I sang songs from preschool ("Puff the Magic Dragon," "The Ants Go Marching"), the pleasure of making music carrying us away and bringing us all back together. Here, in the middle of my life, I had found the rhythm of my family and my place within it.

I've turned out to be an incurable optimist, and I can credit my mother for that. It's because I've soaked up her interminable positive attitude—optimism by osmosis—that I'm so hopelessly hopeful. When I flew for the first time after September 11, I found a kindred spirit in the middle-aged pilot greeting us at the door with a full set of braces on his teeth. I almost laughed out loud at what I took to be his sanguinity. We were not going to die on this flight because he was going to enjoy a long life with straight teeth.

I also appreciate what bell hooks writes in her book *All About Love*: "We can find the love our hearts long for, but not until we let go grief about the love we lost long ago, when we were little and had no voice to speak the heart's longing." This is what I strive for. Although I've searched for it in my past, this elusive love and connection, I am beginning to understand that it is connecting to the present that is making me truly whole.

A month after Cyrus's visit, the four of us sat at the dinner table, Pam and I taking turns reminding the boys of manners and deflecting their bickering. They'd been posturing lately, rankling each other with "Yo Mama." Tonight, after an argument about who got more ice cream in his bowl, Daniel shot it across the table at Ben.

"Yo Mama."

"Yo Daddy," Ben said, not missing a beat.

"You don't have a Daddy."

"Not legally."

"But biologically."

Pam and I followed the ping-pong rally.

"Wow," she said, shaking her head. "They sure do understand the concept."

Recently I had bought Pam an anthology of essays titled *Confessions of the Other Mother: Nonbiological Lesbian Moms Tell All.* That night I overheard Daniel in his room getting ready for bed. "LUKE," he said, his voice gravelly and deep, like I'd heard hundreds of times. I prepared myself for the rest of the line, but this time he changed it. "LUUUKE," he said. "I AM YOUR OTHER MOTHER."

Acknowledgments

Writing this book, my first, has been like running my first marathon. And then running it again. And again. I am so grateful for the coaches, fellow runners, and all the supporters who have lined the route, shouting encouragement.

From the earliest stages, I have been fortunate to have found other writers to train with. My first writing group read my earliest attempts at telling this story. Michele French, Randy Kasten, Sandy Kasten, David Lauver, Mike Shaler, Roxanne Barber, and Sharon Tamm showed me how to get started. Then, my virtual critique group from the Internet Writing Workshop helped me practice.

Holly Rose, Karen Marker, Linda Kilby, Judy Wolff, Nancy Schimmel, Allison Murray, Zachary Mason, Eleanor Vincent, Wendy Coblenz, Richard Bush, Marie Estorage, Peggy Vincent, Meg Jackson-Reinhardt, Christina Eng, Melanie Gideon, Aleta George, and Maureen Duffy helped me discover what I was writing about.

Thanks, also, to the editors who published excerpts in the *San Francisco Chronicle; Brain, Child; hip mama; Offspring;* the *Chicago Tribune; Unbound Press;* flashquake.org; the *Dos Passos Review;* and in the anthologies *Herstory; The Maternal Is Political; Who's Your Mama?;* and *Motif: Writing by Ear.*

Several mentors along the way helped me hone my style and voice. Phillip Lopate at Recoursos; Lan Samantha Chang at the Napa Valley Writers' Conference; and Patricia Hampl at Breadloaf encouraged my nascent attempts at the art of memoir. Dorothy Wall, Janis Cooke Newman, Amanita Rosenbush, and Wendy Lichtman lent their wisdom. My former agent, Randi Murray, believed in this book and worked hard for it. At the Stonecoast MFA program, Michael C. White, Joan Connor, Suzanne Strempek Shea, and especially Barbara Hurd showed me how to go deeper.

The members of my monthly free-writing group, my six adopted sisters, nourished my soul and read pages out of love: Veronica Chater,

B. Lynn Goodwin, Annie Kassof, Suzanne LaFetra, Sybil Lockhart, and Rachel Sarah.

My incomparable critique group, A Good Read, coined the motto "With friends like these, who needs critics?" For their excellent reads and rereads, I thank Colleen Morton Busch, Suzanne LaFetra, and Holly Rose.

My buddies and workshop mates at the Stonecoast MFA program pushed me and cheered me on; Nan Steinley, Jacob Strunk, Pat Hager, Lisa Romeo, and Florence Grende read final drafts. My friend Barbara Weaver helped tidy up the galleys.

It's been such a pleasure working with my Heyday team: Malcolm Margolin, Wendy Rockett, Julian Segal, Susan Pi, Lillian Fleer, Lorraine Rath, Lisa K. Manwill, and my awesome editor Gayle Wattawa, who met me near the finish line and ran the rest of the way with me.

For my writing partner, Michele French, who saw the first scribbles through the last draft and has read almost every word I've written for publication, underlining the good stuff and asking questions nudging me toward better stuff, I am deeply appreciative.

My family, many of whom would prefer to not be written about, I thank for cheering for me despite their wishes to maintain privacy. And to my newly found family, I appreciate your welcoming us into the fold. I'm so glad I found you.

There should be extra compensation for those who live with writers. To my sons, who shared my time and attention with a third sibling, The Book, I offer my never-ending love (and a trip to Hawaii someday). Finally, and especially, to Pam, without whom this story might have been lived but never recorded, my heartfelt thanks. To all of my family members, blood and adopted, among you is where I belong.

About the Author

Kathy Briccetti's work has been featured in literary magazines and anthologies as well as on public radio. An excerpt from *Blood Strangers* was nominated for a Pushcart Prize in 2007, and Briccetti was awarded a residency at the Vermont Studio Center in 2009. She earned a Ph.D. in clinical psychology from the Wright Institute in Berkeley and an MFA in creative writing from the Stonecoast program of the University of Southern Maine. She works as a school psychologist and writer/editor in the Bay Area. She can be reached through her website, kathybriccetti.com.

Since its founding in 1974, Heyday Books has occupied a unique niche in the publishing world, specializing in books that foster an understanding of the history, literature, art, environment, social issues, and culture of California and the West. We are a 501(c)(3) nonprofit organization based in Berkeley, California, serving a wide range of people and audiences.

We are grateful for the generous funding we've received for our publications and programs during the past year from foundations and more than three hundred and fifty individual donors. Major supporters include:

Anonymous; Audubon California; Judith and Phillip Auth; Barona Band of Mission Indians; B.C.W. Trust III; S. D. Bechtel, Jr. Foundation; Barbara and Fred Berensmeier; Berkeley Civic Arts Program and Civic Arts Commission; Joan Berman; Peter and Mimi Buckley; Lewis and Sheana Butler; Butler Koshland Fund; California State Automobile Association; California State Coastal Conservancy; California State Library; Joanne Campbell; Candelaria Fund; John and Nancy Cassidy Family Foundation, through Silicon Valley Community Foundation; Creative Work Fund; Columbia Foundation; The Community Action Fund; Community Futures Collective; Compton Foundation, Inc.; Lawrence Crooks; Ida Rae Egli; Donald and Janice Elliott, in honor of David Elliott, through Silicon Valley Community Foundation; Evergreen Foundation; Federated Indians of Graton Rancheria; Mark and Tracy Ferron; Furthur Foundation; George Gamble; Wallace Alexander Gerbode Foundation; Richard & Rhoda Goldman Fund; Ben Graber, in honor of Sandy Graber; Evelyn & Walter Haas, Jr. Fund; Walter & Elise Haas Fund; James and Coke Hallowell; Cheryl Hinton; James Irvine Foundation; Marty and Pamela Krasney; Robert and Karen Kustel, in honor of Bruce Kelley; Guy Lampard and Suzanne Badenhoop; LEF Foundation; Michael McCone; National Endowment for the Arts; National Park Service; Organize Training Center; Patagonia; Pease Family Fund, in honor of Bruce Kelley; Resources Legacy Fund; Alan Rosenus; San Francisco Foundation; San Manuel Band of Mission Indians; Deborah Sanchez; Contee and Maggie Seely; James B. Swinerton; Swinerton Family Fund; Taproot Foundation; Thendara Foundation; Lisa Van Cleef and Mark Gunson; Marion Weber; Albert and Susan Wells; Dean Witter Foundation; and Yocha Dehe Wintun Nation.

For more information about Heyday Institute, our publications and programs, please visit our website at www.heydaybooks.com.